AF539844

PRICING SOLUTION FOR WATER SUPPLY AND SOLID WASTE MANAGEMENT

PRICING SOLUTION FOR WATER SUPPLY AND SOLID WASTE MANAGEMENT

By

Dr. R. Murugan

Manager
Tamilnadu Urban Finance & Infrastructure Development Cooperation Ltd. (TUFIDCO)
Chennai

&

Dr. X. Antony Thanaraj

Associate Professor
Deptt. of Commerce
Scott Christian College, Nagercoil
Tamil Nadu
(India)

DISCOVERY PUBLISHING HOUSE PVT. LTD.
NEW DELHI-110 002

Published by:
Tilak Wasan
DISCOVERY PUBLISHING HOUSE PVT. LTD.
4831/24, Ansari Road, Prahlad Street
Darya Ganj, New Delhi-110002 (India)
Phone: +91-11-23279245, 43764432
Fax: +91-11-23253475
E-mail: parul.wasan@gmail.com
discoverypublishinghouse@gmail.com
info@discoverypublishinggroup.com
web: www.discoverypublishinggroup.com

First Edition: **2011**
ISBN: 978-81-8356-811-1

Pricing Solution for Water Supply and Solid Waste Management

Printed at:
Shree Balaji Art Press
Delhi

Preface

India's finite and fragile water resources are stressed and depleting while sectoral demands (including drinking water, industry, agriculture and others) are growing rapidly in line with urbanization, population increases, rising incomes and industrial growth. At the same time, urban India is in the midst of transformation. In an era of economic reform, liberalization and globalization, cities and towns are fast emerging as centres of growth.

At independence, India's population was less than 400 million and per capita water availability over 5,000 cubic meters per year. To day, 60 years later, the per capita water availability has fallen to hardly more than 2,000 cubic meters per year and the actual usable quantity is around 1,122 cubic meters per year. Environmental problems include water quality degradation from agro-chemicals, industrial and domestic pollution, groundwater depletion, waterlogging, soil solemnization, salutation, degradation of wetland eco-system impacts, and various health-related problems. In the past, water problem has been developed rather than managed. Management of water has been through a top-down approach and has become virtually a government monopoly.

Water tariff is an important management tool. The important objectives of municipal water tariff design are to balance among four important objectives namely cost recovery, economic efficiency, equity and affordability. There are a number of trade-offs between different objectives and the average price of water supplied by the utility through domestic connections. An efficient tariff will create incentives that ensure for a given water supply cost, that users obtain the largest possible aggregate benefits.

The limited revenues earmarked for the municipalities make them ill-equipped to provide for high costs involved in the collection, storage, treatment and proper disposal of MSW generated which remains unattended and grows into heaps at poorly maintained landfill sites and are prone to contaminate groundwater contamination because of leachate production. Open dumping of garbage facilitates the breeding of disease vectors such as flies, mosquitoes, cockroaches, rats and other pests. Landfill sites also generate gas emissions that are 50 to 60 per cent methane, a greenhouse gas that contributes to global warming. The people in the cities are interested in knowing these problems but are not willing to solve them.

These problems can be solved only by the joint efforts of both government and people. It is highly essential to strengthen the finance of the government to manage the urban water supply and sanitation. Hence, the book focuses on the development of financial model for urban water supply and solid waste management as per the customers' perspectives.

This book has covered all the major segments of the subject and is divided into five chapters spread over the following topics — Introduction, Socio-economic and Demographic profile of respondents, Development of Financial Model for Drinking Water Supply, Solid Waste Management and Its Financial Model, Summary of Findings, Conclusion and Policy Implications. I hope it would serve as a useful text and reference book for all categories of readers, particularly academics, researchers, practitioners and government agencies.

The book earnestly attempts to present the various aspects of financial model as a result of research work carried out by the authors. It is hoped that the readers will not only gain a perspective of the financial model for water supply and sanitation, but also be able to pursue research in the area of pricing of infrastructure services for gaining in depth knowledge.

We are also thankful to Dr. T. Vanniarajan, Associate Professor, Madurai and Dr. Edwin Gnanadhas, Associate Professor in Scott Christian College, Nagercoil giving all-round support for bringing this book.

We are grateful to Shri Tilak Wasan, Director of Discovery Publishing House Pvt. Ltd, New Delhi for having come forward to publish this book.

MURUGAN R.

Antony Thanaraj.X

Contents

Preface

1. **Introduction** 1

Water Resources Quantity and Quality—Evolution of Water and Sanitation Sector Programs—Tariff Structures on the Basic Services—Present Scenario of Water Supply and Solid Waste Management in Chennai—Need for the Study—Statement of the Problem—Review of Previous Studies— Customer Preferences on Drinking Water (Choice Model)—Water Quality—Taste and Odour and Other Aesthetic Judgments—Water Pricing and Metering—Consumer Acceptance of Recycled Water—Willingness to Pay for Drinking Water—Water Pricing—Contingent Valuation (CV) Method—Solid Waste Management—Identification of Research Gap—Research Model—Objectives of the Study—Methodology of the Study—Research Design—Sampling Framework of the Study —Population of the Study—Construct Development—Collection of Data—Framework of Analysis—Limitation of the Study—Scheme of the Report—Reference.

2. **Profile of the Respondents and their Behaviour on Drinking Water Facilities** 32

Annual Income among the Respondents—Gender of the Respondents—Age of the Respondents—Nativity of the Respondents—Occupational Background of the Respondents—Family Size of the Respondents—Number of Earning Members Per Family—House Ownership among the Respondents—Type of House among the Respondents—Drinking Water Pipe Connection among the Respondents—Means used to get Drinking Water—Frequency of Water Supply—Water Availability per Week—Tariff on Drinking Water—Years of Experience with Metro Water System—Usage of Metro Water among the Respondents—Respondents Opinion on other Important Sources of Drinking Water—Frequency of using Bottled Water among the Respondents—Reasons for Buying Bottled Water by the Respondents—Respondents' Expectation from Metro Water Services—Important Expectations among the Respondents—Reliability and Validity of the Important Expectation—Level of Expectation on Important Factors—Level of Perception on Factors among the Respondents—Association between the Profile of Respondents and their SERVQUAL Scale—Monthly Expenditure on Drinking Water—Profile of the Respondents and their Monthly Expenditure on Drinking Water—Association between Profile of the Respondents and their Monthly Expenditure on Drinking Water—References.

3. Development of Financial Model for Drinking Water Supply 68

Willingness to Pay (WTP)—WTP in Different Users Segments—Significant Difference among the Respondents Regarding their WTP—Difference between Monthly Expenditure and WTP for Drinking Water—Profile of the Respondents and their Difference on Monthly Expenditure and WTP—Reasons for Willing-to-pay more for Drinking Water—The Important Reasons for Willing-to-pay More on Drinking Water—Reliability and Validity of the Variables in the Construct—Important Reasons for Willingness-to-pay More—Reasons for Not Willing-to pay more—Important Reasons for Unwillingness-to-Pay More—Reliability and Validity of the Measures in Each Construct—Important Reasons for Unwillingness-to-Pay More—Association between Profile of Respondents and their Importance on three Reasons for not Willing-to-Pay More—Privatization of Drinking Water Services—Reasons for Switching from Public to Private Service Provider—Important Reasons for Switching—Reliability and Validity of the Measures in Each Construct—Important Reason for Switching—Association between the Profile of Respondents and their Level of Importance Attached to Reasons—Impact of Factors of Switching on their Rate of Switching to New Service Provider—Financial Models (Choice Models) on Drinking Water Services—Evaluation of Finance Models by the Respondents —Evaluation of Financial Model on the Basis of Regular Water Supply—Rating of Financial Model on the Basis of Convenient Timing of Water Supply—Evaluation of Financial Models on the Basis of Quality of Water—Rating of Financial Models on the Basis of "Responsiveness"—Evaluation of Financial Models on the Basis of Complaint Handling—Rating of Financial Models on the Basis of 'Reliability' of Water Supply—Evaluation of Financial Model on the Basis of 'Assurance' of Water Supply —Evaluation of Financial Models on the Basis of Quantum of Water Consumed—Rating of Financial Models on the Basis of Government Subsidy—Evaluation of Financial Models on the Basis of Discriminatory Pricing —Evaluation of Financial Models on the Basis of Privatization —Overall Rating on Financial Models—Association between the Profile of Respondents and their Overall Rating of Financial Models—Factors Leading to Choose the Financial Models—Discriminant Factors to Choose the Financial Model (Gender and Age Group of Respondents)—Discriminant Factors among the Respondents Based on their Nativity and Occupational Background—Discriminant Factors among the Respondents (on the basis of their Family Size and Number of Earning Members per Family)—Discriminant Factors among the Respondents with Different Occupancy Status and Type of House—References.

4. Solid Waste Management and Its Financial Model 130

Financing of Solid Waste Management Services—Financed Model in SWM—Awareness on Solid Waste Management among the Respondents—Awareness on Solid Waste Management Index (ASWI) among the

Respondents—Association between Profile of the Respondents and their ASWI—Customers' Expectation from SWM Service—Important Factors in SWM—Reliability and Validity of the Variables in each Factor—Discriminate Validity of the Constructs—Level of Expectation among the Respondents—Level of Perception on Factors in SWM—SERVQUAL Scale on the Factors in SWM—Association between the Profile of Respondents and their SERVQUAL Scale—Models on SWM—Reliability and Validity of the Implications in Each Model—Association between the Profile of Respondents and their Evaluation of Models—Factors Influencing the Model Choice—Discriminate Factors among the Respondents Based on their Nativity and Occupational Background—Discriminate Factors among the Respondents Based on House-ownership and Type of House—Discriminate Factors among the Respondents with Different ASWI—Privatization of SWM—Reasons for Privatization of SWM—Important Reasons for Privatization—Reliability and Validity of the Important Reasons—Discriminate Validity of the Constructs—Respondents' Perception on Important Reasons for Privatization—Association between the Profile of Respondents and their Opinion on Important Reasons—Impact of Important Reasons for Privatization on their Overall Degree of Favour for Privatization among the Respondents—Reasons for not Supporting Privatization—Evaluation of Financial Model for SWM System—Profile of the Respondents and their Choice on Financial Model—Contingent Valuation Model (CVM) —Profile of the Respondents and their WTP—References.

5. **Summary of Findings, Conclusion and Suggestions ... 194**

Conclusion—Policy Implications—Directions for Future Research.

Bibliography 220

Index 231

1 Introduction

Historically, civilizations in India, as around the world, have largely evolved and developed around water bodies as most human activities, including agriculture and industry depend on water. In the five decades since independence, India has witnessed phenomenal development of water resources and has largely successfully met the demand for water for many of the diverse uses in the country. Investments made on infrastructural development in the country have resulted in rapid expansion in urban, energy and industrial sectors. Infrastructure for safe drinking water has been provided to about 85 per cent of India's urban and rural population (Water Supply and Sanitation, 2002)[1].

India's finite and fragile water resources are stressed and depleting while sectoral demands (including drinking water, industry, agriculture and others) are growing rapidly in line with urbanization, population increases, rising incomes and industrial growth. At the same time, urban India is in the midst of transformation. In an era of economic reform, liberalization and globalization, cities and towns are fast emerging as centres of growth. In fact, estimates reveal that urban India contributes more than 50 per cent of the country's GDP at present although it accounts for less than one-third of its population (Natural Human Development Report, 2001)[2]. It is estimated that by 2025, more than 50 per cent of the country's population will live in cities and towns. The growth of urbanization and metro cities is presented in Tables 1.1 and 1.2.

Table 1.1 : Increasing urbanization

Sl. No.	Particulars	1951	1991	2001	2021 (Projected)
1.	Number of urban agglomerations/ towns	2795	3768	4378	—
2.	Urban population	62.0	217.0	285.0	550.0
3.	As percentage of total population	17.3	25.75	27.8	41.00

Source: CPHEEO.

The above table indicates the group of urbanization from 1951 to 2001 and the projected figure in 2021. The growth of metro cities in India is given in Table 1.2.

Table 1.2 : Growth of metro cities

Sl.No.	Particulars	1981	1991	2001
1.	No. of metro cities (Population: 1 million)	12	23	35
2.	Population (in million)	42	70	108
3.	Percentage of urban population	26	32	37.8

Source: CPHEEO.

These figures are indicative of the likely demand for infrastructural facilities, notably water supply and sanitation that could arise due to urbanization.

Water Resources Quantity and Quality

India receives an average annual rainfall of about 4,000 billion cubic metres. This source of water is unevenly distributed both spatially as well as temporally. Most of the rainfall is confined to the monsoon season from June to September, and levels of precipitation vary from 100 mm a year in western Rajasthan to over 9000 mm year in the northeastern state of Megalaya. The uneven geographical distribution of annual rainfall causes severe regional and temporary shortages.

At independence, India's population was less than 400 million and per capita water availability over 5,000 cubic meters per year. 60 years later, the per capita water availability has fallen to 2,000 cubic meters per year and the actual usable quantity is around 1,122 cubic meters per year (Ministry of water resources, 1999)[3].

Environmental problems include water quality degradation from agro-chemicals, industrial and domestic pollution, groundwater depletion, waterlogging, soil solemnization, salutation, degradation of wetland eco-system impacts, and various health-related problems (WQSS, 1997).[4] In the past, water problem has been developed rather than managed. Comprehensive management on a river basin basis, multi-sectorally, conjunctively for surface and groundwater, incorporating both qualitative and quantitative aspects of water is largely lacking. Management of water has been through a top-down approach and has become virtually a government monopoly. A 'supply-side' approach exploiting additional water resources has been pre-dominantly used. This approach has resulted in major economic, social and environmental costs (UWSS, 1999)[5]. In recent years, however, there has been realization regarding the need to address these problems.

Evolution of Water and Sanitation Sector Programs

Water Supply and Sanitation were added to the national agenda during the First Five-Year-Plan period. The Ministry of Water Resources drafted a National Water Policy in 1987 to guide the planning and development of water resources throughout the country. The 1987 policy has been revised and the National Water Policy in the Eighth Five-Year Plan (1992-97), which states: "Safe drinking water and basic sanitation are vital human needs for health and efficiency. The Tenth Plan envisages 100 per cent coverage of rural and urban population with safe drinking water. National Water Policy 2002 has been once again according priority to drinking water. The national policy guiding the water and sanitation sectors in India. It contains the stipulated norms and standards.

The Tenth Plan advocates management of water as an economic asset rather than a free commodity and places the responsibility for regeneration on all user agencies. The Tenth Plan places significant emphasis on Urban Water Supply and Sanitation (UWSS) as opposed to previous plans and emphasizes strong reformative agendas.

Tariff Structures on the Basic Services

Water tariff is an important management tool. The important objective of municipal water tariff design is to balance among four important objectives namely cost recovery, economic efficiency, equity and affordability. There are a number of trade-offs between different objectives and the average price of water supplied by the utility through domestic connections. An efficient tariff will create incentives that ensure for a given water supply cost, that users obtain the largest possible aggregate benefits. A tariff structure is a set of procedural rules to determine the conditions of service and the monthly billing for water users of various categories or classes. The basic types of water tariff structures are—

1. Fixed charge in which the consumers are charged irrespective of the quantity consumed;
2. Water-use charge is levied proportionate to the quantity of water consumed;
3. Fixed charge plus water-use charge that includes consumers are levied a variable charges according to the quantity of water consumed along with a fixed minimum charge.

Present Scenario of Water Supply and Solid Waste Management in Chennai

Water supply in Chennai has been entrusted to Chennai Metropolitan Water Supply and Sewerage Board (CMWSSB) that looks into sources augmentation and distribution of water to consumer. The Board is empowered to collect water connection charges, which is a onetime charge when effecting connection and monthly tariff collected on half yearly basis.

The onetime connection charge is Rs. 3000 for household, Rs.5000 for non-domestic and Rs.10000 for commercial establishment. The tariff is Rs. 50 per month for household. Volumetric basis of tariff is in existence for non-domestic and commercial consumers that varies from Rs. 20 per kilo liter to Rs.60 per kilo liter. The Chennai Metropolitan Water Supply and Sewerage Board (CMWSSB) are in charge of operation and maintenance of water supply and sewerage in Chennai. The amount collected through the connection charges and tariffs are the financial source to manage CMWSSB. CMWSSB has the liability of debt servicing for the borrowed loan to create assets. Financial burden of CMWSSB is increasing day by day due to administered tariff of Government of Tamilnadu.

The solid waste management is with the Chennai Corporation. They are in charge of collection, transportation and disposal of solid waste in Chennai. Out of 10 zones, Chennai Corporation has privatised 5 zones for collection and transportation of solid waste. The staff of Chennai Corporation manages the balance 5 zones' solid waste. Chennai Corporation not followed scientific disposal of solid waste management. Chennai Corporation is not charging fee from household for the solid waste management. The commercial establishments are charged with flat fee ranging from Rs. 100 to Rs. 500 per month. But this is not sufficient to meet the huge operation and maintenance cost incurring for Chennai Corporation.

Need for the Study

The urban water supply and sanitation in India is riddled with so many problems such like inequitable distribution of water in a given city, erratic supply and water quality degrading continuously over time because of high fluoride concentration in good water. Hand pump attached defluoridation and iron removal plants have failed due to inappropriate technology unsuited to community perceptions and community involvement. Desalination plants have been a costly failure mainly due to lapses at different levels such as poor planning and implementation, inappropriate technology to the urban setting and high costs of Operation and Maintenance.

Over the last decade industrial waste and Municipal Solid Waste (MSW) have emerged as the leading causes of the pollution of surface and groundwater. In urban regions, river water is, to a large extent, treated before it is supplied by the municipal authorities to the people for drinking and other domestic purposes. However, Indian rivers today fall short of Central Pollution Control Board's (CPCB) standards due to excessive pollution by untreated sewage and domestic and industrial wastes.

On the urban water supply front, transmission and distribution networks are largely of inferior quality, in addition to being outdated and badly maintained, resulting in higher operating costs. Physical losses are typically high, ranging from 25 to 70 per cent. Low pressures and intermittent supplies lead to back siphoning resulting in contamination in the distribution network. Water is generally available for only two to eight hours a day or on alternative days in most Indian cities. Unsatisfactory service standards have led to low tariff structures, which in turn have resulted in poor resource positions of urban local bodies, poor maintenance and service a vicious circle. Overstaffing and lack of training of the personnel are also the major issues of Urban Water Supply and Sanitation Scheme.

The coverage in terms of organized systems ranges from 35 per cent in class IV cities to 75 per cent in class I Cities. Of the total water generated in the four metros, barely 30 per cent is treated before disposal. Thus, the untreated and partially treated waste water eventually finds its way into fresh water resources such as rivers, lakes and groundwater. The limited revenues earmarked for the municipalities make them ill-equipped to provide for high costs involved in the collection, storage, treatment and proper disposal of Municipal Solid Waste generated which remains unattended and grows into heaps at poorly maintained landfill sites and are prone to contaminate groundwater because of leachate production. Open dumping of garbage facilitates the breeding of disease-vectors such as flies, mosquitoes, cockroaches, rats and other pests. Landfill sites also generate gas emissions that are 50 to 60 per cent methane, a greenhouse gas that contributes to global warming. The people in the cities are interested in knowing these problems but are not willing to solve them. These problems can be solved only by the joint efforts of both government and people. It is highly essential to strengthen the finance of the government to manage the urban water supply and sanitation. Hence, the present study focuses on the development of financial model for Urban Water Supply and Sanitation Scheme as per the customers' perspectives.

Statement of the Problem

The welfare government at a reasonable price should properly and adequately provide the basic infrastructure facilities. At the same time, the people of the countries have to avail and use the services in a proper way. The price paid for the service should be reasonable enough to meet the expenses incurred on the provision of such services. A developing country like India is getting so many grants and loans from various international bodies for the urban development. Even though a huge some of money is invested on such schemes, the final results of the schemes are not up to the expected level. The basic reasons for such failure are the improper assessment of the people's expectations, mismanagement of funds and also non-remunerative schemes. All these reasons are related to peoples' attitude and involvement in their common programmes of public health especially drinking water and solid waste management. The tariff at below cost leads to over utilization of services offered by the local bodies and leads to accumulate loss to the local bodies. Hence, the programmes related to drinking water and control water management are started at high pitch and it faces its own decline in due course of time. This situation forces the local bodies to generate a new financial model, which are creating a consistent social welfare. The financial model should generate substantial revenue to local bodies and also ensure welfare of the people. Hence, the present study focuses on this aspect by generating financial models for drinking water and solid waste management systems and its evaluation on the basis of customers' perspective.

REVIEW OF PREVIOUS STUDIES

Customer Preferences on Drinking Water (Choice Model)

Koss and Sami (2003)[6] found that the consumers expect more on the quality of water and continuity of water supply from their service providers. Bates (2000)[7] revealed that the service provider will provide safe, clean drinking water to their consumers. According to him the key responsibilities of water beverage companies are: supply of clean water, reliable service and value of money.

Meens et al., (2002)[8] found uncertainties related to the knowledge limitations of science to be more acceptable than those stemming from government regulatory activity — or lack of it. They also found that consumers prioritized safe clean drinking water before reliability of supply.

Falahee and Mackae (1995)[9] show that satisfaction with water supplies is valued high compared with most other utilities in terms of price, quality, contract conditions, service quality, customers care, etc.

Water Quality — Taste and Odour and Other Aesthetic Judgments

Drinking Water India (2000) demonstrated that most respondents were relatively satisfied with their drinking water supply especially quality. The quality of water concerns with taste, odour, appearance, hardness, freshness and temperature. It also includes the composition and / or the provenance of the water like natural ingredients, any additives, and the source of water.

Oestman et al., (2004)[10] found that the aesthetic estimations of tap water quality (e.g. taste, colour and odour) will have an impact upon judgments of apparent quality and safety. Taste and odour while being interlinked, tend to relate to different factors, with the sense of taste being most attuned to the inorganic constituents of water, with the sense of smell relating more to organic constituents of water.

Pirion et al., (2004)[11] identified that the taste of chlorine in tap water to be the leading cause of customer complaints and dissatisfaction with drinking water although perceptions are influenced by the chlorine practices of the customers country of residence.

Doria (2002)[12] and Dapont (2005), found both aesthetic preferences and health concerns lead consumers to opt for bottled water, with consumer trust in the water company also influencing consumption choices. Some consumption of bottled water may also occur because of consumer preferences for water that is chilled or sparkling water.

Biswas et al., (2005)[13] carried out a research on potable piped water in Srilanka. They found that the inhabitants continued to use polluted well-water for drinking and cooking purposes, while using the piped water for bathing and washing since they disliked the chlorine odour of the piped water.

Adote et al., (2000) found that consumers who were dissatisfied with the taste, odour, and/or appearance of tap water were willing to pay for bottled water but claimed that they were also doing so to avoid health risks from tap water. They also found that use of water filters tends to be higher amongst consumers who had experienced problems with their municipal tap water.

Water Pricing and Metering

Consumer Council for Water (2005)[14] found it difficult to reconcile the large differences in charges paid for water and beverage services according to where people lived. Issues of water charges were also mentioned on a large scale, national basis according to perceived differences in the quality and cost of services between companies across England and Wales.

Ochoa et al., (1990)[15] found that while responses to new meters were generally positive in their Mexican sample middle-income groups made the greatest savings over the trail period. Similarly differing pricing structures provide incentives for different levels of conservation behaviour and occasionally, as in the case of Japan recently, consumption can be so much reduced that revenue from water charges drop substantially.

Candidate Countries Euro Barometer (2003)[16] revealed that the majority of consumers regard the price of water supplies as fair, which is second highest degree of satisfaction with utility prices after postal services. As for all questions of service pricing those who regard prices as being excessive are generally least able to afford to pay their bills so the figures of those regarding prices as 'excessive' probably reflects low ability to pay rather than a negative response to water prices specially.

Consumer Acceptance of Recycled Water

Stenekes et al., (2006)[17] argued that emotional barriers to recycled water usage need to be considered if there is to be consumer acceptance of recycled water, even if the recycled water is of the highest quality.

Hartley (2006)[18] noted that consumer concern about recycled water usage is tempered by an individual consumer's proximity to the waste water source; consumers are more willing to use their own recycled waste water than waste water drawn from a common source.

Russell and Hampton (2006) cautioned that little is known in general terms about consumer reactions to recycled water usage and thus predicting consumer responses in relation to specific proposals is difficult; local factors make the transfer of results from one to another difficult. They noted that general support for the use of recycled water does not necessarily translate into support for a specific project.

Po et al., (2005)[19] found that 90 per cent of the consumers in Australia accepted using the recycled water for the watering of public parks, golf courses, home lawns and gardens and flushing of toilets. Using recycled water was not considered acceptable for either drinking or cooking by a significant majority of respondents.

Willingness to Pay for Drinking Water

According to Ntengwe (2004)[20] willingness to pay for water services is affected by existing water quality, affordability and ability to pay, together with consumers' level of awareness of water management issues. The status quo can also have a significant effect on willingness to pay amounts, with consumers generally preferring the status quo to charges in service levels and cost structures (Hensker, 2005)[21] .

Raje et al., (2002)[22] argued that consumers have a zero willingness to pay more because of lack of faith in the management system of their water supplier, and only by increasing management transparency and the transparent use of funds are people willing to pay more for improved water services. The affordability of the consumers was also limiting the willingness to pay more for water services.

Calderson et al., (2004) identified the important reasons for willing to pay more for drinking water to be reliability of water supply, water supply for the future generation and sustained environmental services. Whereas the reasons for not willing to pay more for it are poor affordability, and existing high tariff, government irresponsibility and lack of faith in reliable water supply.

Water Pricing

David and Inocencio (2001)[23] revealed that the Government's water pricing policy does not in any way seek to recover the full economic cost of producing water. They identified one of the major weaknesses prevalent in water resource management in metro Manila are "the failure to adopt an integrated, holistic approach in addressing the inherently inter-related issues of water supply planning and operation, demand management, pollution control, watershed and groundwater protection".

Javier (2001)[24] identified the need for a new strategy pricing raw water and other watershed resources based on their true economic values. It emphasizes that this valuation should include the full cost of protecting and harnessing individual resources.

Francisco (2002)[25] underlined the fact that, because of budgetary constraints, the government can no longer afford to subsidize the provision of raw water. Nor should it allow water users to continue thinking that water is abundant and cheap. The very signal it is sending if it does not correctly price raw water. Instead, the price of water should reflect the opportunity costs of competing uses as well as the environmental cost of resources extraction and consumption.

Ebarvia (2003)[26] estimated the marginal opportunity cost of meeting the demand requirements of the industrial sector in metro Manila. This sector draws 80 per cent of its requirements from groundwater and 20 per cent from MWSS.

Yasuo (2005)[27] found that the willingness to pay for services are higher when there is a higher monthly income among the respondents. It is also identified as higher among youngster. The lower the current water usage volume or the shorter the water availability time, the higher the willingness to pay.

Contingent Valuation (CV) Method

Hearth et al., (2007) found that the CV method is widely used to estimate the willingness to pay for the drinking water. The CV method measures the information on (i) what people are currently using; (ii) what improvements are feasible from an engineering, economic, financial and cultural perspective; and (iii) how people view the role of water and sanitation in their daily lives.

Arrow et al., (1993)[28] and Portney (1994)[29], identified seven pillars of designing CV surveys. These are: (i) interview in person rather than over the telephone; (ii) Questions about a future hypothetical occurrence rather than a historical event; (iii) using of a referendum format in which the respondent "votes" on a benefit with a known price; (iv) the interviewer should begin with a scenario describing benefits of a contingent market commodity; (v) the survey should remind that payment for the new commodity may reduce consumption of other goods; (vi) the survey should remind that substitutes exist for the hypothetical commodity in question, and (vii) there should be follow-up questions to make sure that the respondent understands the choices made.

Pattanayak et al., (2004)[30] show that households with reasonably good alternative sources such as wells have low willingness-to-pay and high rejection rates for improved services. In certain cases, quantitative information on water use from different sources is valuable for policy analysis purposes.

Fewtnell et al., (2005)[31] suggested that water, sanitation and hygiene interventions might generate significant gains in health, reducing incidence of diarrhea by approximately 30 per cent in children in developing countries as part of the validity tests. The analysis reveals that the households who have experienced water-related diseases have higher willingness-to-pay.

Whittington (2002) designing the survey to measure willingness-to-pay which consists of five modules. Module-I consists of introductory section, briefly describing background and purpose of the survey; Module-II consists of questions on demographic, socio-economic profile of the households; Module-III contains the questions on current water supply conditions and consumer behaviours; Module-IV contains the contingent valuation market scenarios followed by questions eliciting willingness-to-pay values and Module-V Debriefing questions.

Gunatilake et al., (2006)[32] illustrated that econometric modelling allows undertaking a number of validity tests that adds credibility to the willingness-to-pay estimates. Furthermore, an econometric model can be used to predict the uptake rates with different policy levels such as tariff and connection charges in water and sanitation source studies. The close ended format information provides direct answers to questions related to demand for improved water supply scheme. These additional uses help design suitable tariff and pro-poor water supply scheme service, estimate revenue of the water utility, and provide answers to basic questions on effective demand in water supply scheme project designs.

Cameron et al., (2002)[33] concluded that closed ended elicitation questions are far superior to open ended and payment card methods when compared to welfare estimation from actual choices.

Whillington (1998) suggested the bid amount to predict the willingness-to-pay for WSS. In order to facilitate the econometric modelling of the responses, a range of values (bids) will be presented to different households. The selection of range of bids may be highly influenced by the nearness to actual cost, current bills, range of connection charges and monthly bills. The rule of thumb is that the lowest bid should be low enough that most of the respondents will accept it, while the highest bid should be high enough that most respondents will reject it.

Solid Waste Management

Repetto et al., (1992)[34] used the social costs of waste disposal to estimate user fee. These costs include the risks of air and water pollution, along with noise and other diminutives. They found that in the states they covered, the social costs of waste disposal into a lined landfill with leachate collection were of the same approximate magnitude as the private costs.

Fullerton and Kinnaman (1996)[35] argued that the flat fee pricing of waste disposal is inefficient and does not encourage waste reduction since the marginal cost of waste disposal is zero. Unit pricing as an alternative instrument has been shown empirically to be effective in reducing waste generation by U.S. households.

Miranda et al., (1994)[36] revealed that data from 21 communities with unit pricing schemes show that these schemes reduced garbage by between 17 and 74 per cent and increased recycling by 128 per cent.

Van Houten and Morris (1999)[37] indicated that the Bag Program reduced mixed waste by as much as 51 per cent, while the Can Program by approximately 20 per cent. In both programs the probability of households recycling increased by 18 per cent.

Jenkins (1993)[38] estimated the welfare gains from pricing garbage according to its social marginal cost. He found that this would improve social welfare by as much as US $650 million per year or roughly US $3 per person per year. According to him, municipal waste disposal authorities have suggested that illegal dumping does occur immediately following the implementation of a user charge.

Reschovsky and Stone (1994)[39] revealed that the quantity-based pricing scheme in High Bridge, New Jersey, which a charged communities $2.69 for the first bag and $1.25 per additional bag reported a 25 per cent decline in trash volume. The pay-per-bag pricing scheme promoted the average person to reduce the weight and volume of their garbage by 14 and 37 per cent respectively and to increase the weight of their recyclables by 16 per cent.

Eugenia et al., (2004)[40] found that the demand for solid waste service is inelastic. The cost of waste collection and disposal that can be avoided thanks to unit pricing can be as much as php 3.1 million annually. Recycling costs on the part of government would be minimum because the informal sector is already actively and effectively involved. Welfare gains of the society can be enjoyed if unit pricing replaces a fixed-rate system.

Janal (2002)[41] found that households are willing to pay a premium for improvements in collection frequency, waste disposal methods, and transportation mode attributes. The preferred transportation mode is a mix of compactor and open trucks or a mix of compactor and covered trucks. The households derive positive utility from the provisions of recycling facilities with an implicit price of about MYR 5 (US $1.33) monthly through choice method.

Gottinger (1991)[42] found out that the demand for solid waste collection service depends on the volume of wastes generated, the quantity of refuse the residents want collected and the quality of collection service. Income, price and personal taste influence the amount placed out for collection. For higher disposable personal income levels, a higher level of service will be demanded.

Jerkins (1993)[43] analysed the impact of service-level-based user fees and found that frequency of collection units and location of collection affect waste quantities.

Bennagen (2004)[44] examined the impacts of a unit pricing system in the disposal of solid wastes in Olongapo city. A unit pricing scheme will result in an incremental reduction of about 3,305 tones of waste annually. About PhP 860,000 per year in avoided costs can be realized by the city in SWM in the first 3 years, and savings of up to PhP 2.9 million annually in the succeeding periods.

Cointreau-Levine (2000)[45] points that the collection of user charges enables the service to be financially sustainable. The study revealed that most local governments experience a serious shortfall in meeting their revenue needs from their tax base. User charges, as one means to cover solid waste costs, should not be neglected, even though most solid waste management services are public goods. User charges give the solid waste agency some autonomy by eliminating the need to compete with other government agencies for their share of general revenue.

Laplante (2003)[46] maintained that the fees for solid waste management depends upon the type of solid waste, amount/ volume of taste, distance of the transfer station to the waste management facility, cost of construction, cost of management and type of technology.

Hong et al., (1993)[47] analysed a particular form of volume-based pricing with a survey of 2298 households from Portland and United States. Households pay $12 per container but for an extra container households pay $24 per container. Since price depends on quantity, the price per container is endogenous.

Reschovsky and Stone (1994) measured the price and income elasticities in volume-based pricing. The results showed that the volume of waste declined by 37 per cent and the weight by 14 per cent, while the weight–volume intensity increased with 31.7 per cent. Moreover, the weight of recyclable materials increased with 15.7 per cent. Their estimated price elasticity of the amount of household waste measured in kilograms was rather small.

Choe and Fraser (1999)[48] consider a model in which three agents interact: a firm, a household and a regulator. Four different types of waste were considered. The optional policy combines an environmental tax, a household waste collection charge, and monitoring and imposing fine on illegal waste disposal.

Palmer and Walls (1997)[49] revealed that households use alternatives such as home composting more often. The amount of recyclable materials that can be dropped off free of charge increased substantially. In Bostan weight-base pricing appears to be cost-effective. The problem of illegal dumping is small, due to an effective monitoring and firming system.

Identification of Research Gap

From the previous studies of drinking water (DW) and solid waste Management (SWM) the customer preferences, evaluation of the financial models based on choice model and contingent model have been reviewed and presented. By the review of previous studies, the following research gap is identified. Even though there are so many studies related to DW and SWM, all these studies are related to the developed countries and also to the developing countries except India. The studies in India revealed the cost and benefit of various DW and SWM proposals with the help of the engineering models. The customers' preferences and their willingness to pay for enriched DW and SWM system were not focused upon by any studies. The present study has made an attempt to fill up this research gap with confined objectives and defined research model.

Research Model

The research model has been developed to generate the objectives of the study. The proposed research model for DW and SMW is presented below:

MODEL–I

Product/Quality
Service Quality
Situational Factors
Personal Factors
Socio-Economic Profile
Existing system on DW and SWM
Mix of various attributes
Choice Models
Financial Model
Willingness-To-Pay
Contingent valuation method
Optimum financial model

The aforesaid model is generated to analyse the various financial models, their antecedents, consequences and association with the profile of the customers.

The switching behaviour among the customers has been studied with the help of the following research model.

MODEL–II

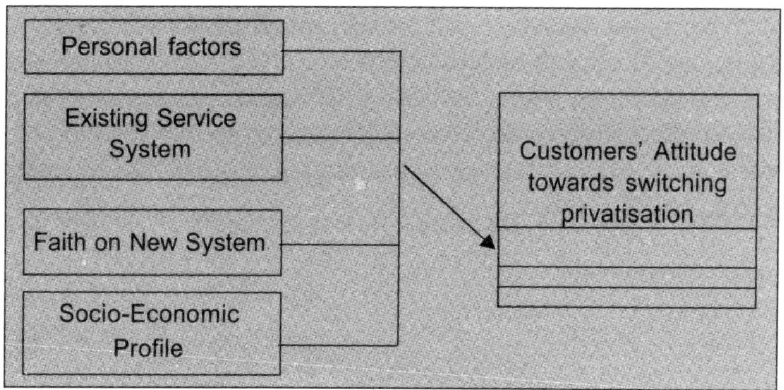

Based on the aforementioned research models, the research objectives have been generated.

Objectives of the Study

The following are the objectives of this study:

(i) To reveal the socio-economic profile of the respondents;

(ii) To study the respondents' perception on the existing system of drinking water;

(iii) To examine the consumers willingness to pay for enriched service on drinking water;

(iv) To generate the financial models and evaluate them on the basis of respondents' perspective;

(v) To study the switching behaviour of the respondents and its correlates;

(vi) To generate the finicial models in solid waste management (SWM) and its evaluation;

(vii) To examine the various pricing methods for solid waste management;

(viii) To analyse the respondents willingness towards the privatization of solid waste management and its reasons and;

(ix) To evaluate the willingness to pay for solid waste management services.

Methodology of the Study

The methodology is the basic framework through which the research objectives have been fulfilled by the researcher. It includes research design, population and sampling framework, construct development, collection of data, framework of analysis, limitation and scheme of the report.

Research Design

A research design is a framework or blueprint for conducting the research project. It details the procedures necessary for obtaining the information needed to structure or solve research problems (Semon, 1996)[50]. Typically a research design involves the following the components namely the type of information needed, the form of research design, measurement and scaling procedures, construct development, data collection, sampling process and plan of data analysis (Kitaeff, 1994)[51] .

The descriptive research is used to describe something; usually market/consumer characteristics or functions. It is conducted for the purposes of describing the characteristics of relevant groups, to estimate the group behaviour, to determine the perceptions of product/service characteristics, and to make specific predictions (Wilson, 1996).

In the present study, the profile of the respondents, their behaviour towards infrastructural facilities and the related aspects, association between their profile and behaviour; and their perception are analysed.

Sampling Framework of the Study

Since the study focuses on the population at Chennai Corporation, the population at Chennai Corporation alone have been included for the study. The sample size is determined as 0.1 per cent of the total population. The determined sample size is distributed to various zones in Chennai Corporation at the proportionate rate. The distribution of sample, their response rate and final sample selected for the analysis are given in Table 1.3.

Table 1.3 : Population, selected, responded and fully responded samples in Chennai city

Sl. No.	Zone	Wards	Total Population	Sample (0.1% on population)	Response rate in per cent	Responded sample	Reusable Questionnaires (Sample)
1.	I	1 to 13	4,10,336	410	32.33	133	74
2.	II	14 to 31	3,75,687	376	24.27	91	65
3.	III	32 to 49	4,59,563	460	23.04	106	81
4.	IV	50 to 63	4,96,777	497	24.57	113	69
5.	V	64 to 78	5,42,132	542	24.17	131	73
6.	VI	79 to 96	3,40,505	341	25.22	86	56
7.	VII	97 to 113	3,49,213	349	21.20	74	49
8.	VIII	114 to 129	4,66,384	466	24.89	116	51
9.	IX	130 to 141	4,15,335	415	25.30	105	59
10.	X	142 to 155	4,87,713	488	25.41	124	62
		Total	43,436,45	4344	24.84	1079	639

The applied sampling procedure is stratified proportionate random sampling. The zones are treated as 'strata'. The total samples are distributed on the basis of the proportionate population in each zone to the total population. The samples in zones are selected at random from the population at each zone. In total 4344 respondents were selected as the sample of the study. But the response rate on the questionnaire is only 24.84 per cent. It varies from 32.33 per cent to 21.20 per cent. Hence the various aspects related to the product/services have been studied through a pre-structured questionnaire and methodology. Hence the present study is purely descriptive in nature.

Population of the Study

The present study focuses on the population at Chennai city only. The Chennai city covers an area of 174.00 sq.km. The total number of wards in the city is 155 with the population of 43.43 lakhs as per the 2001 census. The entire city is classified into ten zones for administration purposes. The number of wards included in each zones varies from 11 wards to 17 wards. The population at 10 zones are given in Table 1.4:

Table 1.4 : Zonewise population at Chennai city as per 2001 Census

Sl.No.	Zone	Including Wards	Area in sq.km.	Population
1.	I	1 to 13	16.19	4,10,336
2.	II	14 to 31	8.40	3,75,687
3.	III	32 to 49	14.10	4,59,563
4.	IV	50 to 63	20.80	4,96,777
5.	V	64 to 78	25.62	5,42,132
6.	VI	79 to 96	8.24	3,40.505
7.	VII	97 to 113	18.12	3,49,213
8.	VIII	114 to 129	17.66	4,66,384
9.	IX	130 to 141	20.27	4,15,335
10.	X	142 to 155	24.60	4,87,313

Source: Chennai Corporation, 2002

Responded questionnaire is only 1079. Out of the 1079 questionnaire, only 639 are in re-usable form. Hence the sample size included for the analysis of data is 639 respondents.

Construct Development

Since the present study is completely based on the primary data, the data have been collected through the structured and pre-tested questionnaire. The questionnaire has been divided into three important parts. The first part of the questionnaire covers the profile of the respondents and their opinion on the existing drinking water facilities at Chennai. The second part of the questionnaire contains various choice models, the respondents' evaluation of various choice models, their willingness to pay for proposed improved drinking water services and respondents' attitude towards privatization. The third part of the questionnaire includes all aspects related to solid waste management.

The various aspects related to the drinking water and solid waste management systems, variables related to the financial models and the attributes related to privatization are generated with the help of previous studies and the views of experts in the relevant field. After the development of questionnaire, the pre-test has been conducted among 10 each respondents in 10 zones at Chennai city, 10 each officials related to metro water system and SWM system at Chennai city. As per the comments of above-mentioned three groups of people, the necessary modification, corrections, inclusion and deletion have been carried out. The final draft has been prepared for data collection.

Collection of Data

The necessary information for the present study has been collected with the help of pre-structured questionnaire. The addresses of the selected respondents have been collected from the zonal office at Chennai Corporation. In total 4344 questionnaires have been mailed to the selected respondents. The sampled respondents have been given 3 months' time to send their filled-in questionnaire. The initial response is very poor being of 11.68 per cent of the total. A reminder with another questionnaire has been sent to the non-responding samples. Another 3 months, time have been given to collect the filled-in questionnaire. The response rate among the remaining 3837 respondents is only 14.91 per cent. In total, the responded sample size is 1079 respondents. Out of the 1079 respondents, only 639 questionnaires are in reusable format. Hence the sample size included for the present study is only 639 respondents.

Framework of Analysis

The collected data were analysed with the help of appropriate statistical tools. The selected statistical tools and the relevance of its applications are given below:

1. One way analysis of variance

The one-way analysis of variance is applied when the intention variable is in interval scale and the group of samples are more than two. The F-statistics is computed by

$$\text{F-Statistics} = \frac{\text{Variance between groups}}{\text{Variance within groups}}$$

It is compared with the table value of F. In the present study, the one-way ANOVA has been examined to find out the significant difference among the three income groups regarding various aspects related to drinking water management and solid waste management system. The association between the profile variables of the respondents and their perception on various attributes related to drinking water management and solid waste management system has been studied.

2. Exploratory Factor Analysis (EFA)

The EFA is one of the multivariate statistical technique to summarise the identical variables into factors whenever the variables are measured in interval scale. The primary purpose of EFA is data reduction and summarization. The factor model may be represented as:

$$Xi = A_i1F_1+A_{i2}F_2+A_{i3}F_3+.....+A_{im}F_m+V_iU_i$$

Whereas

X_i = i^{th} standardized variable

A_{ij} = Standardised multiple regression coefficient of variable I on common factor 'j'

F = Common factor

V_i = Standardized regression coefficient of variable I on unique factor 'i'

U_i = The unique factor for variable 'i'

M = Number of common factors

The unique factors are uncorrelated with each other and with the common factors (Jacques, 1996)[52]. The common factors themselves can be expressed as linear combinations of the observed variables.

$$F_i= W_{i1}X_1+W_{i2}X_2+.....+W_{ik}X_k$$

Where

F_i = Estimate of ith factor

W_i = Weight or factor score coefficient

$_k$ = Number of variables

In the present study, the EFA has been used to narrate variables related to service quality of existing system in DW and SMW, reasons for WTP, reasons for privatization, reasons for switching and reasons for not willing to pay more.

3. Confirmatory Factor Analysis (CFA)

The Confirmatory Factor Analysis is one of the multivariate techniques to test the validity and reliability of the variables in each factor. It is also used to find out the indices of the model (Dale and Murray 2007)[53] . In the present study, the convergent validity, composite reliability and discriminate validity of the factors extracted by EFA are examined with the help of CFA.

4. Multiple Regression Analysis

To find out the cause and effect relationship between the dependent and independent variables, the multiple regression analysis is used when these two variables are in interval scale. (Draper and Smith, 1998). The fitted regression model is:

$$Y = a + b_1X_1 + b_2X_2 + \ldots\ldots + b_nX_n + e$$

Where

Y = Dependent variable

$X_1, X_2 \ldots Xn$ = Independent variables

$b_1, b_2 \ldots bn$ = Regression coefficient of independent variables

A = Intercept and

e = Error term

The ordinary least square method is followed to fit regression equation. In the present study, the multiple regression analysis has been applied to find out the impact of reasons for switching on the rate of switching and also the impact of independent variables on the willingness on privatization.

5. Multiple Discriminate Analysis

Discriminate Analysis is a technique for analysing data when the intention or dependent variable is categorical and the independent variables are interval in nature (Hain et al., 1999)[54] . When three or more categories are involved it is referred to as multiple discriminate analysis (Khan et al., 1995)[55] . In the present study, the MDA have been administered to exhibit the significant discriminate factors leading to choose the finance model in DW and SWM among the different group of respondents with reference to each of their profile.

Limitation of the Study

Since the present study is based on only primary data, it is subject to the following limitations:

1. Even though, the financial model may be generated by the suppliers' perspective and customers' perspective, the present study covers only the customers' perspective.
2. The financial models developed for Drinking Water and SWM system is completely based on two important models namely choice model and contingent valuation method. The other models and methods are beyond the scope of this study.
3. The response rate among the sampled respondents is very poor. Apart from this the sample size is also very limited; of only 0.1 per cent of the population because of the lack of time and references for full survey.
4. The variables related to the many aspects in DW and SWM systems are generated with the help of previous studies and the views of the experts and officials.
5. For the sake of uniformity, the likert–five-point scale has been adopted to measure the respondents attitudes towards various aspects related to DW and SWM system.
6. The applied statistical tools in the present study may be subjected to its own limitations.

Scheme of the Report

For a neat and clear presentation of the report, the present study has been organized into five chapters.

Chapter-I includes introduction, need for the study, statement of the problem, review of previous studies, research gap, objectives methodology, limitations and scheme of the report.

Chapter-II provides profile of the respondents. It includes behaviour on usage of drinking water, expectation and perception on the metro water supply providers, SERVQUAL scale among the respondents, monthly expenditure on drinking water and the association between the profile of the respondents and their monthly expenditure on drinking water.

Chapter-III explains the willingness-to-pay for improved water service, reasons for higher willingness-to-pay, privatization of drinking water services, degree of willingness to switching over to privatisation and the reasons for switching over to privatisation, evaluation of financial models, factors influencing the choice of the financial model and discriminating factors leading to choose the financial model among various groups in each profile variable.

Chapter-IV reveals the awareness of solid waste management (SWM), expectation and perception on various attributes in SWM system at present, evaluation of various choice models, important pricing methods, willingness to pay for enriched SWM system, privatization of SWM and the discriminating factors to choose the finance model among the various groups in each profile variable.

Chapter V explains the summary of findings, conclusions, policy implications and directions for future research.

REFERENCE

1. *Water Supply and Sanitation* (2002), A WHO-UNICEF sponsored study, Planning Commission of India.
2. *Natural Human Development Report* (2001), Planning Commission, New Delhi, 2001.
3. Ministry of Water Resources (1999), *Water Resources Development Plan of India: Policy and Issues*, New Delhi.

4. *Water Quality Status and Statistics* (1996 & 1997), Central Pollution Control Board, New Delhi, 1999.
5. *Urban Water Supply and Sanitation: South Asia Rural Development Services* (1999), The World Bank and Allied Publishers, New Delhi.
6. Koss, P and Sami Khawaja, M (2001), "The value of water supply reliability in California, A contingent valuation study", *Water Policy*, 3(1), pp. 165-174.
7. Bates, A.J., (2000), "Water as consumed and its impact on the consumer—Do we understand the variables?", *Food and Chemical Toxicology*, 38(1), pp. 29-36.
8. Meens, E.G., Tbrueck, L, Dixm, A, Manning, J. Miles, and Patrick, R (2002), "Drinking water quality in the New Millennium: The risk of underestimating public perception", *Journal of the American Waterworks Association*, June, pp. 28-33.
9. Falachee, M and Mackae, A.W (1995), "Consumer Appraisal of Drinking Water: Multidimensional Scaling Analysis", *Food Quality and Preference*, 6(1), pp. 327-332.
10. Oestman, E., Schweitzer, L., Tornbulian, P., Corado, A and Suffet, I.H. (2004), "Effects of chlorine and chloramines on earthy and musty odours in drinking water", *Water Science Technology*, 49(3), pp. 153-159.
11. Pirion, P., Mackey, E.D., Suffet, I.H. and Bruchet, A. (2004), "Chlorinous flavour perception in drinking water", *Water Science and Technology*, 49(4), pp. 321-328.
12. Doria, M.F (2006), "Bottled water versus tap water, understanding consumer preferences", *Journal of Water Health*, 12(3), pp. 271-276.
13. Biswas, A.K., Jayatilaka, R and Tortajada, C (2005), "Social perceptions of the impacts of Colombo water supply projects", *A Journal of the Human Environment*, 34(8), pp. 639-644.
14. Consumer Council for Water (2005), "Shaping the consumer council for water: A report by opinion leader research", http:// www.ofwat.gov.uk/ aptrix/ofwat/publish.nsf/attachment by title/ pdf.
15. Ochoa, A.L et al., (1990), "Informe de proyecho Deteccion y control de fugase. Impact de micro medicion en Guaymas, Sonora internal report, Mexican Institute of water technology, jutepec, Morelos, Mexico. http:/ /billioteca.unesco.org.uy/collect/billiote/import/lileros/effcient water/wochoa.html.
16. Candidate Countries Euro barometer (2003), "Consumer's opinions on services of general interest: Public opinion in the acceding and candidate combines", http://ec.europa.eu/publicopinion/archives/ cceb/2003/cceb2003.3sigfullrep-en.pdf.

17. Stenekes, N., Colebatch, H.K., Waite, T.D. and Ashbolt, N.J. (2006), "Risk and governance in water recycling: Public acceptance revisited", *Science, Technology and Human Values*, 31(4), pp. 107-134.

18. Hartley, T.W (2006), "Public perception and participation in water reuse", *Desalination*, 187(6), pp. 115-126.

19. Po, M., Nancarrow, B., Leviston, Z., Porter, N., Syme, G. and Kaercher, J. (2005), "Predicting Community Behaviour in Relation to Wastewater Reuse: What Drives decisions to accept or reject? Melbourne: CSIRO Stenekes, N., Colebatch, H.K., Waite, T.D and Ashbolt, N.J. (2006), "Risk and Governance in water recycling: Public Acceptance revisited", *Science, Technology and Human Values*, 31(4), pp. 107-134.

20. Ntengwe, F.W. (2004), "The impact of consumer awareness of water sector issues on willingness to pay and cost recovery in Zambia", *Physics and Chemistry of the Earth*, 29(15-18), pp. 1301-1308.

21. Hensker, D., Shore, N. and Train, K. (2005), "Households' willingness to pay for water service attitudes", *Environmental and Resource Economics*, 32(4), pp. 509-531.

22. Raje, D.V., Dhobe, P.S and Deshpande, A.W (2002), "Consumer's willingness to pay more for municipal supplied water: a case study". *Ecological Economics*, 42(3), pp. 391-400.

23. David, C and A.B. Inocencio (2001), "Urban Water Pricing: Metro Manila in enhancing and sustaining stakeholders' participation in watershed management", General Technical report services-9, University of the Philippines, Los Banos.

24. Javier, J.A (2001), "The Philippine strategy for improved watershed resources management in enhancing and sustaining stakeholders' participation in watershed management", General Technical report series-9, University of the Philippines, Los Banos.

25. Francisco, H.A. (2002), "Watershed-Based Water Management Strategy: The Missing Link to sustainable water services", Paper presented during the policy forum on water resource management, Philippine Institute for Development Studies.

26. Ebarvia, M.C.M (2003), "Pricing for Groundwater use of Industries in Metro Manila, Philippines", EEPSEA, Research Report. http://203.116.43.77//publications/research1/ACF4D.html.

27. Yasuo Fujita, Ayumi Fujii, Shgeki Farukawa and Takehiko ogawa (2005), "Estimation of willingness to pay for water and sanitation services through contingent valuation method (CVM) – A case study in Iquitos city, The Republic of Peru", *JBICI Review*, No. 11, pp. 59-87.

28. Arrow, K., R. Solow, P.R. Portney, E.E. Leamer, R. Pedner, and H. Schuman (1993), "Report of the NOAA Panel on Contingent valuation", *Federal Register*, 58(10), pp. 4601-4604.
29. Portney (1994), "The contingent valuation debate: why Economists should care", *Journal of Economic Perspectives*, 8(4), pp. 3-17.
30. Pattanayak, S. K, J. C. Yang, C. Agarwal, H.M. Qunatilake, S.J.H. Bandara and T. Ranasinghe (2004), *Water Sanitation and Poverty in Southwest Srilanka.* RTI. International, Durham, N.C.
31. Fewtrell, L, R.B. Kaufmam, D. Kay, W. Enanoria, L. Haller and J.M. Colford (2005), "Water Sanitation, and Hygiene Interventions to reduce Diarrhea in less developed countries: A systematic review and meta-analysis", *Lancet Infections Diseases*, 5(1), pp. 42-52.
32. Gunatilake, H., J.C. Yang, S.K. Pattanayek, and C. Vandenberg (2006), "*Willingness to pay studies for designing water supply and sanitation project:* A good practice case study. ERD Technical Note, No.17, Economics and Research Department, Asian Development Bank, Manila. Available: http://www.adb.org/documents/erd/technical-notes/tm019.pdf.
33. Cameron, T.A., G.L. Poe, R.G. Emier and W.D. Schulze (2002), "Alternative non-market value elicitation methods: Are the underlying preferences the same?", *Journal of Environmental Economics and Management*, 44(3), pp. 391-425.
34. Repetto, R., R. Dower, R. Jenkins and J. Geoghegan (1992), "Pay-by the Bag household collection charges to Management solid waste." Resources for the future. Inc. November.
35. Fullerton, D. and T.C. Kinnaman (1996), "Household responses to pricing garbage by the Bag", *American Economic Review*, 86(4), pp. 971-984.
36. Miranda, M.C., J.W. Everett, D. Blume and B.A., Roy (1994), "Market based incentives and Residential Municipal Solid Waste", *Journal of Policy Analysis and Management*, 13(4), pp. 681-698.
37. Van Houtven, G.C and Morris, G.E. (1999), "Household Behaviour under alternative Pay-As-You-Throw Systems for Waste Disposal", *Land Economics*, 75(4), pp. 515-537.
38. Jenkins, R.B (1993), "The Economics of Solid Waste Reduction: The impact of user fees." Edward Elgar.
39. Rechovsky J.D. and S.E. Stone (1994), "Market Incentives to Encourage Household Waste Recycling: Paying for what you throw away", *Journal of Policy Analysis and Management*, 13(1), pp. 120-139.
40. M. Eugenia, C. Bemnagen and Vincent Altez (2004), "Impacts of units pricing of solid waste collection and disposal in Alongapo city, Phillippines", Economy and Environment Program for Southeast Asia, Singapore, Available: www.eepsea.org.

41 Janal Othman (2002), *"Household preferences for solid waste management in Malaysia"*, Department of Agricultural and Resource Economics, Faculty of Economics, University Kebanysan, Malaysia, through http://www.eepsea.org.

42 Gottinger, Hans-Werner (1991), *Economic models and applications of solid waste management*, Germany.

43 Jerkins (1993), *The measurement of Environmental and Resource value. Resources for the future*, Washington, D.C., U.S.A.

44 Bennagen, Eugene and V. Altez (2004), "Impacts of unit pricing of solid waste collection and disposal in Alongapo city," Philippines, EEPSEA Research Report No. 2004-RR4.

45 Cointreau-Levine, Sandra and Prasad Gopalan (2000), "Tools for preparing for private sector participation in Municipal Solid Waste Management, Part III."

46 Laplante, Benoit (2003), "Cost-Sharing for solid waste management", *Economy and Environment: selected readings in the Philippines* (2003), H.A. Francisco and M.S delos Angeles (ed.) Phils: REECS-EEPSEA.

47 Hong, S., R. Adams, and H. Love (1993), "An economic analysis of household recycling of solid wastes: The case of Portland, Oregon", *Journal of Environmental Economics and Management*, 25(2), pp. 136-146.

48 Choe, C and I. Fraser (1999), "An economic analysis of household waste management", *Journal of Environmental Economics and Management*, 38(1), pp. 234-245.

49 Palmer, K. and M. Walls (1997), "Optional policies for solid waste disposal: Taxes, subsidies and standards", *Journal of Public Economics*, 65(2), pp. 193-205.

50 Thomas T. Semon (1996), "Marketing Research needs basic Research", *Marketing News*, 28(6), March, p. 34.

51 Kitaeff, R (1994), "Marketing Research Competencies", *Marketing Research: A Magazine of Management and Applications*, 6(3), Summer, pp. 40-41.

52 Jacques Tacq (1996), *Multivariate Analysis Techniques in Social Science Research*, Thousand Oaks, CA: Sage Publications.

53 Dale Fodness and Rrian Murray (2007), "Passengers' expectations of airport service quality", *Journal of Services Marketing*, 21(7), pp.492-506

54 Joseph Hain, Jr. Ralph. E, Runad L.Tatham and W.C. Black, (1999), *Multivariate Data Analysis with Reading*, 5th ed., Prentice Hall, NJ.

55 Zafar Khan, Sudhir K. Chawla and S. Thomas A Cianciolo (1995), "Multiple Discriminate Analysis: Tool for Effective marketing of Computer Information Systems to Small Business Clients", *Journal of Professional Services Marketing*, 12(2), pp. 153-162.

2 Profile of the Respondents and Their Behaviour on Drinking Water Facilities

The development of any financial model on infrastructure facilities offered by the service provider depends upon the profile of their customers, market conditions, nature of their organization, nature of services offered and primary motive of the service provider (Adamowicz, et al., 1994)[1] . Regarding the provision of drinking water supply and solid waste management, the local government is taking charge of provision of all basic amenities and services. Since the government is a welfare government, the primary motive is welfare maximization but not profit maximization (Benmagen and Altez, 2004)[2] . The pricing of the basic services is a great problem to the local governments today since the demand for the services and monitoring up and the pricing of that service are not at all viable. The Government is struggling hard to provide a better service to their people at minimum price. For that purpose, the local governments get so many grants from the various organizations and invest them on the development of such services to the people. But these grants are just enough to invest on overhead cost involved in these projects. The recurring costs in the provision of service are highly problematic today.

Insanitation is increasing the provision for such basic facilities are a serious concern for the local government. The people are ready to pay more but they are expecting assured services from the concerned authorities. Now, the government is facing problem regarding the identification of optimum 'finance model' for these services (Cointreau, 2000)[3]. This 'optimum finance model' highly depends on the people's attitude towards the existing services; present expectations, willingness to pay for it and their switching behaviour. The aforementioned factors are highly related to the profile of the people (Canson, 1992)[4]. Hence, the present study focuses on the profile of the respondents in Chennai city to provide basic information for developing a finance model on the provision of water supply and solid waste management.

Annual Income among the Respondents

The annual income of the respondents indicates the total income earned by the respondents and their family members from all possible services during the period of a year. Since the annual income of the respondents has its own impact on the expectation, perception on the existing services and also their willingness to pay for the improved service in near future, it is included as one of the profile variables. The distribution of the respondents on the basis of their annual income is given in Table 2.1.

Table 2.1: Distribution of respondents on the basis of their annual income

Sl.No.	Annual Income	Number of Respondents	Percentage to the total
1.	Less than Rs.1 lakh	67	10.49
2.	1 – 2.0	124	19.41
3.	2.01– 4.0	198	30.98
4.	4.01 – 6.0	142	22.22
5.	Above 6.0	108	16.90
	Total	639	100

In total a maximum of 30.98 per cent of the respondents have an annual income of Rs.2.01 lakhs to 4.0 lakhs. It is followed by the respondents with annual income of Rs.4.01 to 6.00 lakhs and Rs.1.0 to 2.0 lakhs which constitutes 22.22 and 19.41 per cent to the total respectively. The number of respondents with an annual income of less than one lakh and above 6.0 lakhs constitutes 10.49 and 16.90 per cent to the total respectively. Respondents with an annual income of Rs.2.0 are treated as Lower Income Groups (LIGs) whereas respondents with an annual income of Rs.2.01 lakhs to 6.00 lakhs are considered as Middle Income Groups (MIGs). The respondents with an annual income of above 6.0 lakhs are classified as Higher Income Groups (HIGs).

Gender of the Respondents

Since the gender of the respondents may have its own influence on the willingness to pay for essential services offered by the local government, it is included as one of the profile variables. In general, the male respondents are ready to pay more for the improved services to be offered by the local government than the females. At the same time, the female respondents have better information on the expectation and perception on the services offered by the local government. The distribution of respondents on the basis of their gender is given in Table 2.2.

Table 2.2 : Gender of the respondents

Sl.No.	Gender	Number of respondents			Total
		LIG	MIG	HIG	
1.	Male	138	215	76	429
2.	Female	53	125	32	210
	Total	44	79	20	143

In total, a maximum of 67.14 per cent of the total respondents are males. The male respondents in LIG, MIG and HIG constitute 72.25, 63.23 and 70.37 per cent of the total of 191, 340 and 108 respondents respectively. It reveals that the majority of the respondents are males in the present study.

Age of the Respondents

The age of the respondents may expose their level of awareness and knowledge on the infrastructural facilities offered by the Government. Usually youngsters are having better idea on these and they also compare the services offered by the service provider at par with the service providers at the international level. In general, the young respondents may easily adjust to any new situation. They like improved services even at higher cost. At the same time, the aged customers may have more experience with the existing service providers. Hence, they may disclose a real picture on the service quality of the service provider. In the present study, the age of the respondents is classified into less than 30 years, 30 to 40, 41 to 50, 51 to 60 and above 60 years. The age range of the respondents is presented in Table 2.3

Table 2.3 : Age of the respondents

Sl.No.	Age (in years)	Number of respondents			Total
		LIG	MIG	HIG	
1.	Less than 30	24	41	11	76
2.	30 – 40	46	68	17	131
3.	41 – 50	61	123	39	223
4.	51 – 60	48	66	22	136
5.	Above 60	12	42	19	73
	Total	191	340	108	639

The important age of the respondents is 41 to 50 and 51 to 60 years which constitutes 34.89 and 21.28 per cent to the total respectively. The respondent aged less than 30 years constitute 11.89 per cent of the total. The important age group among LIG is 41 to 50 and 51 to 60 years, which constitute 31.94 and 25.13 per cent of its total. In the case of MIG, these two are 41 to 50 and 30 to 40 years which constitute 36.18 and 10.64 per cent of its total whereas among the LIG, these two are 41 to 50 and 51 to 60 years which constitute 36.11 and 20.37 per cent of its total respectively.

Nativity of the Respondents

The nativity of the respondents indicates their place of origin before they settled in Chennai city. Even though all respondents are in the Chennai city, their nativity indicates that their years of living at Chennai city have its own influence on their experience with the drinking water facilities and solid waste management facilities offered by the local government. The nativity of the respondents may also influence their attitude towards privatization and willingness-to-pay on the essential services in near future. In the present study, the nativity of the respondents is classified into urban, semi-urban and rural. The details of respondents with different nativity in given in Table 2.4

Table 2.4 : Nativity of the respondents

Sl.No.	Nativity	Number of respondents			Total
		LIG	MIG	HIG	
1.	Urban	32	118	49	199
2.	Semi-Urban	94	109	38	241
3.	Rural	65	113	21	199
	Total	191	340	108	639

The important nativity among the respondents is semi-urban which constitutes 37.72 per cent to the total. The respondents belonging to urban and rural areas constitute 31.14 of the total in each. The most important nativity among the LIGs is Semi-urban which constitutes 49.21 per cent of its total followed by rural which constitutes 34.03 per cent of its total. In the case of MIG, the first two nativities are urban and rural which constitute 34.71 and 33.24 per cent of its total respectively. Among the HIG, these are urban and semi-urban which constitute 45.37 and 35.18 per cent of its total respectively. The analysis reveals that more respondents belong to semi urban areas whereas among the HIG, most of the respondents belong to urban areas.

Occupational Background of the Respondents

Since the occupational background of the respondents is one of the important profiles of the respondents, which may be closely associated with the attitude towards the infrastructural facilities provided by the local government, it is included in the present study. The occupational background may indicate the level of annual income and also the consistency of that income. This may have its own impact on the willingness-to-pay for the drinking water services and solid waste management services offered by the local government. The occupational background in the present study is confined to private employment, government employment, business, agriculture and others.

Table 2.5 : Occupational background of the respondents

Sl.No.	Age (in years)	Number of respondents			Total
		LIG	MIG	HIG	
1.	Private Employment	56	104	29	189
2.	Government Employment	49	88	24	161
3.	Business	43	62	37	142
4.	Agriculture	17	29	6	52
5.	Others	26	57	12	95
	Total	191	340	108	639

Table 2.5 explains that the important occupational background among the respondent are private employment and government employment which constitute 29.58 and 25.19 per cent of the total respectively. The respondents with business background constitute 22.22 per cent of the total. The important occupational backgrounds among the LIGs are private employment and government employment which constitute 29.32 and 25.65 per cent of its total respectively. Among the MIGs, it is also same but it constitutes 30.59 and 25.88 per cent of its total respectively. Among the HIG, these two are business and private employment, which constitute 34.26 and 26.85 per cent of its total respectively.

Family Size of the Respondents

The family size of the respondents represents the number of family members living along with the respondents. Since the family size of the respondent has its own influence on their requirement of basic services and also their attitude towards the services offered, it is included as one of the profile variables. A bigger family size leads to less per capita income which may be one of the influencing factors for their willingness-to-pay for essential services and vice-versa. The family size of the respondents in the present study is confined to upto 3, 4 to 5, 6 to 7, and above 7 members. The distribution of respondents on the basis of their family size is given in Table 2.6

Table 2.6 : Family size of the respondents

Sl.No.	Family Size	Number of respondents			Total
		LIG	MIG	HIG	
1.	Upto 3 members	54	78	39	171
2.	4-5 members	81	166	51	298
3.	6-7 members	29	83	10	122
4.	Above 7 members	27	13	8	48
	Total	191	340	108	639

The important family size of the respondents is 4 to 5 and upto 3 members, which constitute 46.64 and 26.70 per cent of the total respectively. The number of respondents with the family size of above 7 members constitutes 7.51 per cent of the total. The first two family sizes among all three groups of respondents are 4 to 5 and upto 3 members. In the case of LIG, these two constitute 42.41 and 28.27 per cent of its total respectively whereas in the case of MIG, these two constitute 48.82 and 22.94 per cent of its total respectively. Among the HIG, these two constitutes 47.22 and 36.11 per cent of its total respectively. The analysis reveals that the important family size of the respondents is 4 to 5 and upto 3 members.

Number of Earning Members Per Family

This analysis indicates the distribution of total earning members per family among the respondents. The higher number of earning members results in higher family income and standard of living. The higher standard of living of the respondents may have its own influence on the expectation and perception on the service offered by the providers and also their willingness-to-pay for better services offered by the service providers. Hence, the number of earning members per family has been included as one of the profile variables. It is confined to one, two and more than two. The distribution of respondents on the basis of the number of family members per family is illustrated in Table 2.7.

Table 2.7 : Number of earning members per family

Sl.No.	Number of earning members	Number of respondents			Total
		LIG	MIG	HIG	
1.	One	72	106	21	199
2.	Two	82	193	68	343
3	More than two	37	41	19	97
	Total	191	340	108	639

In total, a maximum of 53.68 per cent of the total respondents are having two earning members per family which is followed by 31.14 per cent of the respondents with only one earning member in their family. The first two numbers of earning members per family among LIG, MIG and HIG are two and one. These two constitute 42.93 and 37.69 per cent of the total in LIG whereas in MIG, these two constitute 56.76 and 31.18 per cent of its total respectively. Among the HIG, these two constitute 62.96 and 19.44 per cent of its total respectively. The analysis reveals that the most important earning members per family are two.

House Ownership among the Respondents

Since the ownership of the house among the respondents has its own influence on the level of expectation and perception on the services offered by the local government especially drinking water and solid waste management, it is included as one of profile variables. The respondents with own house may differ from the respondents living in rented house. Respondents are categorized as owners, lessees and tenants. The distribution of respondents on the basis of their house occupation is given in Table 2.8.

Table 2.8 : House ownership among the respondents

Sl. No.	House Ownership	Number of respondents			Total
		LIG	MIG	HIG	
1.	Owned house	19	169	65	253
2.	Leased	24	68	31	123
3.	Rent	148	103	12	263
	Total	191	340	108	639

In total, a maximum of 41.16 per cent of the respondents are living in rented house, which is followed by 39.59 per cent of the respondents with owned house. The majority of respondents among LIG live in rented houses, which constitutes 77.49 per cent of the total. Among the MIG, it is owned house which constitutes 49.71 per cent of its total whereas among HIG, it is also owned house which constitutes 60.19 per cent of its total. The analysis reveals that the majority of the respondents live in rented and owned houses.

Type of House among the Respondents

The type of house indicates the nature of the house where the respondents were living at the time of interview. Since the type of house may determine the need level of basic amenities like drinking water and solid waste management among the respondents, it is included as one of the profile variables. The type of house in the present study is classified into individual house and apartments. Since the need of essential services for the resident of these two types of houses are different, it is taken into account in Table 2.9.

Table 2.9 : Type of House among the respondents

Sl. No.	Type of House	Number of respondents			Total
		LIG	MIG	HIG	
1.	Individual	68	126	64	258
2.	Apartments	123	214	44	381
	Total	191	340	108	639

Table 2.9 explains the distribution of respondents on the basis of their type of accommodation. The important type of accommodation among the respondents is 'apartments' which constitutes 59.62 per cent of the total. The most important type of accommodation among LIG and MIG is apartments. Among the LIGs, it constitutes 64.39 per cent of its total whereas among the MIG, it constitutes 62.94 per cent of its total. Among the HIG, it is individual house which constitutes 59.29 per cent of its total. The analysis reveals that the important type of accommodation among the respondents is 'apartments'.

Drinking Water Pipe Connection among the Respondents

It represents the number of pipe connections for drinking water owned by the respondents at their residence. Since the number of water pipe connection may have its own influence on the willingness-to-pay for improved service to be offered by the local governments, it is included as one of the profile variables in the present study. The number of pipe connection is categorised into one, two, three and more than three. The distribution of respondents on the basis of the number of pipe connections is shown in Table 2.10.

Table 2.10 : Drinking water pipe connection among the respondents

Sl.No.	Number of water pipe connection	Number of respondents			Total
		LIG	MIG	HIG	
1.	One	123	114	55	292
2.	Two	56	159	36	251
3.	Three	12	41	10	63
4.	More than three	—	26	7	33
	Total	191	340	108	639

In total, a maximum of 45.69 per cent of the respondents have only one water pipe connection at their residence. It is followed by those respondents with two pipe connections which constitute 39.28 per cent of the total. The most important number of water pipe connection among the LIG is one which constitutes 64.39 per cent of its total whereas among the MIG, it is two pipe connections which constitutes 46.76 per cent of its total. Among the HIGs, it is one pipe connection which constitutes 50.93 per cent of its total. The analysis reveals that the important number of water pipe connection among the respondents is only one.

Means used to get Drinking Water

The local government supplies water only for drinking purposes through pipe line. Because of lesser pressure, some areas are not getting adequate water through pipe line. Hence, they are using stand pipe and trucks for getting their drinking water. If this water is not sufficient, some people use bore water for drinking and cooking purposes also. Since people are using more than one source, the multi-response is alloy. In the present analysis, the means used to get drinking water is confined to pipe, stand pipe, truck and bore-well. The distribution of respondents on the basis of their source used to get drinking water is given in Table 2.11.

Table 2.11 : Means used to get drinking wat er among the Respondents

Sl. No.	Means	Number of respondentsT			otal
		LIG	MIG	HIG	
1.	Pipe	114	262	105481	481
2.	Stand pipe	91	108	36235	235
3.	Truck	102	29	–131	131
4.	Borewell	73	271	108452	452
	Total	380	670	249	1299

At the maximum 75.27 per cent of the respondents use pipe line as their source to get the water supply. The number of respondents who use bore-well water constitutes 70.74 per cent of the total. The number of respondents who use the stand pipe as means to get water constitutes 36.78 per cent of the total. In total, the respondents use two sources to get the drinking water. The LIG use 1.99 tools whereas the MIG use 1.97 tools. The HIG use 2.31 tools to get the water. The analysis reveals that the respondents depend not only on pipeline connection to get their drinking water but also some other means to get it.

Frequency of Water Supply

In order to analyse the frequency of water supply offered by the local government in Chennai, the present study has made an attempt to analyse the frequency of water supply. The respondents were asked to mention the frequency of supplies from their present service provider. The frequency is confined to daily, once in two days, once in three days and irregular. The distribution of respondents based on their views on frequency of water supply they got from the service provider is presented in Table 2.12.

Table 2.12 : Frequency of water supply

Sl. No.	Means	Number of respondents			Total
		LIG	MIG	HIG	
1.	Daily	26	63	14	103
2.	Once in two days	62	72	27	161
3.	Once in three days	17	114	28	159
4.	Irregular	86	91	39	216
	Total	191	340	108	639

At the maximum 33.80 per cent of the respondents say that they are getting irregular drinking water supply from their existing service provider. It is followed by 25.19 per cent of the respondents maintaining that they are getting drinking water once in two days. The number of respondents who are getting daily water supply constitutes 16.12 per cent of the total. The most important frequency of water supply among the LIG and HIG is irregular which constitutes 45.03 and 36.11 per cent of the total of LIG and HIG respectively. Among the MIG, it is once in three days which constitutes 33.53 per cent to its total. The analysis reveals that majority of the respondents are getting only irregular water supply from their existing service provider.

Water Availability per Week

The water availability to the respondents was measured in terms of hours. In total, per week, there are 168 hours. The respondents are asked to mention the total number of hours they are getting drinking water from their service provider per week. The hours of water supply are classified upto 48 hours, 48.01 to 84.0, 84.01 to 120, 120.01 to 168 and above 168 hours. The distribution of respondents on the basis of their water availability per week is given in Table 2.13.

Table 2.13 : Water availability per week in hours

Sl. No.	Weekly water availability in hours	Number of respondents			Total
		LIG	MIG	HIG	
1.	Upto 48	82	58	19	159
2.	48.01 to 84	49	167	41	257
3.	84.01 to 120	42	83	36	161
4.	120.01 to 168	18	32	12	62
5.	Above 168 hours	—	—	—	—
	Total	191	340	108	639

A maximum of 40.22 per cent of the respondents say that they get water from 48.01 to 84.00 hours per week. It is followed by 84.01 to 120 hours and upto 48.00 hours which constitute 25.19 and 24.88 per cent of the total respectively. A maximum of 42.93 per cent of LIG residents view that the availability of water is only upto 48 hours whereas 49.12 per cent of MIG residents maintain that the availability of water is from 48.01 to 84 hours per week. Among the HIG, a maximum of 37.96 per cent say that the weekly availability of water is from 48.01 to 84.00 hours. No respondents are of the opinion that there is an availability of water throughout 24 hours.

Tariff on Drinking Water

The local government imposes drinking water tariff on the users at two different bases namely based on meter and flat rate. Under the meter system, the tariff is imposed on the basis of the quantum of water consumed. Under the flat rate system, the tariff is imposed on a flat rate irrespective of the quantum of water consumed by the respondents. The distribution of respondents on the basis of their tariff system is given in Table 2.14.

Table 2.14 : Tariff on drinking water

Sl. No.	Tariff base	Number of respondents			Total
		LIG	MIG	HIG	
1.	Based on meter reading	52	228	69	349
2.	Flat rate	139	112	39	290
	Total	191	340	108	639

In total, a maximum of 54.62 per cent of the respondents are paying on the basis of the meter reading. The remaining 45.38 per cent of the respondents are paying only a flat rate for drinking water. The most important tariff system among LIG is flat rate whereas among MIG and HIG, it is based on 'meter reading' which constitutes 67.05 and 63.89 per cent of its total respectively.

Years of Experience with Metro Water System

Experience with the services offered by the local government is represented by number of years, since the years of experience among the respondents may present clear picture of their level of expectation and perception on the services offered by the existing service provider. It also reveals their future expectations and their willingness-to-pay for the proposed enriched service. The years of experience in using the service of metro water supply is classified as less than 3, 3 to 6, 7 to 10 years and above 10 years. The distribution of respondents on the basis of their years of experience is illustrated in Table 2.15.

Table 2.15 : Years of experience in using metro water

Sl. No.	Years of Experience	Number of respondents			Total
		LIG	MIG	HIG	
1.	Less than 3 years	6	32	11	49
2.	3 - 6	29	117	32	178
3.	7 - 10	87	102	31	220
4.	Above 10 years	69	89	34	192
	Total	191	340	108	639

In total, a maximum of 34.43 per cent of the respondents have an experience of 7 to 10 years, followed by 30.05 per cent of the respondents with an experience of above 10 years. The number of respondents with less than 3 years of experience constitutes 7.67 per cent of the total. The most important years of experience among LIG is 7 to 10 years which constitutes 45.55 per cent of the total whereas among MIG, it is 3 to 6 years constituting 34.41 per cent of the total. Among the HIG, it is above 10 years which constitutes 31.48 per cent of the total. The analysis reveals that majority of the respondents have an experience of above 6 years in using the metro water.

Usage of Metro Water among the Respondents

The local government supplies drinking water to the people. Because of the cheaper price and flat rate system, the people are using this water for many purposes. This might be one of the important reasons for irregularity in water supply. Hence the present analysis has made an attempt to analyse the nature of metro water usage among the respondents. The usage of water is confined to only drinking, drinking and bathing and all purposes. The distribution of respondents on the basis of their usage of metro water is presented in Table 2.16.

A maximum of 47.89 per cent of the respondents are using the metro water for all purposes. It is followed by 33.65 per cent of the respondents who use it for drinking and bathing purposes. Only 18.46 per cent of the respondents are using

Table 2.16 : Usage of metro water among the respondents

Sl. No.	Usage	Number of respondents			Total
		LIG	MIG	HIG	
1.	Only drinking	23	74	21	118
2.	Drinking and bathing	66	106	43	215
3.	All purposes	102	160	44	306
	Total	191	340	108	639

the metro water exclusively for drinking purpose. The first types usage of metro water among LIG, MIG and HIGs are all purpose, drinking and bathing. Among the LIG, it constitutes 53.40 and 34.55 per cent of the total respectively. Whereas among MIG, these two constitutes 47.06 and 31.18 per cent of the total respectively. Among the HIG, these two constitute 40.74 and 39.81 per cent of the total respectively. This analysis reveals that the respondents are using drinking water for all purposes.

Respondents Opinion on other Important Sources of Drinking Water

The respondents are using not only the metro water from their pipe line but also several other sources of drinking water because of the scarcity and poor quality of water. Even though there are several other sources of drinking water, the present study confines it to buying from neighbours, buying through tanker supplies, engagement of labour to carry water, buying of bottled water and own borewell. The respondents are asked to rate the above-said sources of drinking water at five-point scale according to their order of importance. The assigned marks on these scales are from 5 to 1 respectively. The mean score of each source of water have been computed to exhibit the importance of other sources of drinking water.

The Table 2.17 explains the mean score of other sources of drinking water apart from pipe line. The important other sources of water among LIGs, is buying from neighbours and

Table 2.17 : Opinion on other important sources of drinking water

Sl. No.	Sources of Drinking Water	Meam score Total			
		LIG	MIG	HIG	
1.	Buying from neighbours	3.8414	3.0869	2.6165	3.3344*
2.	Buying through tanker supplies	3.6503	2.4608	2.3302	3.4191*
3.	Engagement of labour to carry water	2.0239	3.3095	3.6165	3.5103*
4.	Buying of bottled water	2.3967	3.8183	4.0664	3.6661*
5.	Own borewell	2.7114	3.9214	3.8145	2.5108

* Significant at five per cent level.

buying through tanker supplies since its mean scores are 3.8414 and 3.6503. Among the MIG, these sources are own borewell and bottled water since their mean scores are 3.9214 and 3.8183 respectively. Among the HIG, these important sources of drinking water are bottled water and own borewell since their mean scores are 4.0664 and 3.8145 respectively. Regarding the importance given to other sources of drinking water, the significant difference among the three income groups of respondents has been identified in the case of buying from neighbours, buying through tanker supplies, engagement of labour to carry water and buying of bottled water since their respective 'F' statistics are significant at five per cent level.

Frequency of using Bottled Water among the Respondents

Now-a-days, the consumption of bottled water for drinking purposes has been increasing at faster rate especially in metro cities. The frequency of consumption of the bottled water indicates the people's capacity to buy such drinking water. Hence, the present study has made an attempt to analyse the frequency consumption of bottled drinking water among the respondents. The respondents are asked to identify among the very frequent, frequent, ordinary, rare and very rare. The distribution of respondents on the basis of their frequency of using of bottled water is given in Table 2.18.

Table 2.18 : Frequency of using bottled water

Sl. No.	Frequency	Number of respondents			Total
		LIG	MIG	HIG	
1.	Very frequent	—	42	74	116
2.	Frequent	3	163	29	195
3.	Ordinary	11	104	5	120
4.	Rare	36	31	—	67
5.	Very rare	141	—	—	141
	Total	191	340	108	639

The important frequencies of consumption of bottled water among the respondents are frequent and ordinary which constitute 30.52 and 18.78 per cent of the total respectively. The number of respondents who are frequently using the bottled water constitutes 18.15 per cent to the total. The most important frequency of usage of bottled water among LIG is very rare which constitutes 73.82 per cent to its total whereas among MIG, it is frequent and ordinary which constitutes 47.94 and 30.59 per cent of the total respectively. Among the HIGs, these are very frequent and frequent which constitutes 68.51 and 26.85 per cent of the total respectively. The analysis reveals that the MIG and LIG are using more bottled water for the drinking purposes than the LIG.

Reasons for Buying Bottled Water by the Respondents

The respondents may purchase and consume bottled drinking water for several reasons. It is highly imperative to analyse the reasons for some policy implications. Even though the reasons for buying bottled water are too many, the present study confines these reasons to lack of confidence on metro water, non-availability of metro water, higher consumption, accessibility of bottled water, branding of bottled water, convenient mode of buying, quality of water, affordability and status. The respondents are asked to rate the above-said reasons at five point scale. The mean scores of the reasons have been computed among the LIG, MIG and HIG separately. The results are presented in Table 2.19.

Table 2.19 : Reasons for buying bottled water

Sl. No.	Reasons	Mean score			F-Statistics
		LIG	MIG	HIG	
1.	Lack of confidence in metro water	2.6114	3.5127	3.8234	3.4143*
2.	Non availability of metro water	3.3445	3.6943	3.9906	0.9226
3.	Higher consumption	3.0113	3.7021	2.6617	3.2144
4.	Accessibility to bottled water	2.6037	3.5919	2.8024	3.3919*
5.	Branding of bottled water	1.8664	2.8114	3.5617	3.9642*
6.	Convenient mode of buying	2.1457	3.0667	3.8673	3.8081*
7.	Quality of water	2.6163	3.5614	3.9166	3.1144*
8.	Affordability	2.0336	2.9917	3.8994	3.9331*
9.	Status	1.6651	2.4103	3.9332	4.1718*

* Significant at five per cent level

The important reasons for buying the bottled water among the LIG is non-availability of metro water and higher consumption since their respective mean scores are 3.3445 and 3.0113. Among the MIG, these reasons are higher consumption and non-availability of metro water since their respective mean scores are 3.7021 and 3.6943. Among the HIG, these reasons are non-availability of metro water and status since their respective mean scores are 3.9906 and 3.9332. Regarding the perception on the reasons for buying the bottled water, the significant differences among three income groups are the perception on lack of confidence on metro water, accessibility of bottled water, branding of bottled water, convenient mode of buying, quality of water, affordability and status since their respective 'F' statistics are significant at five per cent level. In total, the HIG are giving more weightage on the reasons for buying the bottled water for their drinking purposes than the MIG and LIG.

Respondents' Expectation from Metro Water Services

The respondent's attitude towards the current service on drinking water can be measured with the help of their expectation from the service provider and also their perception on the services offered by the service provider. (Teas, 1994[5], Lehtimen and Lehtimen, 1991[6]). Even though the respondents are expecting too many services and attributes from their service providers, the present study reduces them to 17 variables. These are nominal bill, regular water supply, sufficient water supply, pressure of water supply, problem-free pipeline non-mixing of sewage water, non-defective meter, reliability of water service, prompt response from the officials, assurance of service, emphasized service, customer care, colour of the water, taste of the water, treatment of water, time taken for installation of water connection and complaint handling. The respondents are to rate the above-said 17 variables at five-point scale on the basis of their level of expectation. The assigned marks on these scales are from 5 to 1 respectively. The mean scores on the level of expectation on the variables among the LIG, MIG and HIG have been computed separately. The significant difference among the three groups of respondents on their level of expectation on the variables has been computed with the help of one way analysis of variance. The results are given in Table 2.20.

The expectation variables regarding the drinking water supply among the LIG are regular water supply and responsiveness of the officials since their respective mean scores are 3.9088 and 3.8973. Among the MIG these are complaint handling and sufficient water supply since their respective mean scores are 4.1084 and 3.9104. Among the HIG, these variables are reliability of water service and non-defective meter and their respective mean scores are 4.2017 and 4.1764. Regarding the level of expectation on drinking water services, the significant difference among the three income groups has been noticed in the case of nominal bill, non-defective meter and assured service since their respective

'F' statistics are significant at five per cent level. Regarding the level of expectation, the HIGs are expecting more from their service providers compared to the other two income groups.

Table 2.20 : Expectation from metro water services

Sl. No.	Preferences	Means score			Total
		LIG	MIG	HIG	
1.	Nominal bill	3.8916	3.0144	2.6167	3.4433*
2.	Regular water supply	3.9088	3.3473	3.8226	0.6637
3.	Sufficient water supply	3.6617	3.9104	3.9907	0.5133
4.	Pressure of water supply	3.3309	3.7176	3.9883	1.2768
5.	Problem-free pipeline	2.5673	3.0442	3.5684	2.6162
6.	Non-mixing of sewage water	3.1144	3.8186	3.9445	2.4561
7.	Non-defective meter	2.8667	3.9092	4.1764	3.1782*
8.	Reliability of water service	3.6113	3.8997	4.2017	1.8184
9.	Prompt response from the officials	3.8973	4.1140	4.0889	2.1993
10.	Assurance of service	3.4142	3.7337	4.1142	1.9336
11.	Emphasis on service	2.9098	3.5664	4.0117	3.0669*
12.	Customer care	3.6163	3.8224	4.1226	1.5142
13.	Colour of the water	2.9394	3.4209	3.8118	1.6334
14.	Taste of the water	3.0246	3.6168	3.8004	2.0069
15.	Treatment of water	3.1147	3.9039	3.8917	1.8919
16.	Time taken for installation of water connection	2.9903	3.8181	3.6942	2.1446
17.	Complaint handling	3.2045	4.1084	3.9343	0.9168

Important Expectations among the Respondents

The important expectations on drinking water services among the respondents have been analysed using Exploratory Factor Analysis (EFA). The score on level of expectation on 17 variables have been included for the analysis. Initially, the test of validity of data for factor analysis has been conducted with the help of Kaiser-Meyer-Ohlin (KMO) measure of sampling adequacy and Bartletts test of sphericity. The minimum acceptable level of KMO measure is 0.5 whereas the minimum acceptable level of significance of chi-Square value is at five per cent level (Rao and Sahia, 2006[7] and Nunnally, 1978[8]). In the present study, the validity of data for factor analysis has been tested initially. Both the measures satisfy the test of validity. The executed EFA analysis results reveal six important expectations (factors). The variables included in each factor, its reliability, eigen value and the per cent of variation explained by the factors are summarized in Table 2.21

Table 2.21 : Important expectation from metro water services

Sl. No.	Important Expectation	Number of variables	Crownbach alpha.	Eigen value	Per cent of variation explained	Cummulative per cent of variation explained
1.	Quality of water	3	0.7368	4.4089	16.81	16.81
2.	Water supply	3	0.7661	3.6611	14.04	30.85
3.	Service quality	4	0.8144	2.9337	12.52	43.37
4.	Problem-maintenance	3	0.7069	2.0441	10.34	53.74
5.	Customer care	2	0.6911	1.5693	8.45	62.19
6.	Price	2	0.7214	1.0344	6.31	68.50
KMO: Measure of Sampling Adequacy: 0.7314				Bartletts test of sphericity: chi-Square:89.08*		

* Significant at five per cent level.

The narrated six important factors explain the included 17 variables to the extent of 68.50 per cent. The most important expectation among the respondents is 'Quality of water'. It consists of three variables with reliability coefficient of 0.7368. It reveals that the included six variables explain this factor to the extent of 73.68 per cent. The eigen value and the per cent of variation explained by this factor are 4.4089 and 16.81 per cent respectively. The second and third important factors are water supply and service quality and their respective eigen values are 3.6611 and 2.9337. The variations explained by these two factors are 14.04 and 12.52 per cent respectively. The 'water supply and service quality' factors consist of three and four variables with the reliability coefficient of 0.7661 and 0.8144 respectively.

The next two factors identified by the factor analysis are 'problem maintenance and customer care' and their respective eigen values are 2.0441 and 1.5693. These two factors consist of three and two variables with the reliability coefficient of 0.7069 and 0.6911 respectively. The last factor identified by the factor analysis is 'price' factor. It consists of two variables with the reliability coefficient of 0.7214. The factor analysis result in six important expectations on 'drinking water supply' among the respondents for further analysis.

Reliability and Validity of the Important Expectation

The reliability and validity of the variables in all six factors have been examined with the help of Confirmatory Factor Analysis (CFA). The convergent validity and composite reliability of the variables in each factor have been computed to exhibit the level of reliability and validity. The scale convergent validity is related to the high association between the new construct and other similar constructs. If the 't' statistics of the standardized factor loading of the variables in the factor is at the maximum of five per cent level, the convergent validity is assured. (Anderson and Gerhing 1988)[9]. The composite validity indicates the interval consistency demonstrated where the values for all constructs were above the suggested threshold of 0.7 (Fornell and Larcker, 1981)[10]. The more conservative proportion of variance extracted indices indicates the amount of variance captured by a construct in relation to the amount of variance due to the measurement error, demonstrated high validity (Gi et al., 2002)[11]. In the present study, CFA generated via Lisrel 8 (Joreskog and Sor bom, 1993)[12] was used to examine the dimensionality of the service quality of service provider and to analyse the reliability and validity of the measures. The results are given in Table 2.22.

Table 2.22 : Results of confirmatory factor analysis

Sl. No.	Important Expectations	Range of standardized factor loading	Range of 't' statistics	Composite reliability	Average variance extracted
1.	Quality of water	0.6814-0.9124	6.4517*-15.0173*	0.8184	61.44
2.	Water supply	0.6342-0.9317	6.0334*-16.5172*	0.8686	66.05
3.	Service Quality	0.7217-0.9044	6.9907*-14.9108*	0.9134	73.11
4.	Problem-maintenance	0.6459-0.9331	6.1441*-15.0017*	0.7451	57.39
5.	Customer Care	0.6708-0.8919	7.2344*-13.1442*	0.7334	57.42
6.	Price	0.7149-0.9441	8.6911*-17.3342*	0.8346	64.33

* Significant at five per cent level.

The standardized factor loading of the variables in each factor varies from 0.6342 to 0.9441 which are significant at five per cent level. It reveals that there is a convergent validity of each construct and its components. The composite validity of the variables in each factor is greater than 0.7451 which indicates better composite validity. The average variance extracted by each factor varies from 39.39 per cent to 63.11 per cent. The discriminate validity has been examined with the help of inter-correlation between the factors. The discriminate validity has been analysed to show whether the factors are mutually exclusive. The resulting inter-correlation coefficient between the factors are presented in Table 2.23.

Table 2.23 : Inter-relationship between important expectations from metro water service

Factors	Quality of water	Water supply	Service quality	Problem maintenance	Customer care	Price
Quality of water		-0.1417	0.1802	0.2417	-0.2145	-0.1334
Water supply			-0.2617	0.1334	0.1093	0.1667
Service Quality				-0.2142	0.1393	-0.1561
Problem maintenance					-0.2144	0.1091
Customer care						-0.2049
Price						

Higher positive correlation is identified between the quality of water and problem maintenance since its correlation coefficient is 0.2417, whereas higher negative correlation is noticed in the case of water supply and service quality since their respective correlation coefficient is -0.2617. No correlation coefficient is significant at five per cent level. It indicates the discriminate validity of the factors. It shows that the narrated factors are mutually exclusive.

Level of Expectation on Important Factors

The level of expectation on each factor identified by the factor analysis has been computed by the mean score of the level of expectation on the variables in each factor. The mean scores on the level of expectation on all six factors among the LIG, MIG and HIG have been computed separately to exhibit the level of expectation on the factors among the three income groups. Regarding the level of expectation, the significant difference among the three income groups of respondents has been analysed with the help of one way analysis of variance. The results are presented in Table 2.24.

Table 2.24 : Level of expectation on important services of metro water supply

Sl. No.	Important Expectations	Mean score			F-Statistics
		LIG	MIG	HIG	
1.	Quality of water	3.0262	3.6472	3.8346	2.5165
2.	Water supply	3.6338	3.6584	3.9339	0.7338
3.	Service quality	3.4581	3.8285	4.1041	2.0663
4.	Problem-maintenance	2.8907	3.5603	3.7357	1.5661
5.	Customer care	3.4104	3.9654	4.0284	1.3083
6.	Price	3.3792	3.4618	3.3966	0.3616

The highly expected factors among the LIG is water supply and service quality since their mean scores are 3.6338 and 3.4589 respectively. Among the MIG, these factors are customer care and service quality since its mean scores are 3.9654 and 3.8285 respectively. The highly expected factors among the HIG residents are service quality and customer care since their mean scores are 4.1041 and 4.0284 respectively. Regarding the level of expectation, no significant difference among the three income groups has been identified in anyone of the factors. The analysis reveals that all income groups of customers expect at the same level. Even though the HIG group expects more than the MIG and LIG, there is significant difference among the three groups regarding their level of expectation on all six factors.

Level of Perception on Factors among the Respondents

The level of perception on the six important factors among the respondent has been computed by the mean score of the perception on the variables involved in each factor. The mean scores of the perception on six factors among the LIG, MIG and HIG have been computed separately to exhibit the level of perception on the factors among the different income groups. Regarding the level of perception on important factors, the significant difference among the three groups has been examined with the help of one way analysis of variance.

Table 2.25 : Level of perception on important services of metro water supply

Sl.No.	Important services	Mean score			F-Statistics
		LIG	MIG	HIG	
1.	Quality of water	2.4145	2.8616	2.4142	0.8185
2.	Water supply	2.0865	2.3444	2.9044	2.9968*
3.	Service Quality	3.1414	2.6165	2.8816	1.3304
4.	Problem-maintenance	2.6085	2.3441	2.9197	1.9193
5.	Customer care	2.5146	2.8184	2.7614	0.9465
6.	Price	3.4496	3.5336	3.5108	0.4331

* Significant at five per cent level

Table 2.25 explains the level of perception on six important factors related to the drinking water supply among three income group of respondents. The highly valued factors among the LIG is price and service quality since their respective mean scores are 3.4496 and 3.1414 whereas among MIG, these two are price and quality of water. Among the HIG, these two are price and problem maintenance since their respective mean scores are 3.5108 and 2.9197. Regarding the perception on the important services (factors) the significant difference among the three income groups has been identified in the case of water supply since their respective 'F' statistics is significant at five per cent level.

Gap between the Perception and Expectation on Factors

The difference between the perception and expectation of the services among the respondents has been measured to identify the gap between these elements. In the services marketing, this gap is called as SERVQUAL scale (Babakus and Boller, 1992[13]; Parasuraman et al., 1991[14] and Teas, 1994[15]). The mean of SERVQUAL may be positive or negative. The negative SERVQUAL scale indicates that the respondents are not satisfied upto their level of expectation on the drinking water services offered by the service provider. The 'SERVQUAL Scale' on six important factors among LIG, MIG and HIG has been computed separately to exhibit the level of gap between perception and expectation on the factors. Regarding the 'SERVQUAL scale', the significant difference among the three income group of respondents has been analysed with the help of one way analysis of variance. The results are given in Table 2.26.

Table 2.26 : Gap between perception and expectation on important services of metro water supply

Sl. No.	Important services	Mean score			F-Statistics
		LIG	MIG	HIG	
1.	Quality of water	-0.6117	-.7856	-1.4204	2.9996*
2.	Water supply	-1.5473	-1.3140	-1.0295	0.7334
3.	Service Quality	-0.3167	-1.2120	-1.2225	3.8441*
4.	Problem-maintenance	-0.2822	-1.2162	-0.8160	4.1736*
5.	Customer care	-0.8958	-1.1470	-1.2670	2.1632
6.	Price	-0.0704	0.0718	0.1142	0.8142

* Significant at five per cent level.

All SERVQUAL scales on all six factors except the price are in negative among all three group of respondents. It reveals that the respondents are satisfied with the price fixed by the service provider compared to their level of expectation. But in all other cases, they are not satisfied upto their level of expectation. Among the LIG, the higher SERVQUAL scale is noticed in the case of water supply and customer care since their respective SERVQUAL scales are –1.5473 and -0.8958 whereas among the MIG, these two are noticed in the case of water supply and problem maintenance and service quality since their respective mean scores are –1.3140 and -1.2162. Among the HIG, these two are identified in quality of water and customer care since their mean scores are 1.4204 and –1.2670 respectively. Regarding the SERVQUAL scale, the significant difference among the three income groups has been noticed in the case of quality of water, service quality and problem maintenance since their respective 'F' statistics are significant at five per cent level. The analysis reveals that all three groups of respondents are not satisfied upto their level of expectation on first five important services except the price.

Association between the Profile of Respondents and their SERVQUAL Scale

The profile of the respondents may have its own influence on their level of perception and expectation on important services (factors) related to drinking water supply. In order to analyse the association between the profile of respondents and their SERVQUAL scale, the one way analysis of variance has been executed. The included profile variables are gender, age, nativity, occupational background, family size, number of earning members per family, houseownership, type of house, number of water pipe connections and frequency of water supply availed. The important services focused are quality of water, water supply, service quality, problem maintenance, customer care and price. The result of one way analysis of variance are shown in Table 2.27.

Regarding the SERVQUAL scale on the quality of water, the significant difference among the respondents has been identified when they are classified on the bases of their age, nativity, occupational background, family size, number of

Table 2.27 : Association between profile of respondents and the gap between their perception and expectation

Profile Variables	F-Statistics					
	Quality of water	Water supply	Service quality	Problem maintenance	Customer care	Price
Gender	2.4568	3.1454	2.6672	3.9196*	1.8641	4.1446*
Age	3.1731*	2.8606*	2.8144*	2.6162*	2.4508*	3.0818*
Nativity	3.0866*	3.1443*	3.3086*	2.0344	1.9933	2.1146
Occupational background	2.8186*	1.8284	3.6562*	3.4146*	2.5186*	2.8083*
Family size	3.0811	3.6146*	2.8184*	2.0844	1.8863	2.3081
Number of earning members	3.1146*	2.9909*	2.0862	1.4546	2.0233	1.9196
House-ownership	3.2144*	2.0866	2.1144	1.8969	2.7236	2.0644
Type of house	2.8144	3.9197*	2.0369	2.0664	2.8334	3.2146
Number of water pipe connection	2.7147*	3.0617*	2.2727	1.9193	2.1163	2.0863
Frequency of water supply availed	2.8661*	3.1144*	2.8614*	2.7334*	2.6672*	1.7134

* Significant at five per cent level

earning members per family, house ownership, number of water pipe connections and frequency of water supply availed since their respective 'F' statistics are significant at five per cent level. The significantly associating profile variables with the SERVQUAL scale on water supply are age, nativity, family size and number of earning members whereas regarding the SERVQUAL scale on service quality, these profile variables are age, nativity, occupational background, family size and frequency of water supply availed.

The significantly associating profile variables with the SERVQUAL scale of problem maintenance are gender, age, occupational background and frequency of water supply availed whereas regarding the SERVQUAL scale on customer care, these profile variables are age, occupational background and frequency of water supply availed. Regarding the SERVQUAL scale on price, the significantly associating profile variables are gender, age and occupational background. The analysis reveals that the important profiles associating with the gap between their level of perception and expectation on the important services related to the drinking water are their age, occupational background and frequency of water supply availed.

Monthly Expenditure on Drinking Water

The respondents in the study area are getting their drinking water from several possible sources. For that, they are spending a portion of their monthly expenditure. It is highly essential to analyse the monthly expenditure on drinking water among the respondents to create an optimum 'finance model' for the infrastructural facilities. Hence the present study focuses on the monthly expenditure on drinking water incurred by the respondents. The mean and standard deviation of monthly expenditure incurred on drinking water among the three income groups have been computed and presented in Table 2.28.

Table 2.28 : Monthly expenditure on drinking water

Sl. No.	Income groups	Mean	Standard deviation	Coefficient of variation (in per cent)
1.	LIG	82.39	13.45	16.32
2.	MIG	191.46	38.68	20.20
3.	HIG	265.24	25.69	9.68
	Overall	171.33	27.36	18.13

The mean of monthly expenditure on drinking water incurred among the LIG is Rs.82.39 which is subject to the standard deviation of 13.45. Among the MIG, the mean of expenditure is Rs.191.46 whereas among the HIG, it is Rs.265.24. The lesser coefficient of variation in the monthly expenditure on drinking water is identified as 9.68 per cent among the HIG. It assumed that the HIG are spending nearly three fold times greater than the amount spent by the LIG. The higher consistency in incurring such expenditure is also identified among HIG. In total, the respondents included in the present study are spending an average of Rs.171.33 for their drinking water during the period of 1 month.

Profile of the Respondents and their Monthly Expenditure on Drinking Water

Since the profile of the respondents plays an important role in the expenditure on drinking water, the present study has made an attempt to analyze the monthly expenditure on drinking water among the different groups of respondents regarding each profile variable. The mean, standard deviation and coefficient of variation of monthly expenditure on drinking water are presented in Table 2.29.

The male respondents estimate their monthly expenditure on drinking water to be Rs.134.69 whereas among the female respondents, it is Rs.252.27. The higher level of consistency on the expenditure on drinking water is seen among the female respondents compared to male respondents. Regarding the age of the respondents, the lesser aged respondents state that they are spending more on drinking water than the aged respondents. In the present study, it is found that the respondents less than 30 years are spending an average of Rs.189.36 whereas the respondents aged of above 60 years are spending an average of Rs.107.24. The respondents of age 30-40 years are spending an average of Rs.183.08, which is declining to Rs.165.84 among the age group of 51-60 years.

The urban respondents spend an average of Rs.215.83 for drinking water per month whereas among the semi-urban and rural respondents, it is only Rs.183.62 and Rs.119.95 respectively. The occupational background among the

Table 2.29 : Monthly expenditure on Drinking Water in different customer segments

Sl. No.	Profile	Mean	Standard deviation	Coefficient of variation (in per cent)
I	**Gender**			
	Male	134.69	18.66	13.85
	Female	252.27	26.73	10.59
II	**Age**			
	Less than 30 years	189.36	25.04	13.22
	30-40 years	183.08	20.99	11.46
	41-50 years	182.61	33.69	18.45
	51-60 years	165.84	19.33	11.66
	Above 60 years	107.24	32.62	30.42
III	**Nativity**			
	Urban	215.83	26.44	12.25
	Semi-urban	183.62	19.37	10.55
	Rural	119.95	17.25	14.38
IV	**Occupational background**			
	Private employment	205.68	31.44	15.29
	Government employment	183.11	23.62	12.89
	Business	176.45	19.34	10.96
	Agriculture	79.21	8.69	10.97
	Others	125.79	12.61	10.02

respondents also reflects the difference in monthly expenditure on drinking water among the respondents. The respondents in private employment spend an average of Rs.205.68 whereas the respondents engaged in agriculture are spending only an average of Rs.79.21 per month. The government employee spends an average of Rs.183.11 for drinking water whereas the businessman spends an average of Rs.176.45 per month.

The distribution of monthly expenditure on drinking water among the respondents based on their family size, number of earning members per family, houseownership, type of house, number of water pipe connections and frequency of water supply availed is shown in Table 2.30.

Table 2.30 : Monthly expenditure Incurred on drinking water by different customer segments

Sl. No.	Profile	Mean	Standard deviation	Coefficient of variation (in per cent)
1.	**Family size**			
	Upto 3 members	182.49	31.08	17.03
	4-5 members	176.06	19.44	11.04
	6-7 members	157.68	24.03	15.24
	Above 7 members	136.87	15.32	11.19
2.	**Number of earning members** per family			
	One	126.83	11.36	8.96
	Two	172.69	18.05	10.45
	More than two	257.81	32.46	12.59
3.	**House**			
	Owned	183.62	19.08	10.39
	Leased	173.08	24.72	14.28
	Rented	158.69	20.44	12.88
4.	**Type of house**			
	Individual	213.09	22.65	10.63
	Apartment	143.05	41.08	28.72
5.	**Number of pipe connections**			
	One	186.46	13.09	7.02
	Two	166.11	17.25	10.38
	Three	146.33	10.89	7.44
	More than three	124.91	11.33	9.07
6.	**Frequency of water supply**			
	Daily	76.08	8.42	11.07
	Once in 2 days	142.35	14.15	9.94
	Once in 3 days	169.69	19.42	11.44
	Irregular	239.55	41.08	17.15

The increased family size of the respondents reduces their monthly expenditure on the drinking water. This may be because the respondents with higher family size depend more on metro water at lesser cost. At the same time, the respondents with smaller family size may have better standard of living. They may depend more on bottled water. The mean of monthly expenditure among the respondents with the family size of upto 3 members is Rs.182.49 whereas it is only Rs.136.87 among the respondents with the family size of above 7 members.

The increase in number of earning members per family results in an increase in the monthly expenditure on drinking water. The respondents with one earning member per family spent Rs.126.83 for drinking water whereas the respondents with more than two members spent Rs.257.81 per month. Based on the house category, the mean of monthly expenditure on drinking water among the respondents with owned house is Rs.183.02 whereas among the respondents living in leased and rented houses, it is Rs.173.08 and Rs.158.69 respectively. At present, the respondents in apartments are spending an average of Rs.143.05 for their drinking water every month but it is subject to higher fluctuations since its coefficient of variation is 28.72 per cent. The average amount spent on drinking water by the respondents in individual house is Rs.213.09.

The respondents with only one water pipe connection spent Rs.186.46 per month for drinking water. The increase in the number of water pipe connections reduces the monthly expenditure on the drinking water among the respondents. Respondents with more than three water pipe connections spent Rs. 124.91 for their drinking water. Respondents facing irregular water supply spent Rs. 239.55 per month on drinking water whereas the respondents getting daily water supply spent Rs. 76.08 per month.

Association between Profile of the Respondents and their Monthly Expenditure on Drinking Water

The association between the profile of the respondents and their monthly expenditure on drinking water is examined using one way analysis of variance. The included profile variables are gender, age, nativity, occupational background, family size, number of earning members per family, house category, type of house, number of pipe connections and frequency of water supply availed. The results are given in Table 2.31.

Table 2.31 : Significant difference in monthly expenditure on drinking water supply among different customer segments

Sl. No.	Profile variables	F-Statistics	Table value of 'F' at 5 per cent level	Result
1.	Gender	4.8127	3.84	Significant
2.	Age	3.6073	2.37	Significant
3.	Nativity	4.1142	2.99	Significant
4.	Occupational background	2.6069	2.37	Significant
5.	Family size	2.5161	2.60	Insignificant
6.	Number of earning members per family	3.9692	2.99	Significant
7.	House category	2.9969	2.99	Significant
8.	Type of house	2.8064	3.84	Insignificant
9.	Number of pipe connection	2.9808	2.60	Significant
10.	Frequency of water supply availed	2.7331	2.60	Significant

The significantly associating profile variables with their average amount spent on drinking water supply is gender, age, nativity, occupational background, number of earning members per family, house category, number of pipe connections and frequency of water supply availed since their respective 'F' statistics are significant at five per cent level. The analysis reveals the impact of profile of the respondents on their average monthly expenditure on the drinking water.

REFERENCES

1. Adamowicz, W., J. Lauviere, and M. Williams (1994), "Combining revealed and stated preference methods for valuing: Environmental Amenities", *Journal of Environmental Economics and Management*, 26(1), pp. 271-292.
2. Benmagen, Engene and V. Alterz (2004), "Impacts of Unit Pricing Solid Waste Collection and Disposal in Olongopo city, Phillippines, EEPSEA Research Report, No. 2004-RR4.
3. Cointreau-service, Sandra and Gopalan (2000), Tools for preparing for private sector participation in Municipal solid waste management, part-III.
4. Carson, R (1992), "A contingent Valuation study of Lost Passive use value Resulting from the Exxon Valdez oil spill", Appendices A-D-A Report to the Assorney General of the State of Alaska.
5. Teas, K.R. (1994), "Expectations as a comparison standard in measuring Service Quality: An Assessment of Reassessment", *Journal of Marketing*, 58(2), pp.132-139.
6. Lehtinen, U. and Lehtine, J.R (1991), "Two approaches to service quality dimensions", *The Services Industries Journal*, 11(1), pp. 287-303.
7. Prasada Rao, P and Vedantam Sahia (2006), "Mutual Funds: Exploring the Retail Customer Expectations", *The ICFAI journal of services marketing*, 4(2), June, pp. 25-33.
8. Nunnally, J.C (1978): *Psychometric Theory*: Mc.Graw, Hill, New York, NY.
9. Anderson, J.C and Gerhing (1988), "Structural Equation Modeling in Practice: A Review and Recommended Two-step Approach", *Psychological Bulletin*, 103(3), pp. 411-423.
10. Fornell, G and Larcker, D.M (1981), "Evaluating structural equation modeling with unobservable variables and measurement error", *Journal of Marketing Research*, 18(1), pp. 39-50.
11. Gi-Du Kang, Ferrey Fames and Kostas Alexandis (2002), "Measurement of Internal Service Quality: application of the SERVQUAL battery to Internal Service Quality", *Managing Service Quality*, 12(5), pp. 278-291.
12. Joreskog, K.G. and Sorbom, D. (1993), "LISREL 8: Structural Equation Modeling with the SIMLIS Command Language, Scientific Software, Maple, IN.
13. Babakus, E., and Boller, G.W. (1992), "An Empirical assessment of the SERVQUAL scale", *Journal of Business Research*, 24(3), pp.253-268.
14. Parasuraman, A, Zeithaml, V.A and Berry, L.L. (1991), "Refinement and reassessment of the servqual scale", *Journal of Retailing*, 67(4), pp. 420-450.
15. Teas, R.K. (1994), "Expectations as a Comparison Standard of Measuring Service Quality: An assessment of a reassessment", *Journal of Marketing*, 58(October), pp. 132-141.

3 Development of Financial Model for Drinking Water Supply

The contingent valuation method (CVM) is widely used to the take key decisions in the water sector in developing countries. The specific objective of CVM is to elicit the potential service users' maximum willingness–to–pay (WTP) for carefully selected water supply service options. Carefully constructed contingent valuation scenarios describe a hypothetical market where the user 'buys' a particular level of service, using a specified payment method. The water system can be managed by a choice of institutions. Therefore, the CVM survey can collect useful data on individuals' preferences for the exact type of improved water supply, their ability and willingness to pay for this system. This information can then be used to determine an appropriate tariff policy and financial package for the improved water supply system, often involving the allocation of appropriate subsidies to poorer households.

Willingness to Pay (WTP)

The financial sustainability of a project is most important for project designers and planners. It involves predicting what users will be able and willing to pay for water in the future. Consumers are often willing to pay a higher price for water than the tariffs charged. There are three ways to estimate WTP (Alison and Kevin, 2003).[1]

1. Observe the prices that people pay for goods in various markets (i.e., water, vending, buying, from neighbours, paying local taxes).

2. Observe individual expenditure of money, time, labour etc., to obtain goods, or to avoid their loss. This might involve the household surveys
3. Ask people directly what they are willing-to pay for goods or services in the future.

The CVM methodology includes all three ways to measure the WTP.

The present study has made an attempt to analyse the WTP among the respondents for the improved drinking water service in near future. The respondents are asked to mention their own WTP per month on drinking water service. The mean of the WTP among the income groups, its standard deviation and the co-efficient of variation are illustrated in Table 3.1.

Table 3.1 : Willingness to pay for drinking water for a month

Sl.No.	Income Groups	Mean	Standard Deviation	Co-efficient variation (in %)
1.	LIG	61.32	22.04	35.94
2.	MIG	117.03	26.91	16.11
3.	HIG	232.42	31.07	13.37
	Overall	146.48	24.16	17.19

The mean of WTP among the LIG is only Rs. 61.32, which is subject to more fluctuations since their respective co-efficients of variation is 35.94 per cent. The mean of WTP among MIG and HIG is Rs. 167.03 and Rs. 232.42 respectively with the co-efficient of variation of 16.11 and 13.37 per cent respectively. In total, the mean of WTP for drinking water service per month is Rs. 146.48 with the co-efficient of variation of 17.19 per cent. The analysis reveals that HIG residents are ready to pay more on improved drinking water service in near future compared to the other two income groups.

WTP in Different Users Segments

The contingent valuation methodology allows planners to assess people's willingness to pay for service options and provides the necessary basis for projecting sales and revenues. This information is essential to support community participation and enable 'informed choice' at the household level as well as at the community level. WTP surveys provide the parameters to underpin financial models needed to evaluate expansion plans and to set tariffs. The WTP survey provides more information on the willingness-to-pay for water services among the various user segments. Since the users belong to various segments, the WTP is changing. In general, the user of drinking water is segmented into household, business firms and industries.

The household is again segmented on the basis of their profile. In the globalised scenario, the discrimination strategy is essential to position the product/service among different group of consumers. On the basis of the profile, the consumers are classified by their gender, age, nativity, occupational background, family size, number of earning members per family, house category, type of house, number of water pipe connections and frequency of water supply availed so far. It is highly important to analyse the WTP among the different group of customers in each profile for some policy implications. The mean score of WTP, its standard deviation and its co-efficient of variation have been examined and shown in Table 3.2.

The mean of WTP for drinking water per month among the male respondents is Rs. 165.34 whereas among females, it is Rs. 107.96. Lesser consistency in the view on WTP is identified among the females since their respective co-efficient of variation is 19.53 per cent. The age is an important criterion on the view on WTP among the respondents. The lesser aged respondents are willing to-pay more than the aged customers. The respondents with the age of less than 30 years are willing to pay for a month of Rs. 163.34 whereas it is only Rs. 130.97 among the respondents aged above 60 years. The respondents in the age group of 30 to 40 and 41 to 50 years are having a WTP of Rs. 152.08 and Rs. 149.73 respectively. The higher consistency in their view on WTP is identified among the respondents with the age of less than 30 years.

Table 3.2. Willingness to pay among different user segments

Sl. No.	Profile	Mean	Standard Deviation	Co-efficient of Variation
I.	**Gender**			
	Male	165.34	15.44	9.34
	Female	107.96	21.08	19.53
II.	**Age in years**			
	Less than 30	163.34	21.33	13.06
	30 – 40	152.08	33.18	21.82
	41 – 50	149.73	27.69	18.49
	51 – 60	134.68	24.17	17.95
	Above 60	130.97	38.08	29.08
III	**Nativity**			
	Urban	173.34	32.44	18.71
	Semi-urban	158.25	27.39	17.31
	Rural	105.38	21.73	20.62
IV	**Occupational background**			
	Private employment	192.25	29.09	15.13
	Government employment	145.08	21.43	14.77
	Business	136.33	18.55	13.61
	Agriculture	65.44	9.32	14.24
	Others	117.36	10.68	9.10

Regarding the nativity of the respondents, the urban respondents are willing to spend Rs.173.34 for the drinking water per month whereas the rural respondents are willing to pay only Rs. 105.38. The WTP among the semi-urban respondents is Rs. 158.25. Based on the occupational background, the mean of WTP among the respondents with private and government employment of WTP is noticed among the respondents engaged in agriculture since their respective mean of WTP is Rs. 65.44 only. The higher consistency of WTP is identified among the respondents with other occupations whereas lesser consistency is noticed among the respondents with private employment.

The WTP among the respondents in different customers segments based on their family size, number of earning members per family, house category, types of house, number of pipe connections and frequency of water supply availed is given in Table 3.3.

Table 3.3. Willingness to pay in different customer segments

Sl. No.	Profile	Mean	Standard Deviation	Co-efficient of Variation
I.	**Family Size (members)**			
	Upto 3	165.36	17.66	10.68
	4 – 5	141.99	23.02	16.21
	6 – 7	139.42	19.17	13.75
	Above 7	125.08	21.65	17.31
II.	**Number of earning members per family**			
	One	108.69	11.07	10.18
	Two	161.96	19.36	11.95
	More than Two	169.31	18.52	10.94
III.	**House Ownership**			
	Owned House	167.51	21.06	12.57
	Lease	144.06	17.33	12.03
	Rental	127.39	12.54	9.84
IV	**Type of House**			
	Individual	171.88	10.62	6.18
	Apartments	129.29	11.37	8.79
V	**Number of Pipe Connection**			
	One	165.27	29.08	17.59
	Two	136.02	17.14	12.60
	Three	120.73	13.99	11.59
	More than three	109.04	10.24	9.39
VI	**Frequency of water supply**			
	Daily	60.07	8.51	14.17
	Once in 2 days	129.16	17.27	13.37
	Once in 3 days	140.24	18.39	13.11
	Irregular	205.55	31.42	15.29

The respondents with the family size of upto 3 members are willing to spend a higher amount of Rs. 165.36 whereas the minimum of WTP of Rs. 125.08 is identified among the respondents with the family size of above 7 members. The increase in number of earning members per family results in an increase in their WTP on drinking water. In our study, the respondent with the only one earning member is willing to pay an average of Rs. 108.69 only whereas the respondents with more than two earning members are willing to pay an average of Rs. 169.31.

By the house category, the respondents living in are ready to pay an average of Rs. 167.57 per month for their drinking water whereas the respondents living in rented house is ready to pay an average of Rs. 127.39. The respondents living in leased house are willing to pay an amount of Rs. 144.06. The respondents residing in individual house are willing to pay an average of Rs. 171.88 whereas the respondents in apartments are ready to pay only Rs. 129.29 per month.

The increase in the number of pipe connections owned by the respondent results in a decrease in their WTP. The respondents with one connection are willing to pay an average of Rs. 165.27 whereas the respondents with more than three connections are willing to pay an average of Rs. 109.04. The respondents with irregular drinking water supply at their residence are willing to pay more than others. The mean of WTP among them is Rs. 205.55 whereas among the respondents with daily drinking water supply, it is only Rs. 60.07. It reveals the role of the profile of the respondents on their WTP for their drinking water.

Significant Difference among the Respondents Regarding their WTP

The profile of the respondents plays its own role in the WTP for the drinking water among them. Hence, the present study has made an attempt to analyze the significant differences among the different group of respondents under different profile regarding their WTP using one-way analysis of variance. The results are given in Table 3.4.

Table 3.4 : Willingness to pay per month on drinking water in different customers Segments

Sl. No.	Profile Variables	F-Statistics	Table Value of 'F' at rive pre cent level	Result
1.	Gender	4.1745	3.84	Significant
2.	Age	2.1606	2.37	Significant
3.	Nativity	3.2067	2.99	Significant
4.	Occupational Background	2.6814	2.37	Significant
5.	Family Size	2.4143	2.60	Insignificant
6.	Number of earning members per family	3.0669	2.99	Significant
7.	House Category	2.6881	2.99	Insignificant
8.	Type of house	3.6144	3.84	Insignificant
9.	Number of pipe connection	3..2673	2.60	Significant
10.	Frequency of water supply availed	2.9168	2.60	Significant

The significantly associating profile variables with the WTP among the respondents are their gender, age, nativity, occupational background, number of earning members per family, number of pipe connections and frequency of water supply availed since their respective 'F' statistics are significant at five per cent level. The result of one-way analysis of variance indicates the importance of profile of respondents in their willingness-to-pay for the drinking water facilities.

Difference between Monthly Expenditure and WTP for Drinking Water

There are two different approaches in CVM. The first one is 'Revealed Preference' whereas the second one is 'Stated Preferences'. In the revealed preference approach, the monthly expenditure on the drinking water among the respondents is measured whereas in the stated preferences approaches, the respondents are directly asked to mention their WTP (Lund 1995[2] ; Griffin and Mjelde, 2000[3]). The respondents are actually spending more money on getting drinking water every month but their WTP for it may be lesser since they are willing to reduce their offered price. Hence, the comparison on these two prices have been analysed to show the mindset of the respondents. The results are given in Table 3.5.

Table 3.5 : Difference between monthly expenditure and willingness to pay for drinking water per month

Sl. No.	Income Groups	Mean of the difference between monthly expenditure and their WTP	Standard Deviation (in %)	Co-efficient variation
1.	LIG	21.07	2.49	11.82
2.	MIG	24.43	3.06	12.53
3.	HIG	32.82	5.13	15.63
	Overall	24.85	3.29	13.24

While the respondents are spending more on drinking water per month, they are willing to pay only less of it. For example, the LIG residents are spending a monthly amount of Rs.82.39 for drinking water whereas they are willing to pay only Rs.61.32, the difference being Rs.21.07 per month. Similarly, the differences between MIG and HIG are identified as Rs.24.43 and 32.82, respectively. In total, the respondents are trying to reduce Rs.25.00 from their monthly expenditure on drinking water. It is generally seen among all respondents.

Profile of the Respondents and their Difference on Monthly Expenditure and WTP

The difference between monthly expenditure and WTP among the respondents has been computed. Since the profile of the respondents may be associated with such difference, the association between the profile of the respondents and their difference in monthly expenditure and WTP is analyzed using with the help of one-way analysis of variance. The results are given in Table 3.6.

Table 3.6 : Significant difference between different groups of customers in each profile variable regarding their WTP

Sl. No.	Profile Variables	F-Statistics	Table Value of 'F'	Result
1.	Gender	3.9194	3.84	Significant
2.	Age	2.6693	2.37	Significant
3.	Nativity	3.2762	2.99	Significant
4.	Occupational Background	2.8086	2.37	Significant
5.	Family Size	2.4517	2.60	Insignificant
6.	Number of earning members per family	3.1233	2.99	Significant
7.	House ownership	2.4542	2.99	Insignificant
8.	Type of house	3.0617	3.84	Insignificant
9.	Number of pipe connection	2.8664	2.60	Significant
10.	Frequency of water supply availed	2.7331	2.60	Significant

Table 3.6 shows the computed 'F' statistics and table value of 'F' regarding the difference between monthly expenditure and WTP among the different groups of respondents regarding each profile variable. Regarding the differences, the significant difference among the different groups of respondents has been noticed when they are classified on the basis of their gender, age, nativity, occupational background, number of earning members per family, number of pipe connection and frequency of water supply availed since their respective 'F' statistics are significant at five per cent level. It reveals the importance of the profile variables in their differences between monthly expenditure and WTP.

Reasons for Willing-to-pay more for Drinking Water

The consumers of essential goods and services especially the drinking water and solid waste management are ready to pay more than what they actually do at present. At the same time, they are revealing their expectations for the future services as their conditions for WTP to pay more for it. The reasons for their willing to pay more have been identified by

Levallois et al., (1999)[4], Merrett (2002)[5] and Kontogianni et al., (2004)[6]. The identified reasons for their willingness-to-pay more are reliability of water service, quality of water, environment service, water service for future generation, environmental awareness, problem with local government, affordability, accessibility, labour problem, management of water and assured service. The respondents are asked to rate the above-said 11 reasons at five-point scale according to their order of importance. The assigned scores on these scales are from 5 to 1 respectively. The mean score of the reason among three income groups have been computed separately to exhibit the level of importance attached with each reason for their willingness-to-pay-more.

The results are given in Table 3.7.

Table 3.7 : Reasons for willing to pay more for drinking water

Sl. No.	Reasons	Mean Score			F-statistics
		LIG	MIG	HIG	
1.	Reliability of water service	3.1143	3.6586	4.0345	3.1142*
2.	Quality of water	3.0499	3.7236	4.1087	3.2769*
3.	Environment service	2.7642	2.8142	3.1447	1.3308
4.	Water service for future generation	2.6508	2.8208	3.2478	1.7179
5.	Environmental awareness	3.1447	3.0869	3.6509	1.4433
6.	Problem with local government	2.7869	3.4562	3.8551	1.8186
7.	Affordability	2.6166	3.1486	4.2145	3.3446*
8.	Accessibility	2.7376	2.9193	3.0568	1.0441
9.	Labour problem	2.8082	3.6968	4.1191	3.3991*
10.	Management of water	2.7109	3.2414	3.6168	2.9039
11.	Assured service	3.0869	3.4136	3.9234	2.9993*

* Significant at five per cent level.

The important reasons for their greater willingness to pay for drinking water among the LIG are environmental awareness and reliability of water service since their respective mean scores are 3.1447 and 3.1143. Among the MIG, these reasons are quality of water and labour problem since their respective mean scores are 3.7236 and 3.6968 whereas among the HIG, these are affordability and labour problem since their means scores are 4.2145 and 4.1191 respectively. Regarding the perception on reasons for their willingness to pay more, the significant difference among the three group of respondents have been seen in the case of their perception on reliability of water service, quality of water, affordability, labour problem and assured service since their respective 'F' statistics are significant at five per cent level. In total, the HIG are highly rating the reasons for their willingness to pay more for the drinking water service than the other two income groups.

The Important Reasons for Willing-to-pay More on Drinking Water

Eleven variables have been used to measure the reasons for willing-to-pay more on the drinking water. The scores on these eleven variables have been included in the Exploratory Factor Analysis (EFA) to narrate the reasons into important reasons. The test of validity of data for factor analysis has been performed with the help of KMO measure of sampling adequacy and Bartletts test of sphericity. Since the KMO measure of sampling adequacy is greater than 0.5 i.e. 0.7123 and the level of significance of chi-square is at five per cent level, the EFA has been executed to narrate the reasons. The identified important reasons and the reasons in each, its reliability, eigen value and the per cent of variation explained by these important reasons are given in Table 3.8.

The narrated two important reasons for the willingness-to-pay more are 'Environment' and 'Service'. These two important reasons explain eleven reasons to the extent of 67.16 per cent. The first important reason identified by the factor analysis is 'Environment'. It consists of seven reasons with the reliability co-efficient of 0.8149. The eigen value and the per cent of variation explained by this 'environment' is 3.8963 and 40.84 per cent respectively. The second important reason is 'service' since its eigen value and the per cent of variation explained by it are 1.5426 and 26.32 respectively.

Table 3.8 : Important reasons for willing-to-pay more

Sl. No.	Important Reasons	No. of variables	Cronbach Alpha	Eigen Value	%t of variation explained	Cumulative % of variation explained
1.	Environment	7	0.8149	3.8963	40.84	40.84
2.	Service	4	0.7664	1.5426	26.32	67.16
KMO measure of sampling adequacy:0.7123			Bartletts test of sphercity: Chi-square Value: 76.08*			

* Significant at five per cent level.

Reliability and Validity of the Variables in the Construct

In total, seven and four reasons are reflected in 'Environment' and 'Service' factor. In order to analyse the convergent and composite reliability, the confirmatory factor analysis has been administered. The range of standardized factor loading of the various reasons in 'Environment' and 'Service', its statistical significance, composite reliability and the average variance extracted are illustrated in Table 3.9.

Table 3.9 : Reliability and validity of the variables in the factors (Important Reasons)

Sl. No.	Important Reasons	No. of variables	Cronbach Alpha	Eigen Value	% of variation explained	Cumulative % of variation
1.	Environment	0.7237-0.9098	4.1142*-16.86	0.8184	59.68	0.2462
2.	Service	0.6861-09231	3.8466-17.04	0.7906	44.06	

* Significant at five per cent level.

The standardized factor loading of the reasons in 'Environment' is varying from 0.7237 to 0.9098 whereas all factor loadings are significant at five per cent level. It reveals the convergent validity of the variables in the construct. A similar situation is identified in the case of variables in 'service' since their factor loadings are significant at five per cent level. The composite reliability of the 'Environment' and service are greater than the minimum of 0.50. The average variances extracted by these two important reasons are 59.68 and 44.06 per cent. The lesser insignificant correlation between the two important reasons (0.2462) indicates the mutual exclusiveness of these two reasons.

Important Reasons for Willingness-to-pay More

The respondents compute the mean score of the two important reasons for the willingness-to-pay more for drinking water facilities in near future to exhibit the level of the importance attached to environment and service. The score of the two important reasons for willingness-to-pay more is computed by the mean score of the various reasons in it. The results are given in Table 3.10.

Table 3.10 : Important reasons for willingness to pay more on drinking Water

Sl. No.	Important Reasons	Mean Score			F-statistics
		LIG	MIG	HIG	
1.	Environment	3.1143	3.6586	4.0345	3.1142*
2.	Service	2.8298	3.1286	3.6255	2.9939*

* Significant at five per cent level.

The LIG gives more importance to the 'Environment' factor source; its mean score is 2.9155 whereas among MIG and HIG, it is also 'Environment' reasons since its mean scores are 3.5199 and 3.9038 respectively. The HIG rated the environment and service reasons at a higher level compared to the other two income groups for their willingness-to-pay more. Regarding the importance given to these two reasons, the significant difference among the three income groups has been noticed since their respective 'F' statistics are significant at five per cent level.

Reasons for Not Willing-to pay more

Out of 639 respondents, 117 respondents are not willing to pay more for their improved drinking water facilities in near future. Out of 117 respondents, 76.00 per cent of the respondents belong to LIG. The reasons for their un-willingness-to-pay more is analysed to exhibit the important reasons for it. The mean score on each reason among the LIG, MIG and HIG has been computed separately. Regarding the level of importance given to these reasons, the significant difference among the three income groups has been analysed with the help of one way analysis of variance. The results are given in Table 3.11.

Table 3.11 : Reasons for not willing-to-pay more for drinking water

Sl. No.	Important Reasons	Mean Score			F-statistics
		LIG	MIG	HIG	
1.	Unaffordability	3.9897	3.1462	2.8144	3.2465*
2.	High tariff	3.8614	3.2143	2.6166	3.0192*
3.	Government irresponsibility	2.9103	3.6869	3.8644	2.9968*
4.	Not caring about the environment	3.5684	3.2143	3.0143	1.3441
5.	Government mismanagement of resources	3.0441	3.6162	4.3868	3.6868*
6.	Non-reliability of Government service	3.2445	3.9193	4.2346	3.1449*
7.	Poor service quality	2.7183	3.8644	3.9391	3.2173*
8.	Political intervention	3.0668	3.7733	4.1155	3.5069*

* Significant at five per cent level.

The important reasons identified by the LIG are unaffordability and high tariff since their respective mean scores are 3.9897 and 3.8614. Among the MIG these reasons are non-reliability on Government service and poor service quality since their mean scores are 3.9193 and 3.8644 respectively whereas among the HIG, these are Government mismanagement of resources and non-reliability of

Government service since their mean scores are 4.3868 and 4.2346 respectively. Regarding the level of importance given to the reasons, the significant difference among the three income groups has been identified in the case of unaffordability, high tariff, Government irresponsibility, Government mismanagement of resources, non-reliability of Government services, poor service quality and political intervention since their respective 'F' statistics are significant at five per cent level.

Important Reasons for Unwillingness-to-Pay More

The scores on the reasons for unwillingness-to-pay more for the drinking water service in future have been included for the factor analysis to identify the important reasons for unwillingness-to-pay more. Initially, the test of validity of data for factor analysis has been performed with the help of KMO measure of sampling adequacy and Bartletts test of sphericity. Both these two tests satisfy the validity of data. The executed EFA analysis results in three important reasons. The number of variables in each important reason, its reliability co-efficient, eigen value and the per cent of variation explained by the three important reasons are given in Table 3.12.

Table 3.12 : Important reasons for not paying more on drinking water

Sl. No.	Important Reasons	No. of variables in	Cronbach Alpha	Eigen Value	% of variation explained	Cumulative % of variation explained
1.	Political	3	0.7233	2.9197	33.68	33.68
2.	Mismanagement	3	0.6869	1.8886	14.36	48.04
3.	Economic	2	0.7914	1.1144	12.69	60.73
KMO measure of sampling adequacy: 0.6972			Bartletts test of sphericity: Chi-square value: 69.08*			

*Significant at zero per cent level.

The narrated three important reasons explain the willingness-to-pay more to the extent of 60.73 per cent. The

economic reasons since their respective 'F' statistics are significant at five per cent level.

Association between Profile of Respondents and their Importance on three Reasons for not Willing-to-Pay More

Since the profile of the respondents may have its own influence on the level of importance attached to their non willingness-to-pay more for the improved drinking water service in near future, the present study has made an attempt to analyse the association between the profile of the respondents and their level of importance attached to Political, Mismanagement and Economic factors. The one-way analysis of variance has been executed to analyse such associations. The included profile variables are gender, age, nativity, occupational background, family size, members of earning members per family, houseownership, type of house, number of pipe connections and frequency of drinking water availed. The results are given in Table 3.15.

Table 3.15 : Association between the profile of the respondents and their important Reasons for not paying more

Sl. No.	Profile variables	F-Statistics		
		Political	Mismanagement	Economic
1.	Gender	2.4568	3.0244	3.5686
2.	Age	2.7901*	2.6403*	2.8084*
3.	Nativity	2.0966	2.3144	2.2969
4.	Occupational background	2.5147*	2.8286*	3.1486*
5.	Family size	2.4562	2.0149	3.2449*
6.	Number of earning members per family	3.5686*	3.2143*	3.8687*
7.	House Category	2.5158	2.0868	2.9143
8.	Type of house	2.8188	3.4543	3.6504
9.	Number of pipe connections	2.6869*	2.9197*	3.1147*
10.	Frequency of water supply availed	2.9334*	3.0458*	2.8446*

* Significant at five per cent level.

Regarding the level of importance attached to the political reasons, the significant associating profile variables are age, occupational background, number of earning members per family, number of pipe connections and frequency of drinking water supply availed since their respective 'F' statistics are significant at five per cent level. The significantly associating profile variables with the level of importance attached to the 'economic' reasons are age, occupational background, family size, number of earning members per family, number of pipe connections and frequency of drinking water availed. The analysis reveals the importance of profile variables namely age, occupational background, number of earning members per family, number of pipe connections and frequency of drinking water availed and the level of importance attached to the important reasons for their unwillingness-to-pay more for the improved drinking water service in near future.

Privatization of Drinking Water Services

Over the last decade the global movement towards involvement of the private sector in the provision of drinking water supply and sanitation services has been rapidly gaining momentum and as has met political opposition. Efforts to privatize metro water services have become a lightening rod for groups struggling against the economic and political forces pushing globalization and a potent symbol of what is wrong with the development approach advocated by the World Bank and other multilateral agencies to bring global market forces to bear on economies in developing countries (Stiglitz, 2002)[7].

Proponents of private sector involvement in the metro water sector cite three main benefits (Water Manifesto 2000)[8]. First, the private sector is able to deliver services more efficiently than public sector providers, thus lowering the real cost of service provision. Second, the private sector can mobilize capital to finance much needed service improvements for both existing populations and population growth. Third and perhaps most important, it is argued that privatization offers the only politically feasible avenue open to replace the corrupt, rent-seeking management teams ensured in many water utilities in developing countries.

The people's perception on the privatization of the metro water and sanitation management is a pre-requisite for the success of the privatization (Dumol, 2000)[9]. The people may be afraid about high tariff and discriminatory service in the private sector. Social welfare is a big concern on the privatization of essential services (Hanemann, 1984)[10]. Hence, it is highly essential to conduct a survey on the people's attitude towards the privatization of essential services. It is the only remedy to solve the problems of privatization of essential services (Cameson and James, 1987)[11]. Hence the present study has made an attempt to analyse the switching behaviour of the respondents regarding their drinking water services.

In the present study, the willingness of the respondents to switch over from public sector providers to private service providers has been measured at five-point scale namely very-high, high, moderate, low and very low. The distribution of respondents on the basis of their willingness to accept privatization is presented in Table 3.16.

Table 3.16 : Willing to switch over to private agencies

Sl. No.	Rate of Willingness to Switchover	Number of respondents			Total
		LIG	MIG	HIG	
1.	Very high	27	55	46	128
2.	High	36	117	34	187
3.	Moderate	63	102	21	186
4.	Low	42	39	7	88
5.	Very low	23	27	–	50
	Total	191	340	108	639

In total, a maximum of 29.26 per cent of the respondents are highly willing to switch over to private service providers which is followed by 29.10 per cent with moderate willingness. The number of respondents with very high willingness to switch over constitutes 20.03 per cent to the total. The respondents with low and very low willingness to switchover constitute 21.59 per cent to the total. A higher number of LIG are having a moderate view on privatization. The number of respondents with low and very low switching behaviour constitutes 34.03 per cent to its total whereas among the MIG and HIG, it constitutes 19.41 and 6.48 per cent to its total respectively. The analysis reveals that majority of the respondents are willing to switch over to the private sector providers.

Reasons for Switching from Public to Private Service Provider

The people are willing to switch over from public service provider to private service provider because of their bitter experience with the existing service provider, their service quality and also the higher expectation from the private service providers. The respondents perceive that the improved services provided by the private operator would entail substantially higher water bills. It is highly essential to analyse the reasons the respondents behaviour for switching to improve the existing service and permit the private operator in the field. The reasons for their switching are drawn from reviews Cronin et al., 2000[12] ; MC Fadden, 1976[13] ; Whittington, 2002[14] ; and Othsman 2002). In the present study, in total 27 reasons for their switching have been identified. The respondents are asked to rate the 27 reasons at five point scale from highly agreeable to highly disagreeable. The assigned scores on these scales are from 5 to 1 respectively.

The mean scores of the reasons among the LIG, MIG and HIG have been computed to exhibit the important reasons for privatization. The results are given in Table 3.17.

The important reasons for the switching among the LIG are lesser switching cost, complaint handling of present service provider and lesser opportunity cost since their mean scores are 3.6617, 3.6163 and 3.6116 respectively. Among the MIG, these reasons are losing of confidence on the existing suppliers, reputation of the new service providers and feedback from foreign practices since their mean scores are 4.1146, 4.1144

Table 3.17. Mean score of reasons for switching

Sl. No.	Reasons for Switching	Mean Score			F-Statistics
		LIG	MIG	HIG	
1.	Good quality of water	2.6817	3.45021	3.9903	3.6908*
2.	Normal fees	2.9098	3.0144	3.3361	2.1146
3.	Good service	2.5161	3.6861	4.1144	3.8081*
4.	Poor service of present service provider	3.1442	3.8089	4.2096	3.3617*
5.	Complaint handling of present service provider	3.6163	3.9192	4.1134	1.3322
6.	Knowledge about the new services	2.1449	3.3861	3.8186	3.4566*
7.	Mental effort to accept the changes	2.4334	3.6869	4.1089	3.7309*
8.	Reputation of the new service providers	3.0624	4.1144	3.9903	3.8962*
9.	Privatization is good	3.2145	3.9089	4.1186	2.3568
10.	Feedback from foreign practices	3.5168	4.0862	4.2447	1.9197
11.	Losing confidence on the existing supplies	3.2718	4.1146	3.9806	2.4413
12.	High cost of present supplier	3.0339	2.9333	2.5144	1.3903
13.	High cost of other sources compared with existing cost	3.5084	3.9193	3.6868	0.8182
14.	Lesser switching costs	3.6617	3.7327	3.5681	0.4502
15.	Cost on water holidays	3.4103	3.8189	4.2342	0.6861
16.	Social cost greater than social welfare	2.6804	3.6804	3.9037	3.2917*
17.	Simple procedure to get connection	3.1448	3.5862	3.6163	1.0864*
18.	Simple procedure to make complaints	3.4503	3.6166	3.8182	0.7316
19.	Lesser cost of maintenance	3.5661	3.4503	3.6883	0.4307
20.	Lesser opportunity cost	3.6116	3.5311	3.7184	0.5114
21.	Affordability	3.3311	3.8684	4.1786	2.0676
22.	Method of payment of tariff	2.9091	3.7909	4.0991	3.3969*
23.	Tariff is based on consumption	3.4143	3.6163	3.9092	1.2041
24.	Acceptance of electronic payment	3.6062	3.5664	3.3994	0.7339
25.	Services other costs	3.1773	3.2146	3.5619	0.6417
26.	Taste of water	3.2144	3.3191	3.9818	2.0142
27.	Colour of water	3.3147	3.2146	3.8446	1.3669

* Significant at five per cent level.

and 4.0862 respectively. Among the HIG, these reasons are feedback from foreign practices, cost of water holidays and poor service of present service provider since their mean scores are 4.2447, 4.2342 and 4.2096 respectively. Regarding the importance attached to the reasons, the significant difference among the three income groups has been noticed in the case of good quality of water, good service, mental effort to accept the changes, reputation of the new services providers, social cost greater than social welfare, simple procedures to get connection and method of payment of tariff since their respective 'F' statistics are significant at five per cent level.

Important Reasons for Switching

The score of the 27 reasons for switching has been included for the factor analysis in order to narrate the important reasons for switching. The validity of data for factor analysis was tested with the help of KMO measure of sampling adequacy and Bartletts test of sphericity. The above said two tests justify the validity of data for factor analysis since the KMO measure of sampling adequacy is greater than 0.5 and the chi-square value is significant at zero per cent level. The executed Exploratory Factor Analysis (EFA) results in seven important reasons namely price, office management, new service provider, supplementary cost, present service provider, personal and quality of water. The factors in various important reasons for switching, its reliability co-efficient, eigen value and the per cent of variation explained by the important reasons are given in Table 3.18.

The narrated seven important reasons for switching among the respondents explain the various reasons to the extent of 75.90 per cent. The most important reason for switching is price since its eigen value and the per cent of variation explained by this reason is 4.0345 and 16.82 per cent respectively. It consists of five variables with the reliability co-efficients of 0.7671. The second and third important reasons are office management and new service provider since their

Table 3.18 : Important reasons for switching

Sl. No.	Important Reasons	No. of variables	Cronbach Alpha	Eigen Value	% of variation explained	Cumulative % of variation explained
1.	Price	5	0.7671	4.0345	16.82	16.82
2.	Office management	5	0.8103	3.7145	14.33	31.15
3.	New service provider	4	0.6994	3.1408	11.09	42.24
4.	Supplementary cost	4	0.7039	2.8086	10.38	52.62
5.	Present service provider	3	0.8334	2.3144	8.97	61.59
6.	Personal	3	0.7108	2.0667	7.36	68.95
7.	Quality of water	3	0.6405	1.5768	6.95	75.90
KMO measure of sampling adequacy: 0.8139				Bartletts test of sphericity: Chi-square Value: 103.08*		

* Significant at five per cent level.

eigen values are 3.7145 and 3.1408 respectively. The per cent of variation explained by these two reasons are 14.33 and 11.09 per cent respectively. The office management consists of five factors with the reliability co-efficient of 0.8103 whereas the new service provider consists of four factors with the reliability co-efficient of 0.6994. The other important reasons namely supplementary cost, present service provider, personal and quality of water consists of 4, 3, 3 and 3 factors with the reliability co-efficient of 0.7039, 0.8331, 0.7108 and 0.6405 respectively. The factor analysis results in seven important reasons for their switching behaviour.

Reliability and Validity of the Measures in Each Construct

The reliability and validity of the factors in each important reason have been examined with the help of Confirmatory Factor Analysis (CFA). The convergent validity and the composite reliability have been estimated with the help of standardized factor loading of the factors in each important reason and its statistical significance. The range of computed standardized factor loading; its statistical significance, composite reliability and average variance extracted by each important factor are summarized in Table 3.19.

Table 3.19 : Reliability and validity of the variables in each construct

Sl. No.	Important Reasons	Range of Standardised factor loading	Range of 't' statistics	Composite Reliability	Average Variance Extracted
1.	Price	0.7511-0.9317	3.9145*-13.9163*	0.8147	55.08
2.	Office management	0.7511-0.9317	4.3906*-15.1762*	0.8696	61.32
3.	Service provider	0.6199-0.8568	3.8081*-11.0869*	0.7331	48.84
4.	Supplementary cost	0.7024-0.8991	4.1142*-10.6861*	0.7149	47.32
5.	Present service provider	0.7517-0.9408	5.2344*-15.9068*	0.8686	60.17
6.	Personal	0.6339-0.8517	4.0011*-10.9968*	0.7417	51.14
7.	Quality of water	0.6108-0.8116	3.5622*-9.3993*	0.6646	43.49

* Significant at zero per cent level.

The range of standardized factor loading of the variables in 'price' is 0.6308 to 0.9026 which is significant at five per cent level. The range of standardized factor loading of the variables in office management is 0.7511 to 0.9317 whereas in service provider it varies from 0.6199 to 0.8568 which is significant at five per cent level. The standardized factor loading of the variables in supplementary cost varies from 0.7024 to 0.8991 whereas in present service provider, it varies from 0.7517 to 0.9408 which is significant at five per cent level. In case of personal and quality factors, the standardized factor loading of the variables is significant at five per cent. It reveals the convergent validity of the variables in each construct. The composite reliability of the variables in each important factor is greater than the minimum threshold of 0.5. The average variance extracted by the important factor varies from 61.32 per cent to 43.49 per cent. It reveals the reliability and validity of the variables in each constant.

The discriminant validity of the constructs has been tested with the help of inter-correlation between these important factors. The inter-correlation matrix is given in Table 3.20.

Table 3.20 : Inter-correlation between the factors

Factors	Price	Office management	Service provider	Supplementary cost	Present service provider	Personal	Quality of Water
Price		–0.2445	0.1094	0.0968	0.1748	0.2144	–0.1894
Office Management			0.2411	0.1339	0.0868	0.1341	–0.1737
Service provider				0.2142	0.1917	–0.1236	0.1088
Supplementary cost					–0.2868	–0.1802	0.0969
Present service provider						0.1916	0.2304
Personal							0.2144
Quality of water							

The higher inter-correlation co-efficient is identified between the supplementary cost and present service provider since its correlation co-efficient is –0.2868 whereas the lesser correlation co-efficient is noticed between price and service provider since its correlation co-efficient is 0.1094. No correlation co-efficient is significant at five per cent level. It reveals the discriminant validity of the constructs. It shows that the important factors for switching have a mutual exclusiveness.

Important Reason for Switching

The important reasons for switching are exhibited by the mean scores of the important factors. The score of the important reasons for switching is computed by the mean score of the various reasons in each important factor. The mean scores of the important reasons for switching among LIG, MIG and HIG have been exhibited in Table 3.21.

The important reasons for their switching among LIG are office management and present service provider since their respective mean scores are 3.4758 and 3.3441. Among the MIG,

Table 3.21 : Important factors leading to switching among different customers groups

Sl. No.	Important factors	Mean Score			F-statistics
		LIG	MIG	HIG	
1.	Price	3.0889	3.3139	3.4885	1.8443
2.	Office management	3.4758	3.5501	3.6481	1.2109
3.	New service provider	3.0685	3.9489	4.1170	3.1774*
4.	Supplementary cost	3.3152	3.7878	3.8482	0.9197
5.	Present service provider	3.3441	3.9476	4.1012	2.1744
6.	Personal	2.6365	3.6471	4.0354	3.6887*
7.	Quality of water	3.0703	3.3282	2.4571	2.4339

*Significant at five per cent level.

these reasons are new service provider and present service provider since their mean scores are 3.9489 and 3.9476 respectively whereas among the HIG, these are new service provider and present service provider since their mean scores are 4.1170 and 4.1012 respectively. Regarding the importance given to reasons, the significant difference among the three income groups has been identified in the case of new service provider and personal factor since their respective 'F' statistics are significant at five per cent level.

Association between the Profile of Respondents and their Level of Importance Attached to Reasons

The profile of the respondents plays an important role in the importance given to the various reasons for their switching. For some policy implications, it is imperative to analyse the association between the profile of the respondents and the level of importance attached to each important reason with the help of one way analysis of variance. The included profile variables are gender, age, nativity, occupational background, family size, number of earning members per family, house ownership, type of house, number of water pipe connections and frequency of water supply availed. The result of the one-way ANOVA is given in Table 3.22.

Table 3.22 : Association between the profile of respondents and their perception on reasons for switching

Sl. No.	Profile Variables	F-Statistics						
		Price	Office Management	New Service Provider	Supplementary Cost	Present Service Provider	Personal	Quality of Water
1.	Gender	2.9108	1.8676	2.2146	1.0889	2.5656	3.1483	3.5334
2.	Age	2.5209*	2.6163*	2.0414	3.1443*	2.7306*	2.3641*	2.5086*
3.	Nativity	3.1142*	3.6604*	2.9991*	3.0464*	3.3309*	2.0896	2.5616
4.	Occupational background	2.4568*	2.6861*	2.7308*	1.8644	2.0414	3.1408*	2.5604*
5.	Family size	2.5144	1.9196	2.7336*	2.5616	2.6969*	1.8448	2.8106*
6.	Number of earning members per family	3.2086*	2.6117	2.3968	2.8184	2.4403	2.6617	3.1466*
7.	House ownership	1.8441	2.1718	2.5038	2.3819	2.9108	2.9949*	3.0868*
8.	Type of house	2.0433	1.8486	2.4406	2.1718	2.6617	3.1718	3.2344
9.	Number of water pipe connection	2.1141	2.5142	2.8183*	2.4146	2.5038	2.1142	1.8617
10.	Frequency of water supply availed	2.8108*	1.3345	2.6465*	2.0217	2.8184*	1.6684	2.0314

* Significant at five per cent level.

Regarding the level of importance attached to the 'price' as the reason for switching, the significantly associating profile variables are age, nativity, occupational background, number of earning members per family and frequency of water supply availed. The significantly associating profile variables with the 'office management' are age, nativity and occupational background since their respective 'F' statistics are significant at five per cent level. Regarding the importance attached to the new service provider, these profile variables are nativity, occupational background, family size and frequency of water supply availed.

The significantly associating profile variables with the perception on 'supplementary cost' are age and nativity whereas in the case of 'present service provider', these profile variables are age, nativity, family size and frequency of water supply availed. Regarding the perception on 'personal' factor, the significantly associating profile variables are age, occupational background and houseownership whereas regarding the perception on quality of water, these profile variables are age, occupational background, family size, number of earning members per family and houseownership. This analysis reveals the importance of profile of the respondents and their level of importance attached to their reasons for switching.

Impact of Factors of Switching on their Rate of Switching to New Service Provider

The rate of switching to new service provider (Private Operator) has been measured at five-point scale. It is treated as the dependent variables. The level of importance attached to each important reason namely price, office management, new service provider, supplementary cost, and present service provider, personal and quality of water are treated as the independent variables. The impact of the level of importance attached to important reasons for switching to private operator and on the rate of switching to private operator has been analysed with the help of multiple regression analysis. The ordinary least square method has been followed to fit the regression equation. The fitted regression model is:

$$Y = a + b_1X_1 + b_2X_2 + b_3X_3 + b_4X_4 + b_5X_5 + b_6X_6 + b_7X_7 + e$$

Y - Rate of switching to private operator

Where X_1 - Level of importance attached to 'office management'

X_2 - Level of importance attached to 'New Service Provider'.

X_3 - Level of importance attached to 'Supplementary Cost'.

X_4 - Level of importance attached to 'Present Service Provider'

X_5 - Level of importance attached to 'Present Service Provider'

X_6 - Level of importance attached to 'Personal'

X_7 - Level of importance attached to 'Quality of water'

$b_1, b_2 \ldots b_n$ - Regression coefficients of independent variables

a - Intercept and

e - Error term

The impact of the factors leading to switching on their rate of switching to new service provider (Private Operator) has been examined among LIG, MIG, HIG and also for pooled data separately. The results are given in Table 3.23.

Table 3.23. Impact of factors leading to switching on their rate of switching to new service provider

Sl. No.	Independent Variables	Regression co-efficients in			
		LIG	MIG	HIG	Pooled
1.	Price	–0.1033	0.0454	–0.0616	–0.0421
2.	Office management	0.0911	0.1066	0.1868*	0.1233
3.	New service provider	0.1344*	0.1408*	0.1913*	0.1571*
4.	Supplementary cost	0.0834	0.1939*	0.1334*	0.1201
5.	Present service provider	0.1443*	0.2417*	0.2108*	0.2246*
6.	Personal	0.1047	0.1133	0.1517*	0.1117
7.	Quality of water	0.1566*	0.1886*	0.2816*	0.2049*
	Constant	0.8991	1.3894	2.1081	1.8184
	R^2	0.7569	0.7147	0.6867	0.8142
	F-statistics	10.2644*	8.9617*	8.0944*	13.4644*

* Significant at five per cent level.

The significant influencing factors on the rate of switching to new service provider among the LIG are level of importance attached to new service provider present service provider and quality of water. A unit increase in the level of importance attached to the service provider, the experience with the present service provider and quality of water results in an increase in the rate of switching to new service provider by 0.1344, 0.1443 and 0.1566 units among the LIG. The changes in the level of importance attached to the seven important factors explain the changes in the rate of switching to new service provider to the extent of 75.69 per cent.

The significantly influencing factors on the rate of switching to new service provider among the MIG are level of importance attached with new service provider, supplementary cost, present service provider, personal and quality of water. The analysis of pooled data reveals that a unit increase in the level of importance attached to the new service provider, present service provider and quality of water result in an increase in rate of switching to new service provider by 0.1571, 0.2246 and 0.2049 units respectively. The changes in the level of importance attached to these factors explain the changes in the rate of switching to new service provider to the extent of 81.42 per cent.

Financial Models (Choice Models) on Drinking Water Services

The 'Finance Model' indicates the way in which the service provider determines the price of drinking water supplied. It also includes the various stages in the price determination. There are two basic approaches to building models, the 'downward' approach and the 'upward' approach. Under the upward approach, higher priority is given to field data and the ability and willingness-to-pay for drinking water among the respondents. It implies that this method might ignore the cost of processing and distribution of water and also the fixed overheads on drinking water management in the determination of its price. It is simply based on the opinion of the respondents, as the basic objective is maximization of social welfare. It is also called as "Bottom up" modeling. (Bathurst and O'Connell, 1992[15]; Beven, 1989[16]; Grayson and Bloschl, 2000[17]).

In the downward approach, the water suppliers determine the various costs involved in the processing and distribution of water to the people. The suppliers determine the 'cost plus' pricing for the drinking water supplied to the people. In the downward approach, there is no need for field data about the peoples' opinion on the pricing of drinking water. Even though the public operators are fixing the price which at least covers the cost of drinking water, it is also called as 'Top down' modeling (Beck, 1987[18]; Jabesman and Hronberger, 1993[19]).

In the present study, the upward approach alone is used to develop the financial model for drinking water since it is highly customer centric and frequently used in developing countries. In total, five financial models have been developed by the research with the help of previous studies, views of experts and the idea of the ministry of urban development. The financial model developed is given in Fig 3.1.

Financial Model – 1

Fig. 3.1 Financial model–1

In the above financial model, the Central/State Government has to give grant to local bodies for providing drinking water supply to the people. The local body has to supply water to the people at below the cost incurred by ULB. This financial model aims at only social welfare of the people.

Financial Model – 2

Under the financial model-2, the discriminatory pricing for the water supply is introduced. The model is given in Fig. 3.2

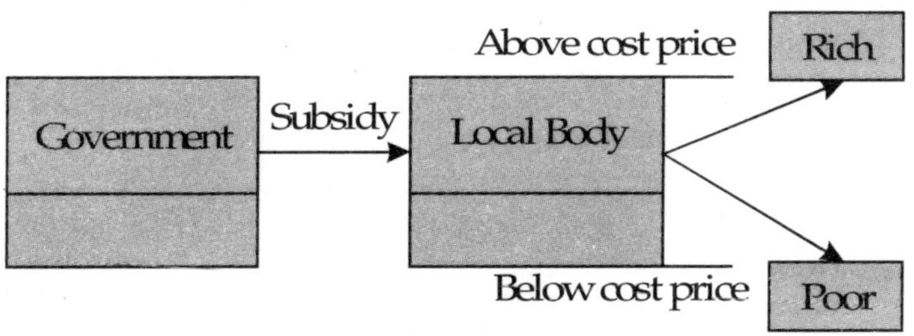

Fig. 3.2 Financial Model–2

In the model 2, the Central/State Government grants subsidy to the local body for providing water supply. The local body is empowered to fix different prices for supplying water (Two-tariff system). The affluent consumers have to pay above the cost whereas the poor will be charged below cost incurred to ULB. In this model, both the social welfare and the survival of ULB have been focused.

Finance Model-3

Finance model-3 represents the privatization of drinking water supply services. The price of drinking water is under the control of the Government, which is called as regulated price. The finance model-3 is presented in Figure 3.3.

Fig. 3.3 Finance Model–3.

In the above-said model, the Government hands over the power to the local body to select the private enterprise for providing drinking water services to the people. Both Government and local bodies may decide the selection criteria for the private enterprise. The local body permits the private enterprise to supply the drinking water to the people at the regulated price fixed by the local body.

Finance Model-4

Under the finance model-4, the privatization regulated pricing and social welfare have been considered. The proposed finance model-4 is illustrated in Figure 4.

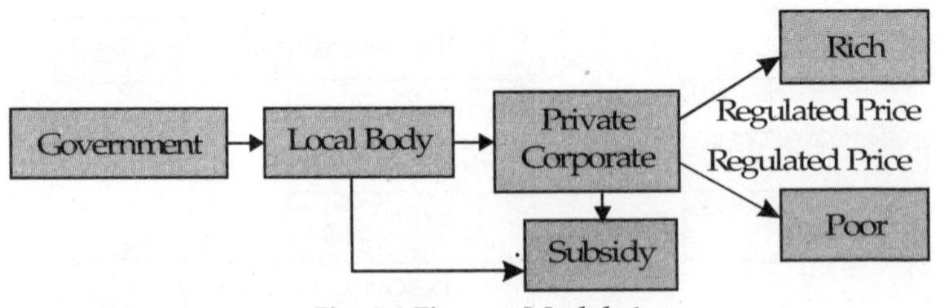

Fig. 3.4 Finance Model–4

Under this finance model, the local body permits the private enterprise to supply drinking water to the people. The private corporate has to classify the people into rich and poor on the basis of their documented annual income. The private enterprise has been permitted to fix a uniform price on the rich and the poor alike. The loss incurred by the provision of service to the people by the private services is set off by the subsidy granted by the local body.

Finance Model-5

Finance model-5 includes the privatization discriminating regulated pricing and also social welfare. The proposed model-5 is shown in Figure 3.5.

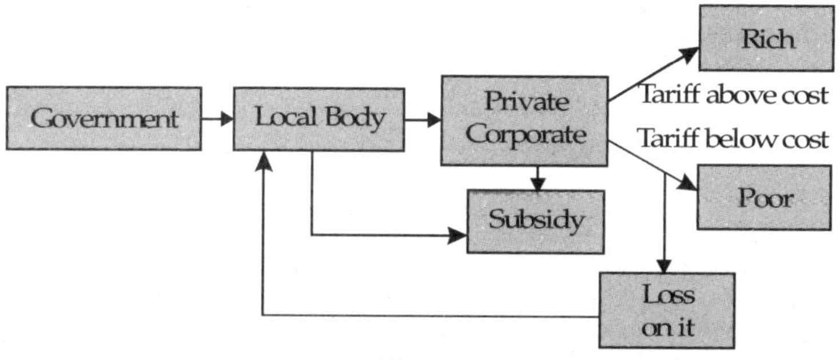

Fig. 3.5

Under this finance model, the local body permits the private enterprise to supply the drinking water to the people. The private enterprise has to classify the people into rich and poor on the basis of their documented annual income. The private supplier is permitted to fix a tariff above the cost for the rich whereas a tariff below cost for the poor. The enterprises are asked to equalize the loss from tariff below cost by the tariff above cost. Even if there is a loss, that loss is compensated by the local body by granting subsidy.

Evaluation of Finance Models by the Respondents

The finance models may be generated by the Government/ Local bodies/experts according to their feasibility studies and based on people's expectations (Willis et al., 2005[20]; Voloerbergh et al., 2007[21]; Turgeon et al., 2004[22]). The optimum financial model can be identified by the appropriate evaluation of the models on the basis of customer preferences (Nielson et al., 2003[23]; and Owen et al., 1999[24]). Even though the evaluation criteria are too many, the present study confines it to low tariff, regular water supply, convenient timing of water supply, quality of water, responsiveness, complaint handling, reliability of supply, assurance of supply, quantum of water consumed, Government subsidy, discrimination of pricing and privatization. The respondents are asked to rate the all five models at five point scale on the basis of each criterion of evaluation. The mean score of each finance model among the three income groups on the basis of low tariff has been computed to exhibit the respondents' attitude towards the financial models on the basis of low tariff. Regarding the perception on each financial model the significant difference among the three groups of respondents has been examined with the help of one-way analysis of variance. The results are given in Table 3.24.

Table 3.24 : Rating of finance models on the basis of low tariff

Sl. No.	Models	Mean Score			F-statistics
		LIG	MIG	HIG	
1.	Model-I	4.1568	3.8684	2.5168	3.9168*
2.	Model-II	3.7633	3.5026	3.7171	1.0144
3.	Model-III	3.0445	3.1419	3.8163	1.2761
4.	Model-IV	3.1234	3.0861	2.8186	0.7362
5.	Model-V	2.6566	2.9446	3.7174	3.0164*
	F. Statistics	4.4563*	3.0143*	3.2514*	—

* Significant at five per cent level.

The highly rated financial models among the LIG is model-I and Model-II since their respective mean scores are 4.1568 and 3.7633. Among the MIG, the highly rated financial models are model-I and model-II since their mean scores are 3.8684 and 3.5026 respectively. Among the HIG, these financial models are model-III and V since their respective mean scores are 3.8163 and 3.7174. Regarding the rating of financial models on the basis of low tariff, the significant difference among five models has been noticed among LIG, MIG and HIG since their respective 'F' statistics are significant at five per cent level. Regarding the rating on each financial model, the significant difference among the three income groups has been noticed since their respective 'F' statistics are significant at five per cent. It reveals that all respondents rate the five financial models with different weightage.

Evaluation of Financial Model on the Basis of Regular Water Supply

On the basis of regular water supply, all the five models have been evaluated by the respondents at five point scale. The mean score of the financial models among the LIG, MIG and HIG has been computed separately to show the level of importance attached to the financial models on the basis of the regular water supply. One-way analysis of variance has been administered to find out the significant difference among the three income groups regarding evaluation of each financial model and among the five models regarding their evaluating LIG, MIG and HIG separately.

Table 3.25 : Rating of finance models on the basis of regular water supply

Sl. No.	Models	Mean Score			F-statistics
		LIG	MIG	HIG	
1.	Model-I	2.4564	2.8162	2.3661	1.2491
2.	Model-II	3.0568	3.2661	3.0482	0.5262
3.	Model-III	3.8969	3.4541	3.6569	0.7341
4.	Model-IV	3.3342	3.4886	3.4144	0.4562
5.	Model-V	3.1451	3.5684	3.8184	2.4565
	F. Statistics	3.2546*	0.9147	2.9967*	—

* Significant at five per cent level.

The Model-III is highly regarded by LIG regarding the regular water supply since its mean score is 3.8969 whereas by MIG, it is model-V, since its mean score is 3.5684. The HIG highly rates the financial model-V since its mean scores is 3.8184. Regarding the evaluation of all five models, there is no significant difference among the three income groups. Regarding the evaluation by LIG and HIG there is a significant difference among the five financial models since their respective 'F' statistics is significant at five per cent level.

Rating of Financial Model on the Basis of Convenient Timing of Water Supply

The timing of water supply is one of important service expected by the consumer from the service providers. The consumers expect 24 hours drinking water supply but it is not possible for the service provider to provide such services because of the scarcity of drinking water. Hence, the service provider has to fulfill the maximum requirements of the consumers regarding their timing of water supply. In the present study, the respondents are asked to rate the financial models regarding the convenient timing of water supply at five-point scale. The results are given in Table 3.26.

Table 3.26 : Rating of financial models on the basis of convenience timing of water supply

Sl. No.	Models	Mean Score			F-statistics
		LIG	MIG	HIG	
1.	Model-I	2.8148	2.5086	2.3441	0.9197
2.	Model-II	2.6681	2.9196	2.7276	0.4508
3.	Model-III	2.8145	3.6864	3.6502	1.7366
4.	Model-IV	3.0718	3.4561	3.8914	0.8443
5.	Model-V	3.5684	3.5889	3.3445	0.7317
	F. Statistics	3.0146*	3.2784*	3.5142*	—

* Significant at five per cent level.

The LIG prefer model V regarding the convenient timing of the water supply since its mean score is 3.5684 whereas the MIG and HIG consider model-III and model-IV as the best in this regard since their respective mean scores are 3.6864 and 3.8914. Regarding the rating on financial models, there is no significant difference among the three income groups. Among all the three income groups, there is a significant difference on rating of financial models on the basis of the convenient timing of water supply since their respective 'F' statistics are significant at five per cent level.

Evaluation of Financial Models on the Basis of Quality of Water

The quality of water is the essential part of the drinking water service since it is the necessary and basic commodity. It is imperative to evaluate the financial model that will provide such quality water to the consumers. It represents the channels through which the consumers are getting quality water. The respondents are asked to rate the five financial models on the basis of the quality of water at five-point scale. The mean score of each model among the three income groups has been computed to exhibit the level of importance given on financial models by the respondents.

Table 3.27. Rating of finance models on the basis of quality of water

Sl. No.	Models	Mean Score			F-statistics
		LIG	MIG	HIG	
1.	Model-I	3.0244	2.6861	2.4562	1.3344
2.	Model-II	3.1782	2.7093	2.5149	2.1627
3.	Model-III	3.3308	3.8684	3.0866	2.0449
4.	Model-IV	3.2961	3.3446	3.6869	1.0961
5.	Model-V	3.4542	3.6117	3.8145	0.6861
	F. Statistics	0.9331	3.3089*	3.4181*	—

* Significant at five per cent level.

Table 3.27 exhibits the mean score of the financial models and their respective 'F' statistics. Regarding water quality, Model-V is highly rated by LIG whereas the MIG and HIG rate Model-III and V since their respective mean scores are 3.8684 and 3.8145. Regarding the rating on financial models, there is no significant difference among the three income groups. Regarding the rating on five financial models by LIG there is no significant difference among the five models. Since their respective 'F' statistics is not significant at five per cent level. Among the MIG and HIG, the significant differences on rating of five financial models have been noticed since their respective 'F' statistics are significant at five per cent level.

Rating of Financial Models on the Basis of "Responsiveness"

Responsiveness is one of important service quality factors identified by Parasuraman et al., (1985[25], 1990[26], 1993[27] and 1988[28]). The service providers have to respond to the appeal of their customers in a pleasing manner to improve their service quality. In the present study, the people are expecting same type of responsiveness from their service providers of drinking water and other basic amenities. In order to evaluate the financial models generated by the present study, the respondents were asked to rate the given financial models at five-point scale on the basis of responsiveness. The results are given in Table 3.28.

Table 3.28 : Rating of financial models on the basis of responsiveness

Sl. No.	Models	Mean Score			F-statistics
		LIG	MIG	HIG	
1.	Model-I	2.7178	2.4503	2.3911	0.4517
2.	Model-II	2.6109	2.9691	2.5089	0.6991
3.	Model-III	3.4542	3.4541	3.1143	0.3969
4.	Model-IV	3.6768	3.9296	3.5648	0.5108
5.	Model-V	3.5089	3.7122	3.8909	0.4917
	F. Statistics	3.1408*	3.3416*	3.2717*	—

* Significant at five per cent level.

The highly rated financial model on the basis of the responsiveness of the service providers among the LIG is model-IV since its mean score is 3.6768. Among the MIG and HIG, these models are model IV and model V since their mean scores are 3.9296 and 3.8906 respectively. Regarding the rating on the financial models, there is no significant difference among the three income groups since their respective 'F' statistics are not significant at five per cent level. Among the LIG, MIG and HIG significant differences on the rating of five financial models have been noticed since their respective 'F' statistics are significant at five per cent level. It reveals that the levels of importance attached to the five financial models are significantly different among all respondents.

Evaluation of Financial Models on the Basis of Complaint Handling

Regarding the public services namely drinking water and solid waste management, the service provider has to handle the complaints raised by the customers within a stipulated time. The response and handling procedures on complaints is one of the successful factors to determine the service quality of the service providers. In the present study, the respondents were asked to rate the five financial models on the basis of their faith on the complaint handling in these models at five-point scale. The results are given in Table 3.29.

Table 3.29 : Rating of financial models on the basis of complaint handling

Sl. No.	Models	Mean Score			F-statistics
		LIG	MIG	HIG	
1.	Model-I	2.6071	2.4044	2.3908	0.5908
2.	Model-II	2.4143	2.3917	2.6119	0.4773
3.	Model-III	2.8239	3.5089	3.4568	1.3969
4.	Model-IV	3.1339	3.2345	3.6969	0.8142
5.	Model-V	3.0868	3.4541	3.8184	2.1408
	F. Statistics	2.3402	3.1146*	3.4084*	—

* Significant at five per cent level.

The highly rated financial models among the LIG is model-IV since its mean score is 3.1339 whereas among the MIG and HIG, these are Model-III and V since their mean scores are 3.5089 and 3.8184 respectively. Regarding the rating of financial models, there is no significant difference among the three income group of respondents since their respective 'F' statistics are not significant at five per cent level. Between the MIG and HIG, significant difference among the rating of five different financial models has been noticed since their respective 'F' statistics are significant at five per cent level.

Rating of Financial Models on the Basis of 'Reliability' of Water Supply

The 'reliability' of the water supply is one of the important service quality factors. In general, consumers are expecting more 'reliability' on the water service from their service providers. On the basis of the reliability of water supply, the respondents were asked to rate the proposed five financial models at five point scale. The score on the financial models among the three income groups have been computed separately. The significant difference among the three groups of customers regarding their evaluation on each financial model and also the evaluation of five models by each customers group were analysed with one-way analysis of variance.

Table 3.30 : Rating of financial models on the basis of reliability of water supply

Sl. No.	Models	Mean Score			F-statistics
		LIG	MIG	HIG	
1.	Model-I	2.6568	2.4409	2.2908	0.4913
2.	Model-II	2.8184	2.6331	2.4541	0.6339
3.	Model-III	3.5086	3.6889	3.6904	0.5147
4.	Model-IV	3.3341	3.7126	3.9221	1.2133
5.	Model-V	3.4908	3.5969	3.7338	0.6519
	F-Statistics	2.8145	3.1245*	3.4906*	—

* Significant at five per cent level.

Table 3.30 reveals the mean scores of the financial models and their respective 'F' statistics. The highly rated financial models among the LIG, MIG and HIG are model III, model IV and model IV since their respective mean scores are 3.5086, 3.7126 and 3.9221. Regarding the evaluation of five financial models, the significant differences among the three income groups have not been identified since their respective 'F' statistics are not significant at five per cent level. Among the MIG and HIG, the significant differences on the evaluation of five financial models have been noticed since their respective 'F' statistics are significant at five per cent level.

Evaluation of Financial Model on the Basis of 'Assurance' of Water Supply

Regarding the assurance on the water supply, the proposed five financial models have been rated by the respondents at five point scale in order to identify the important financial model regarding the assurance of water supply. The one-way analysis of variance has been executed to find out the significant difference among five models among LIG, MIG and HIG separately. The significant differences among the LIG, MIG and HIG have also been analysed in evaluation of each financial model.

Table 3.31 : Rating of financial models on the basis of assurance of water supply

Sl. No.	Models	Mean Score			F-statistics
		LIG	MIG	HIG	
1.	Model-I	2.4568	2.2969	2.1442	0.8186
2.	Model-II	2.7339	2.3043	2.6559	0.5963
3.	Model-III	3.2144	3.4547	3.7308	0.8124
4.	Model-IV	3.0868	3.6908	3.9617	1.2441
5.	Model-V	3.4544	3.7376	3.8144	0.9596
	F. Statistics	3.1409*	3.3308*	4.1716*	—

* Significant at five per cent level.

The highly rated financial model among the LIG is model-V since its mean score is 3.4544 whereas among MIG and HIG, they are model-V and model-IV since their mean scores are 3.7376 and 3.9617 respectively. Among the LIG, MIG and HIG, the significant differences among the evaluation on five financial models have been identified since their respective 'F' statistics are significant at five per cent level. Regarding the evaluation of each financial model, there is no significant differences among the three income group of respondents since their respective 'F' statistics are not significant at five per cent level.

Evaluation of Financial Models on the Basis of Quantum of Water Consumed

The quantum of water consumed by the respondents is one of the important criteria to evaluate the proposed financial models. The respondents who are consuming greater quantity of water usually prefer the flat rate model proposed by the local bodies since their average cost of drinking water per litre is very less. The consumers who consume only lesser quantity of water prefer the price based on quantity, discriminatory pricing, quality of water and also the service provider who renders better service quality. Hence, the present analysis has made an attempt to evaluate all five financial models among the three income groups. The results are given in Table 3.32.

Table 3.32 : Rating of financial models on the basis of quantum of water consumed

Sl. No.	Models	Mean Score			F-statistics
		LIG	MIG	HIG	
1.	Model-I	3.6843	2.5779	2.3093	3.1457*
2.	Model-II	3.1109	2.4041	2.2596	2.8086
3.	Model-III	2.5969	3.0964	3.2145	1.4507
4.	Model-IV	2.3446	3.1469	3.5886	3.0969*
5.	Model-V	2.6561	3.2273	3.7174	3.1144*
	F. Statistics	3.1142*	3.7108*	3.9663*	—

* Significant at five per cent level.

The highly rated financial model among the LIG is model-I since its mean score is 3.6843 whereas among the MIG and HIG, it is model-V since its mean scores are 3.2273 and 3.7174 respectively. Regarding the rating of financial models, the significant differences among the three income groups have been identified in the case of evaluation on model-I, IV and V since their respective 'F' statistics are significant at five per cent level. Among the LIG, MIG and HIG, the significant differences among the evaluation of all five financial models have been identified since their respective 'F' statistics are significant at five per cent level.

Rating of Financial Models on the Basis of Government Subsidy

The Central/State Government grants subsidy to the local Government for the provision of drinking water to the people at a subsidized rate. If the system is handed over to the private enterprises, the granting of subsidies will be highly questionable. Hence, people may have some idea before evaluating the financial models. Hence people use the subsidy as one of the important criterion to evaluate the financial models. The mean scores of all five financial models on the basis of Government subsidy among the LIG, MIG and HIG and their respective 'F' statistics are given in Table 3.33.

Table 3.33 : Rating of financial models on the basis of government subsidy

Sl. No.	Models	Mean Score			F-statistics
		LIG	MIG	HIG	
1.	Model-I	3.8919	3.5089	3.7371	0.469
2.	Model-II	3.6394	3.4144	3.8662	0.5082
3.	Model-III	2.5089	3.0661	2.9109	1.2447
4.	Model-IV	2.3444	2.5059	2.5664	0.3917
5.	Model-V	2.4224	2.4417	2.4147	0.1249
	F. Statistics	4.1718*	3.9096*	3.8617*	—

* Significant at five per cent level.

Among the LIG, the highly rated financial model on the basis of Government subsidy is model-I since its mean score is 3.8919 whereas among the MIG and HIG, it is also model-I since its mean scores is 3.5089. Among the HIG, it is Model-III. Among the LIG, MIG and HIG the significant difference among the rating of five financial models have been noticed since their respective 'F' statistics are significant at five per cent level.

Evaluation of Financial Models on the Basis of Discriminatory Pricing

The discriminatory pricing represents the different prices on the same drinking water supplies to different groups of people. Usually, the price may be charged on the basis of the income and quantity consumed of the households. In the present system, there is a uniform pricing. The purposed finance model consists of both uniform and discriminatory pricing. The respondents are asked to rate the five financial models on the basis of discriminatory pricing on water. The results are given in Table 3.34.

Table 3.34 : Rating of financial models on the basis of discriminatory pricing

Sl. No.	Models	Mean Score			F-statistics
		LIG	MIG	HIG	
1.	Model-I	2.6869	2.8184	2.5144	0.6867
2.	Model-II	3.7334	3.6679	3.4568	0.5146
3.	Model-III	2.5089	3.1144	2.9091	0.7331
4.	Model-IV	2.4142	2.7089	2.5124	0.4964
5.	Model-V	2.9884	3.1081	3.4509	0.9691
	F. Statistics	3.4504*	3.3969*	4.1086*	—

* Significant at five per cent level.

On the basis of discriminatory pricing, the highly rated financial model among the LIG is model-II since its mean score is 3.7334 whereas among the MIG and HIG, these are also model-II since its mean scores are 3.6679 and 3.4568. Regarding the evaluation of all financial models, there is not significant difference among the three income groups since their respective 'F' statistics are not significant at five per cent level. Among the LIG, MIG and HIG, the significant difference on evaluation of five financial models have been noticed since their respective 'F' statistics are significant at five per cent level.

Evaluation of Financial Models on the Basis of Privatization

The privatization of public services is one of the important criterions to evaluate the financial models. The people may have their own opinion on privatization. Some of them may be for the privatization to get enriched service even at higher prices. Some may not be favour to privatization because of fear on higher tariffs and discrimination. Hence the respondents are asked to rate the proposed five financial models at five point scale on the basis of privatization. The results are given in Table 3.35.

Table 3.35 : Rating of financial models on the basis of privatization

Sl. No.	Models	Mean Score			F-statistics
		LIG	MIG	HIG	
1.	Model-I	2.4508	2.3399	2.1406	0.3996
2.	Model-II	2.6114	2.4106	2.3441	0.4547
3.	Model-III	3.2911	3.1987	3.2516	0.4086
4.	Model-IV	3.0986	3.8664	3.4544	0.6889
5.	Model-V	3.6164	3.9337	3.8996	0.4024
	F. Statistics	3.1408*	3.5969*	3.9091*	—

* Significant at five per cent level.

The highly rated financial model among the LIG is model-V since its mean score is 3.6164 whereas among the MIG and HIG, this is model-V since their respective mean scores are 3.9337 and 3.8996. Regarding the evaluation of all five financial models, there is no significant difference among the three income groups since their respective 'F' statistics are not significant at five per cent level. Among the LIG, MIG and HIG, the significant difference among the evaluation on five financial models have been identified since their respective 'F' statistics are significant at five per cent level.

Overall Rating on Financial Models

The overall rating indicates the summative rating of all five financial models on the basis of all dimensions namely low tariff, regular water supply, convenience timing of water supply, quality of water, responsiveness, complaint handling, reliability of water supply, assurance of water supply, quantum of water consumed, Government subsidy, discriminatory pricing and privatization. The mean score of each financial model at 12 criterion variables among the respondents have been computed to exhibit the overall rating. The results are presented in Table 3.36.

Table 3.36 : Overall rating of financial models

Sl. No.	Models	Mean Score			F-statistics
		LIG	MIG	HIG	
1.	Model-I	2.9671	2.8697	2.5501	0.8906
2.	Model-II	3.0534	2.8827	2.8471	0.5711
3.	Model-III	2.8483	3.3944	3.3998	0.9143
4.	Model-IV	3.0216	3.3476	3.4232	1.3436
5.	Model-V	3.1707	3.4101	3.6196	2.2765
	F. Statistics	1.0143	2.9904*	4.2152*	—

* Significant at five per cent level.

The highly rated financial model among the LIG is model-V since its mean score is 3.1707. The difference between the mean score of all five financial models among LIG is not statistically significant. It reveals that the LIG may be favour on model-V but at the some time they may adjust with other four financial models also. The highly rated financial model among the MIG is model-V since its mean score is 3.4104. It is followed by the model-III since its mean score is 3.3944. Among the MIG, the significant difference on the rating on five financial models have been identified since their respective 'F' statistics are significant at five per cent level. It reveals that the MIG study prefers the model-V and it is followed by model III and IV. The highly rated financial model among the HIG is model-V since its mean score is 3.6196. It is followed by model-IV and model-III since its mean scores are 3.6196 and 3.3998 respectively. Regarding the evaluation on all five financial models the significant difference among the five finance models have been noticed since their respective 'F' statistics is significant at five per cent level. The analysis reveals that the HIG is highly favour model-V and it is followed by model-IV and III.

The model-I is highly rated by LIG since its mean score is 2.9617 whereas among MIG and HIG, it is 2.8697 and 2.5501 respectively. The difference among the three income groups is not statistically significant regarding the overall rating of financial model-I. The same situation is also identified in financial model-II. In the case of financial model-III, it is highly rated by the HIG since its mean score is 3.3998 whereas among the MIG and LIG, it is 3.3944 and 2.8483 respectively. Regarding the evaluation of the financial model-III, there is no significant difference among the three income groups. The same trend is identified in the case of financial model-IV and V. The analysis reveals that the MIG and LIG is strongly prefer the financial model-V whereas, the LIG is also preferring it but they are in different to select any one of the financial models.

Association between the Profile of Respondents and their Overall Rating of Financial Models

The profile of the respondents may be associated with their rating of financial models. It is highly imperative to analyse such association to find out the significance of the profile variables in rating of financial models. The one way analysis of variance has been administered to analyse the association between the profile of respondents and then for overall rating of five financial models separately. The results are given in Table 3.37.

Regarding the evaluation of Model-I, the significantly associating profile variables are age, occupational background, family size, number of earning members per family and house category since their respective 'F' statistics are significant at five per cent level. The significantly associating profile variables on the evaluation of model-II are age, occupational background, house category and type of house. Regarding the evaluation of model-III, the significantly associating profile variables are age, nativity, occupational background, family size, number of earning members per family and house category since their respective 'F' statistics are significant at five per cent level. The significantly associating profile variables with the evaluation of financial model-IV are age, occupational background, family size, houseownership, type of house, number of pipe connections and frequency of water supply

Table 3.37 : Association between profile of respondents and their rating on financial models

Sl. No.	Profile variables	F-Statistics				
		Model-I	Model-II	Model-III	Model-IV	Model-V
1.	Gender	3.1414	3.0816	3.3993	3.7874	4.1445*
2.	Age	2.8696*	2.70218	2.7694*	2.7089*	2.7317*
3.	Nativity	2.0414	2.9142	3.6061*	2.9196	3.0664
4.	Occupational background	2.9902*	3.1411*	2.9192*	2.8184*	2.9197*
5.	Family size	2.6061*	2.1517	2.6069*	2.7671*	2.8082*
6.	Number of earning members per family	3.3046*	3.0644	3.4424*	3.0646	3.0144
7.	House Category	2.5779*	2.6861*	2.6869*	2.5859*	2.6884*
8.	Type of house	2.9143	3.2344*	2.9017	3.2168*	2.7089
9.	Number of pipe connections	2.4082	2.7139	2.6566	3.0917*	2.9604*
10.	Frequency of water supply avails	2.6342	2.5396	2.4314	2.8664*	2.8184*

* Significant at five per cent level.

availed whereas in the case of evaluation of model-V, these profile variables are gender, age, occupational background, family size, house category, number of pipe connections and frequency of water supply availed. The study reveals the role of the profile variables namely age, occupational background, house category and family size in the evaluation of the financial models.

Factors Leading to Choose the Financial Models

The proposed financial models are rated by 12 intention variables to evaluate the financial models. The important factors leading to select the financial models have been analysed separately to exhibit the important attributes of drinking water supply among the respondents. Even though the factors are too many, the present study confines itself to tariff, quality of water, regular water supply, service quality, customer care, nature of service provider and proper maintenance. The mean scores of each factor among the respondents under different groups in each of their profile have been computed to exhibit the level of importance attached to each factor. The multi-discriminant analysis has been examined to identify the important discriminant factors among the different groups of respondents in each profile variables. The results are given in Table 3.38.

Table 3.38 : Mean score and standardized discriminant coefficient of factors to choose the finance model

Sl. No.	Factors	Mean score among			Standard discriminant co-efficient
		LIG	MIG	HIG	
1.	Tariff	3.8184	3.2094	2.5168	1.04*
2.	Quality of water	2.5065	3.4608	3.7331	1.29*
3.	Regular water supply	3.2143	3.5142	3.8994	0.34
4.	Service quality	3.0664	3.4033	3.7669	0.49*
5.	Customer care	3.1147	3.3229	3.5045	0.29
6.	Nature of service provider	2.7664	2.8085	2.8144	0.04
7.	Proper maintenance	2.9193	2.9944	3.4324	0.18
8.	Cluster size	191	340	108	
9.	Eigen value		16.34		
10.	Per cent of variance explained		81.36		
11.	Canonical correlation		0.6789		

* Significant at five per cent level.

Three distinct clusters namely LIG, MIG and HIG were constructed on the basis of the income of the respondents. The important factors leading to the choice of the financial model among them are tariff and regular water supply since their respective mean scores are 3.8184 and 3.2143 whereas among the MIG, these are regular water supply and quality of water source since their respective mean scores are 3.5142 and 3.4608. Among the HIG, these factors are regular water supply and service quality since their respective mean scores are 3.8994 and 3.7669. The income of the respondents influences the three group of respondents regarding their importance attached to the factors leading to choose the financial model.

The significant and strongest discriminators were tariff, quality of water and service quality since their respective standardized discriminant coefficients are significant at five per cent level. The eigen value, per cent of variance explained and canonical correlation confirm the reliability of the established multiple discriminant analysis (Capon et al., 1994)[29] . The analysis reveals that the tariff, quality water and service quality are the important discriminators to choose the financial model among the three income groups. The LIG residents give more importance to tariff and the MIG and HIG give more importance to quality of water and service quality.

Discriminant Factors to Choose the Financial Model (*Gender and Age Group of Respondents*)

The male respondents may differ from female respondents regarding the level of importance attached with the selection of financial model. It is highly imperative to analyse the level of importance attached to these factors and also to identify the significant discriminant factors to choose the model among them. Based on the age of the respondents, they are classified into less than 30 years, 30 to 40, 41 to 50, 51 to 60 and above 60 years; the level of importance attached to the factors to choose among them may differ. It is more important to examine this aspect to reveal the importance of factors among youngsters and elders. The mean scores of each factor among different group of respondents have been computed separately. The multiple discriminant analysis has been executed to identify the significant discriminant factor among them. The results are given in Tables 3.39 and 3.40.

The highly regarded factors among the male respondent is nature of service provider and quality of water since their mean scores are 3.8244 and 3.8184 respectively. Among the female respondents, these are quality of water and regular water supply since their mean scores are 3.7341 and 3.6639 respectively. The significant discriminant factors to choose the financial model among the male and female respondents are tariff, customer care, nature of service provider and proper

Table 3.39 : Mean score and standardized discriminant coefficients of factors (Gender)

Sl. No.	Factors	Gender		
		Male	Female Discriminant coefficient	Standardized
1.	Tariff	2.9143	3.6143	-0.84*
2.	Quality of water	3.8184	3.7341	-0.13
3.	Regular water supply	3.5549	3.6639	-0.09
4.	Service quality	3.6861	3.4159	0.26
5.	Customer care	3.8178	3.0611	1.24*
6.	Nature of service provider	3.8244	3.144	0.59*
7.	Proper maintenance	3.0914	3.2455	0.72*
8.	Cluster size	429	210	
9.	Eigen value		15.43	
10.	Per cent of variation explained		73.36	
11.	Canonical correlation		0.6566	

* Significant at five per cent level.

maintenance since their respective standardized discriminant co-efficient are significant at five per cent level. The eigen value, per cent of variance explained and canonical correlation of the multiple discriminant function is greater than the minimum threshold (Zafar khan et al., 1995)[30].

The most important factor reading to choose the financial model by the respondents aged less than 30 years is service quality since their respective mean score is 3.8224. Whereas among the respondents with the age of 30 to 40 years and 41 to 50 years, it is regular water supply since its mean score is 3.8142 and 3.5046 respectively. Among the respondents aged between of 51 and 60 years and above 60 years the most important factor is nature of service provider since their respective mean scores are 3.8164 and 3.5617. The significant discriminant factors among the different age groups leading to choose the financial model are tariff, quality of water, service quality, customer care, nature of service provider and proper

Table 3.40 : Mean score and standardized discriminant coefficients of factors (Age)

Sl. No.	Factors	Age (in years)					
		<30	30-40	41-50	51-60	>60	Standardized discriminant coefficient
1.	Tariff	2.4511	2.6514	2.8991	3.0239	3.5169	-1.39*
2.	Quality of water	3.6861	3.6441	3.5042	3.1419	2.8646	-1.07*
3.	Regular water supply	3.5994	3.8142	3.5046	3.2443	3.0686	0.29
4.	Service quality	3.8224	3.5662	3.4144	3.2168	2.9661	1.17*
5.	Customer care	3.7993	3.8108	3.3919	3.1817	3.0669	0.42*
6.	Nature of service provider	3.0441	2.9692	3.1417	3.8164	3.5617	0.56*
7.	Proper maintenance	3.5994	3.4114	3.2092	3.0919	2.8186	0.39*
8.	Cluster size	76	131	223	136	73	
9.	Eigen value				18.01		
10.	Per cent of variation explained				89.43		
11.	Canonical correlation				0.7147		

* Significant at five per cent level.

maintenance since their respective discriminant coefficients are significant at five per cent level. The estimated discriminant function justifies its validity since then respective eigen value, per cent of variation explained and canonical correlation are greater than the minimum threshold.

Discriminant Factors among the Respondents Based on their Nativity and Occupational Background

On the basis of nativity, the respondents are classified into urban, semi-urban and rural (Table 3.41) whereas on the basis of occupational background, they are classified into

Table 3.41 : Mean score and standardized discriminant coefficient of the factors (Nativity)

Sl. No.	Factors	Nativity			
		Urban	Semi-urban	Rural	Standardized Disc. coefficient
1.	Tariff	2.5081	2.8196	3.3417	–0.58*
2.	Quality of water	3.4117	3.6861	3.8664	–0.14
3.	Regular water supply	3.6086	3.4514	3.7311	–0.05
4.	Service quality	3.8085	3.4142	3.0861	0.39*
5.	Customer care	3.9214	3.2626	2.9141	1.45*
6.	Nature of service provider	3.4516	3.0891	2.4541	1.33*
7.	Proper maintenance	3.6165	3.0811	3.2156	–0.24
8.	Cluster size	109	241	199	
9.	Eigen value		17.67		
10.	Per cent of variation explained		88.43		
11.	Canonical correlation		0.7562		

respondents in private employment, government employment, business, agriculture and others. The level of importance attached to the factors among different group of respondents has been examined to exhibit the level of importance on each factor. The MDA have been applied to identify the significant discriminant factors.

The highly rated factors by the urban respondents are customer care and service quality since their respective mean scores are 3.9214 and 3.8085 whereas among the semi-urban respondents, these are quality of water and regular water supply since their mean scores are 3.6861 and 3.4514 respectively. The important factors identified by the rural respondents are quality of water and regular water supply since their respective mean scores are 3.8664 and 3.7311. The significant discriminant factors among the three groups of respondents regarding the level of importance attached to

Table 3.42 : Mean score and standardized discriminant co-efficients of factors (Occupational Background)

Sl. No.	Factors	Occupational Background					Standar-dized disc. coeffi-cient
		Private employ-ment	Govt. employ-ment	Busi-ness	Agri-culture	Other	
1	Tariff	2.6819	2.9192	2.9029	3.5686	3.0141	-0.49*
2.	Quality of water	3.4541	3.2664	2.9196	2.8441	3.2626	0.22
3.	Regular water supply	3.6865	3.8191	3.4554	2.9961	3.1445	-0.67*
4.	Service quality	3.8185	3.2696	3.0144	2.8661	3.3349	-0.91*
5.	Customer care	3.7479	3.4546	3.3441	3.0669	3.1457	0.36
6.	Nature of service provider	3.5884	3.6869	3.0441	2.6614	2.8108	0.74*
7.	Proper maintenance	3.6189	3.0844	3.2449	2.5994	2.9069	0.15
8.	Cluster size	189	161	142	52	95	
9.	Eigen value			18.68			
10.	Per cent of variation explained			92.04			
11.	Canonical correlation			0.8144			

* Significant at five per cent level.

these factors are tariff, service quality, customer care, and nature of service provider since their respective standardized discriminant coefficients are significant at five per cent level.

The significant discriminant factors among the differently occupied respondents are tariff, regular water supply, service quality and nature of service provider since their respective discriminant coefficients are significant at five per cent level. The most important factors among the private and government employed are regular water supply and service quality since their respective mean scores are 3.8185 and 3.8191. Among the businessmen and agriculturalists, these factors are regular water supply and tariff since their respective mean scores are 3.4554 and 3.5686. Among other respondents, it is service quality since its mean score is 3.3349.

Discriminant Factors among the Respondents (on the basis of their Family Size and Number of Earning Members per Family)

On the basis of the family size, the respondents are classified into the family size of upto 3, 4 to 5, 6 to 7 and above 7 members (Table 3.43) whereas on the basis of the number of earning members per family, they are classified into the respondents with one, two and more than two earning members (Table 3.44). Since the level of importance attached to the factors leading to choose the financial model among the different group of respondents in each profile are different, the present study has made an attempt to identify the level of importance attached to each factor by different groups of respondents and also the significant discriminant factors among the different groups.

Table 3.43 : Mean and discriminant coefficient of the factors (Family Size)

Sl. No.	Factors	Family Size				
		Upto3	4-5	6-7	Above 7	Standardized disc. Coefficient
1.	Tariff	2.4568	2.5144	2.8986	3.5644	1.43*
2.	Quality of water	3.6868	3.4504	3.2344	3.0861	0.8101*
3.	Regular water supply	3.7121	3.5611	3.4599	3.3444	0.2462
4.	Service quality	3.8688	3.6108	3.2089	2.9196	1.6803*
5.	Customer care	3.9144	3.6564	3.0869	2.8243	1.7141*
6.	Nature of service provider	2.4514	2.7131	2.9696	3.4514	–0.9717*
7.	Proper maintenance	3.4516	3.6817	2.9194	2.5656	1.2616*
8.	Cluster size	171	298	122	48	
9.	Eigen value			16.49		
10.	Per cent of variation explained			75.04		
11.	Canonical correlation			0.6448		

Table 3.44 : Mean and discriminant coefficient of the factors (Number of earning members per family)

Sl. No.	Factors	Number of earning members			
		One	Two	Above two	Standardized disc. Coefficient
1.	Tariff	3.5614	3.0119	2.4562	1.23*
2.	Quality of water	3.3144	3.5667	3.8183	0.49*
3.	Regular water supply	3.4504	3.6860	3.5059	0.13
4.	Service quality	3.6183	3.4514	3.8184	–0.42
5.	Customer care	3.4133	3.7189	3.8026	–0.38
6.	Nature of service provider	2.6869	3.3811	3.9193	–1.41*
7.	Proper maintenance	3.1414	3.5089	3.8564	–0.52*
8.	Cluster size	199	343	97	
9.	Eigen value	18.04			
10.	Per cent of variation explained	81.89			
	Canonical correlation	0.7996			

The highly regarded factors among the respondents with the family size of upto 3 and 4 to 5 members is customer care and proper maintenance since their respective mean scores are 3.9144 and 3.6817. For those respondents with the family size of 6 to 7 and above 7 members, these are regular water supply and tariff since their respective mean scores are 3.4599 and 3.5644. The significant discriminant factors among these four groups on the basis of family size are tariff, quality of water, service quality, customer care, nature of service provider and proper maintenance since their respective discriminant coefficients are significant at five per cent level.

The most important factor identified by respondents with only one earning member is service quality since its mean score is 3.6183 whereas among the respondents with two earning members, it is customer care since their respective mean score is 3.7189. Among the respondents with more than two earning members, it is nature of service provider since its mean score is 3.9193. The significant discriminant factors among the three group of respondents are tariff, quality of water, nature of service provider and proper maintenance since their respective discriminant coefficients are significant at five per cent level. The analysis reveals the importance of tariff, quality of water, nature of service provider and proper maintenance in presenting different financial models to respondents with different number of earning members per family.

Discriminant Factors among the Respondents with Different Occupancy Status and Type of House

On the basis of occupancy status, the respondents are classified into the respondents living in owned house, leased house, and rented house whereas on the basis of type of house, they are grouped into the respondents living in individual house and apartments. Since the level of importance attached to each factor among the different groups are different, the present study has made an attempt to analyze the level of importance attached to each factor among different groups of respondents with its mean score. The multiple discriminant analysis (Kathryn and Diane, 1996)[31] has been employed to identify the significant discriminant factors among these groups. The results are given in Tables 3.45 and 3.46.

The highly rated factors among the respondents with owned house and leased house are tariff and quality of water since their mean scores are 3.8186 and 3.7182 respectively. Among the respondents living in rented house, it is 'customer care' since its mean score is 3.9297. The significant discriminant factors among the above said three groups are tariff, service quality, customer care, nature of service provider and proper maintenance since their respective discriminant coefficients are significant at five per cent level.

The most important factors among the respondents living in individual house and apartments are tariff and service quality since their mean scores are 3.6446 and 3.8778 respectively. The significant discriminant factors among the two group of respondents are tariff, service quality, customer

Table 3.45. Mean score and discriminant coefficients of factors (House Ownership)

Sl. No.	Factors	House ownership			
		Owned house	Leased house	Rented house	Standardized disc. Coefficient
1.	Tariff	3.8186	2.8684	2.6168	1.39*
2.	Quality of water	3.4503	3.7182	3.6962	0.12
3.	Regular water supply	3.2449	3.6604	3.7173	–0.38
4.	Service quality	3.1408	3.2641	3.8081	–0.76*
5.	Customer care	2.9961	3.4408	3.9297	–1.43*
6.	Nature of service provider	2.3917	3.0768	3.5149	–1.31*
7.	Proper maintenance	3.1411	3.3396	3.8911	–0.61*
8.	Cluster size	253	123	263	
9.	Eigen value		18.64		
10.	Per cent of variation explained		85.96		
11.	Canonical correlation		0.8336		

Table 3.46. Mean score and discriminant coefficients of factors (Type of House)

Sl. No.	Factors	Type of House		Standardized Disc. coefficient
		Individual	Apartment	
1.	Tariff	3.6446	2.7184	1.17*
2.	Quality of water	3.5994	3.6168	–0.12
3.	Regular water supply	3.4508	3.4103	–0.09
4.	Service quality	3.1491	3.8778	–0.67*
5.	Customer care	3.2446	3.7449	–0.53*
6.	Nature of service provider	3.5844	2.6843	1.03*
7.	Proper maintenance	3.5021	3.6169	–0.07
8.	Cluster size	258	381	
9.	Eigen value		16.33	
10.	Per cent of variation explained		72.41	
11.	Canonical correlation		0.6554	

care and nature of service provider since their respective discriminant coefficients are significant at five per cent level. The respondents living in individual house consider tariff, quality of water and nature of service provider as important whereas the respondents living in apartments consider the service quality, customer care and quality of water to be the deciding factors in choosing the financial model.

REFERENCES

1. Alison Wedgwood and Kevin Sanson, (2003), *Willingness-to-pay surveys – A Streamlined approach*, Water, Engineering and Development Centre, Lough Borough University, UK, p. 6.
2. Lund, J.R., (1995), "Derived estimation of Willingness to pay to avoid prolalistic shortage", *Water Resources Research*, 31(5), pp. 1367-1372.
3. Griffin, R.C., and Mjelde, J.W. (2000), "Valuing water supply reliability", *American Journal of Agricultural Economics*, 82(2), p. 414.
4. Levallois, P., Grondin, J., and Gingras, S., (1999), "Evaluation of consumer attitudes on taste and tap water alternatives in Quebec", *Water Science and Technology*, 40(4), pp. 135-139.
5. Merret, S., (2002), "Deconstructing Household's Willingness–to– pay for water in low income countries", *Water Policy*, 4(2), pp. 157-172.
6. Kontogianni, A., Longford, I.H., Papandreou, A., and Skourfos, M.S., (2004), "Social preferences for improving water quality: An Economic analysis of benefits from waste water treatment", *Water Resources Management*, 17(1), pp. 317-336.
7. Stiglitz, J., (2002), "Globalison's Discontents", *The American Prospect*, 13(1), January, pp. 1-14.
8. Water Manifesto (2000), 30 Rue Manrose, 1030 Brussels, Belgium, http: //www.f1 boat.com/99/water manifesto.html.
9. Dumol, M., (2000), "*Manila Water Concession: A Key Government Officials' Daisy of the World's Largest Water Privatisation*", World Bank Publication, Washington, D.C. July.
10. Hanemann, W.M., (1984), "Welfare Evaluations in Contingent Valuation Experiments with Discrete Responses", *American Journal of Agricultural Economics*, 66 (3), pp. 332-341.
11. Cameson, J., and James, M., (1987), "Efficient Estimation Methods for 'Closed-Ended' Contingent Valuation Surveys", *Review of Economics and Statistics*, 69(2), pp. 269-276.

12. Cronin, J.J., Muchael, B.K., and Thomas, M.K.G., (2000), "Assessing the Effects of Quality, Value and Customer Satisfaction on Consumer behavioural intentions in service environment", *Journal of Retailing,* 76 (2), pp. 116-123.

13. MC Fadden, D., (1976), "The Revealed Preferences of a Government Bureaucracy: Empirical Evidence", *Journal of Economics,* 7(1), pp. 55-72.

14. Whittington, Dale (2002), "Improving the Performance of Contingent Valuation Studies in Developing Countries", *Environmental and Resource Economics,* 22(4), pp. 323-367.

15. Bathurst, J.C. and O'Connel, P.E. (1992), "The future of distributed modeling: The system hydrologique", *European, Hydrol.Proc.,* 6(1), pp. 265-277.

16. Beven, K.J. (1989), "Changing ideas in water pricing – the case of physically based models", *Journal of Hydrology,* 105(4), pp. 157-172.

17. Grayson, R.B. and Bloschl, G., (2000), *"Spatial Patterns in Drinking Water Pricing: Observation and Modelling"*, Cambridge University Press, p. 404.

18. Beck, M.B., (1987), "Water Pricing Model: A Review", *Water Resource Research,* 23(2), pp. 1393-1442.

19. Jebesman A., and Hornberger, G.M. (1993), "Complexity in 'Financial Model' for drinking water", *Water Resource Research,* 26(4), pp. 2659-2666.

20. Willis, K.G., Scarpa, R., Acust, M., (2005), "Assessing water company customers preferences and willingness to pay for service improvements: A stated choice analysis", *Water Resources Research,* 41(2), pp. 1-11.

21. Voloerberch, I., Kelay, T., Chenoweth, J., Fife-Schaw, C., Morrison, G., and Lundehn, C., (2007), Measuring customer preferences for drinking water services: Methods for water utilities", Techneau Report, www.techneau.org.

22. Turgeon, S., Rodriguez, M.J., Theniault, M., and Levallois, P., (2004), "Perception of drinking water in Quebec region (Canada): The influence of water quality and consumer location in the drinking water system", *Journal of Environmental Management,* 70(3), pp. 363-373.

23. Nielsen, J.B., Gyrd-Hanson, D., Kristiansen, I.S., Nexpe, J., (2003), "Impact of Socio-demographic factors on Willingness-to-pay for the reduction of a future health risk", *Journal of Environmental Planning and Management,* 46(1), pp. 39-47.

24. Owen, A.J., Colbourse, J.S., Clayton, C.R.I., Fife-Sahaw, C., (1999), "Risk Communication of hazardous processes associated with drinking water quality – a mental models approach to customer perception; part-1-a methodology", *Water Science and Technology*, 39(10), pp. 183-188.

25. Parasuraman, A., Zeithammal, V.A., and Berry, L.L., (1985), "A Conceptual model for service quality and implications for future research", *Journal of Marketing*, 49(Fall), pp. 41-50.

26. Ibid. (1988), "SERVQUAL: A Multiple – Item Scale for measuring consumer perceptions of service quality", *Journal of Retailing*, 64(1), pp. 12-40.

27. Ibid. (1990), "A Empirical examination of relationship in an extended service quality model", Cambridge, MA: Marketing Science Institute.

28. Ibid. (1993), "More on improving service quality measurement", *Journal of Retailing*, 69(1), pp. 140-147.

29. Noel Capon, Gavan, J, Fitzsimons and Rick Weingarte (1994), "Affluent investors and mutual fund purchases", *International Journal of Bank Marketing*, 12(3), pp. 17-25.

30. Zafar Khan, Sudhi, K.Chawla and S.Thomas A. Cianuiolo (1995), "Multiple Discriminant Analysis: Tool for effective marketing of computer information systems to small business elicits", *Journal of professional services marketing*, 12(2), pp. 153-162.

31. Kathryn, H, Dansky and Diane Brannon (1996), "Discriminant Analysis: A technique for adding value to patient satisfaction surveys", *Hospital and Health Services Administration*, 41(4), Winter, pp. 503-513.

4 Solid Waste Management and Its Financial Model

The local bodies have been responsible for Solid Waste (SW) management services. However, over the years, various weaknesses in the institutional, financial and technical aspects, have led to inefficiency in the provision of services at various levels. These contrast with the increasing waste generation rates and environmental awareness among the general public. The local bodies are not collecting any fees and tax on SW management among the public. The local bodies are sharing a certain proportion of property tax to spend on SW management which is insufficient to manage the SW.

Cities in developing and industrialized countries in general do not spend more than 0.5 per cent of their per capita Gross Natural Product on urban waste services (World Bank, 1999)[1]. Expenditure in SWM also serves as a reliable proxy to service levels for collection and disposal. Maintenance and operation costs in low-income countries show that about 20 to 50 per cent of city revenues are spent for SWM, while in high-income countries, it is 1 to 10 per cent of their revenues. SWM costs less to governments of high-income countries because of private sector participation, high labour and vehicle productivity and greater efficiency (Cointreau and Gopalan, 2000)[2].

Financing of Solid Waste Management Services

Sumalde (2005)[3] mentioned three main options for financing the recurrent cost of municipal SWM: user charges, local taxes and inter-governmental transfers. To promote the responsiveness of the supplying agency to user needs and ensure that collected funds are actually spent on waste management, it is preferable to finance operations through user charges rather than general tax revenues. Adding solid waste charges to utility charges may increase collection efficiency. User charges should be based on the actual cost of SWM, and related to the volume of collection service provided. Among the larger waste generators, variable fees may be used to manage the demand for waste services by providing incentive for waste minimization. To achieve equity of waste service access, some cross–subsidization and/or financing out of general revenue will be required (Kneith, 1994)[4].

Financed Model in SWM

There are two methods for financing SWM. These are choice model (CM) and contingent valuation (CV). The aim of CM was to identify marginal values for SWM activities. This allows identification of a desirable SWM plan from the demand side perspective. (Morrison et al., 1998)[5]. The purpose of CV was to assess the value of a total SWM package. In the CV method, respondents are asked to reveal their maximum willingness-to-pay (WTP) to obtain some degree of environmental improvement or to avoid a loss, relative to some baseline situations (Kwabena et al., 2001[6]; Adamovicz et al., 1994[7]).

The customers' choice and willingness-to-pay more on SWM have to be properly assessed to generate an optimum financial model to avoid environmental problem. Hence it is essential to analyze the customer choice of the proposed model and their WTP in the present study. Since, the basic information on the awareness of SWM among the people is essential, the present study focuses on this aspect initially to provide basic information.

Awareness on Solid Waste Management among the Respondents

The peoples' responsibility is to be aware of the SWM in their area. It will be highly helpful for conserving their environment. Even though the variables related to SWM are too many, the present study confines to 11 variables. The respondents are asked to rate the variables according to their level of awareness on these variables at five point scale. The mean scores of the variables among the LIG, MIG and HIG have been computed separately. The results are given in Table 4.1.

Table 4.1 : Awareness on solid waste managements

Sl. No.	Variables in Solid Waste Management	Mean score			F-Statistics
		LIG	MIG	HIG	
1.	Collection point	2.6568	2.9193	3.4517	2.4568
2.	Collection timing	2.7103	3.1086	3.6508	2.5681
3.	Disposal system	2.4417	2.6866	3.3316	2.9903*
4.	Complaint system	2.6034	2.7331	3.086	0.9644
5.	Street sweeping	2.4509	2.3087	2.9174	1.6877
6.	Type of solid waste	2.8611	3.1459	3.3962	2.0244
7.	System of collection in foreign countries	2.3032	3.0466	3.7086	2.4586
8.	Collection fees	2.7184	3.1144	3.3094	2.5081
9.	Cost incurred to local government	2.0618	2.2149	2.5161	1.9197
10.	Importance of solid waste management	2.1144	2.0433	2.6562	1.8021
11.	Government programmes on solid waste management	2.0893	2.8144	3.1443	3.0446*

*Significant at five per cent level.

The highly regarded variables in SWM among the LIG is type of solid waste, collection fees and collection timing since their respective mean scores are 2.8611, 2.7184 and 2.7103. Among the MIG, these variables are type of solid waste, collection of fees and collection timing since their respective mean scores are 3.1459, 3.1144 and 3.1086. Among the HIG, these are system of collection in foreign countries, collection timing and collection point since their respective mean scores are 3.7086, 3.6508 and 3.4517. Regarding the level of awareness on SWM, the significant differences among the three income groups have been identified in the level of awareness on disposal system and government programmes on solid WM since their respective 'F' statistics are significant at five per cent level.

Awareness on Solid Waste Management Index (ASWI) among the Respondents

The awareness on solid waste management among the respondents is summated with the help of an Index called as awareness on solid waste management index (ASWI). The ASWI is computed as

$$ASWI = \frac{\sum_{i=1}^{n} SSW\ V_i}{\sum_{i=1}^{n} M\ SSW\ V_i} \times 100$$

Where

SSWV - Score on Solid Waste Management Variables

MSSWV - Maximum score on Waste Management Variables

i=1-n - Number of variables in Waste Management Variables

Table 4.2 : Awareness on solid waste management index (ASWI) among the respondents

Sl. No.	ASWI (%)	Number of respondents			Total
		LIG	MIG	HIG	
1.	Less than 21	136	146	8	290
2.	21 – 40	47	132	17	196
3.	41– 60	7	30	54	91
4.	61– 80	1	25	21	47
5.	Above 80	—	7	8	15
	Total	191	340	108	639

As a maximum 45.38 per cent of the respondents are having an ASWI of less than 21 per cent. It is followed by 30.67 per cent of the respondents with an ASWI of 21 to 40 per cent. Respondents with the ASWI of above 80 per cent constitute 2.34 per cent to the total. The number of respondents with an ASWI of above 60 per cent constitutes 0.50, 9.41 and 26.85 per cent to the total of LIG, MIG and HIG respectively. The analysis reveals the level of awareness on solid waste management among the HIG is greater than MIG and LIG.

Association between Profile of the Respondents and their ASWI

The profile of the respondents may be associated with their level of awareness on SWM. Hence, the present study has made an attempt to analyse the association between these two variables. The included profile variables are gender, age, nativity, and occupational background, and family size, number of earning members per family, house ownership and type of house. The one-way analysis has been employed to analyse the associations. The results are given in Table 4.3.

Table 4.3 : Association between profile of respondents and their ASWI

Sl. No.	Profile variables	F-Statistics	Table value of 'F' at 5 per cent level	Result
1.	Gender	2.6342	3.84	Insignificant
2.	Age	2.7346	2.37	Significant
3.	Nativity	3.1403	2.99	Significant
4.	Occupational background	2.6604	2.37	Significant
5.	Family size	2.5114	2.60	Insignificant
6.	Number of earning members per family	2.6603	2.99	Insignificant
7.	Houseownership	2.5142	2.99	Insignificant
8.	Type of house	2.9193	3.84	Insignificant

The significantly associating profile variables with their ASWI among the respondents are their age, nativity, and occupational background service and their respective 'F' statistics are significant at five per cent level. The analysis reveals that there is a significant difference among the respondents regarding their ASWI when they are classified on the basis of their age, nativity and occupational background.

Customers' Expectation from SWM Service

The customers' expectation on SWM service from their service provider is defined as the control of waste generation, storage, collection, transfer and transport, processing and disposal of solid wastes consistent with the best practices based on public health, economics, and financial, engineering, administrative, legal and environmental considerations. Managing solid waste refers to solid waste produced by households, commercial entities and institutions. They are highly heterogeneous and are influenced by socio-geographical factors. The variables in SWM are identified with the help of previous Studies (Othman, 2002[8]; Gutting, 1991[9]; Van Houten and Morris, 1999[10]). The confined variables related to SWM is collection time, separation of wastages, provision of packets, frequency of collection, street sweeping, disposal of wastages, number of workers engaged, street bins for collection of wastages, complaint handling, reliability of service, responsiveness to the customer call, assured service, accessible employees, empathized service, discriminatory pricing, fine on violation of rules and regulations and strict implementation of rules and regulations.

The respondents are asked to rate the above-said variables at five point scales according to their level of expectation. The mean scores of the variables among the three income groups have been computed to exhibit their level of expectation attached to each variable. The results are shown in Table 4.4.

Table 4.4 : Level of expectation on Solid Waste Management (SWM) in the present system

Sl. No.	Variables in SWM	Mean score			F-Statistics
		LIG	MIG	HIG	
1.	Collection time	3.1843	3.8033	4.1089	3.1084*
2.	Separation of wastages	2.6432	3.0692	3.7334	3.0662*
3.	Provision for packets	3.2464	3.6671	3.8189	2.9147
4.	Frequency of collection	3.6343	3.8084	4.0917	1.4033
5.	Street sweeping	2.9194	3.1663	3.9608	3.1642*
6.	Disposal of wastages	2.4142	2.8554	3.8186	3.8171*
7.	Number of workers engaged	2.6639	3.4137	3.9044	3.5089*
8.	Street Bins for collection of wastages	3.4143	3.6889	3.9902	1.0842
9.	Complaint handling	3.3142	3.8089	4.3642	3.1193*
10.	Reliability of service	3.4046	3.6168	4.2911	2.9908*
11.	Responsiveness to the customers' call	3.5166	3.9193	4.4144	1.2149
12.	Assured service	3.6084	3.9897	4.0861	1.0334
13.	Approvable employees	3.2143	3.6866	3.9168	2.1143
14.	Empathized service	3.3939	3.7184	4.1144	2.0896
15.	Discriminatory pricing	2.6934	3.8144	4.0451	3.4152*
16.	Fine on violation of rules and regulations	2.8604	3.9142	4.2663	3.6069*
17.	Strict implementation of rules and regulations	3.1149	3.8646	3.9936	2.8142

* Significant at five per cent level.

The highly expected variables in SWM among the LIG is frequency of collection, assured service and responsiveness to the customers' call since their respective mean scores are 3.6343, 3.6084 and 3.5166. Among the MIG, these variables are assured service, responsiveness to the customers' call and fine on violation of rules and regulations since their respective mean scores are 3.9897, 3.9193 and 3.9142. Among the HIG, these variables are responsiveness to customers' call complaint handling reliability of service and imposing of fine on violation of rules and regulations since their respective mean scores are 4.4144, 4.3642, 4.2911 and 4.2663. Regarding the level of expectation on the variables in SWM, the significant differences among the three income group of respondents have been noticed in the expectation on collection time, separation of wastages, street sweeping, disposal of wastages, number of workers engaged, complaint handling, reliability of service, discriminatory pricing and fine on violation of rules and regulations since their respective 'F' statistics are significant at five per cent level. In total, the level of expectation on SWM among the HIG residents is greater than that among the MIG and LIG.

Important Factors in SWM

The score of the level of expectation on various variables in SWM has been included for factor analysis in order to convent the variables into factors. Exploratory factor analysis has been executed to identify the factors in SWM. Initially, the validity of data for factor analysis has been examined with the help of KMO measure of sampling adequacy and Bartletts test of sphericity. Both these two tests satisfy the validity of data for factor analysis and the EFA has been executed. The EFA results in four important factors in SWM. The variables in each factor, its eigen value, per cent of variation explained and cronbach alpha are summarized in Table 4.5.

The important factors in SWM are service quality, system, facilities and price. All these four factors explain the variables in SWM to the extent of 79.52 per cent. The most important factor is service quality since its eigen value and the per cent of variation explained by this factor are 3.8143 and 26.44 per cent respectively. It consists of six variables with the reliability co-efficient of 0.8189. The second and third important factors

Table 4.5 : Important expectation from the SW Management Service Provider

Sl. No.	Important Factors in SWM	Number of variables	Crown-bach alpha	Eigen value	% of variation explained	Cummu-lative per cent of varia-tion explained
1.	Service Quality	6	0.8189	3.8143	26.44	26.44
2.	System	5	0.7443	3.2069	22.28	48.72
3.	Facilities	4	0.7904	2.5691	19.34	68.06
4.	Price	2	0.8244	1.0844	11.46	79.52
KMO: Measure of Sampling Adequacy: 07647			Bartletts test of sphericity: Chi-Square:81.49*			

* Significant at zero per cent level.

are system and facilities since their eigen values are 3.2069 and 2.5691 respectively. The above-mentioned two factors consist of five and four variables with the reliability co-efficient of 0.7443 and 0.7904 respectively. The last factor identified by EFA is price. It consists of two variables with the reliability co-efficient of 0.8244. The factor analysis results in four important factors in SWM.

Reliability and Validity of the Variables in each Factor

In order to analyze the reliability and validity of the variables in each factor, the confirmatory factor analysis has been executed. The convergent validity, composite reliability and the average variance have been found to prove its reliability and validity. The convergent validity was assessed by the significance of 't' statistics (Chau, 1997)[11]. The minimum household of composite (construct) reliability is 0.5 (Nunnally, 1978)[12]. The suggested criterion of average variance extracted (AVE) is 0.5 (Fornell and Larcker 1981)[13].

In the present study, the convergent validity of the variables in each factor is confirmed since their respective 't' statistics are significant at five per cent level. The construct or composite validity is also confirmed since the composite reliability of each factor is greater than the minimum threshold. Apart from this AVE values are all above the suggested criterion of 0.5. These results provide sufficient evidence for convergent validity of the scales.

Table 4.6 : Reliability and validity of the variables in each factor

Sl. No.	Factor	Range of standardized factor loading	Range of 't' statistics	Composite reliability	Average variance extracted
1.	Service quality	0.7247–0.8645	5.4565*–10.4621*	0.8443	61.09
2.	System	0.6535–0.9239	4.6142*–13.1917*	0.7826	49.54
3.	Facilities	0.7647–0.9344	7.0891*–14.7637*	0.8169	52.42
4.	Price	0.6144–0.9299	4.0863*–13.9364*	0.8344	59.03

Discriminate Validity of the Constructs

Discriminate validity of these factors can be assessed by AVE and the squared correlation co-efficient between the constructs (Segar and Grova, 1993[14]; Skerlavaj et al., 2007[15]). It is also examined with the help of the inter-correlation co-efficient between the factors and its level of significance (Chan, 1997). The significant correlation co-efficient between the constructs indicate lesser discriminate validity. The results are given in Table 4.7.

Table 4.7 : Inter relationship between the factors in SWM

Factors	Service Quality	System	Facilities	Price
Service Quality		0.1346	–0.2723	–0.1582
System			0.1891	0.2036
Facilities				–0.1339
Price				

Table 4.7 explains the inter correlation between the factors extracted by the EFA. The correlations co-efficient are ranging

from -0.2723 to -0.1339. But no correlations co-efficient are statistically significant. It reveals the mutual exclusiveness of the factors in SWM. It confirms the discriminate validity of the factors.

Level of Expectation among the Respondents

The level of expectation on the factors in SWM is derived from the mean score of the level of expectation on all variables in each factor. The mean of expectation on each factor in SWM is computed to exhibit the level of expectation on factors in SWM among the LIG, MIG and HIG separately. Regarding the level of expectation, the significant differences among the three income groups have been examined with the help of one way analysis of variance. The results are presented in Table 4.8.

Table 4.8 : Level of expectation on factors in SWM

Sl. No.	Factors	Mean score			F-Statistics
		LIG	MIG	HIG	
1.	Service quality	3.4087	3.7899	4.1978	82.3674
2.	System	3.0992	3.5424	3.9777	3.1086*
3.	Facilities	2.9347	3.4063	3.8830	3.0674*
4.	Price	2.7769	3.8643	4.1557	3.6543*

*Significant at five per cent level.

The highly expected factor in SWM among the LIG is 'service quality' since its mean score is 3.4087 whereas among the MIG, it is 'price' since its mean score is 3.8643. Among the HIG, this factor is 'service quality' since its mean score is 4.1978. In short, the HIG are expecting more in all four factors in SWM compared to MIG and LIG. Regarding the level of expectation on factors in SWM, the significant differences among the three income groups have been noticed in the case of system, facilities and price since their respective 'F' statistics are significant at five per cent level.

Level of Perception on Factors in SWM

The level of perception on the variables in SWM has been also measured at five-point scale. The level of perception on important factors in SWM is derived from the mean score of the level of perception on variables in each factor. The mean of perception on four factors in SWM has been computed to exhibit the respondents' perception on it. Regarding the level of perception, the significant differences among the three income groups have been computed with the help of one way analysis of variance. The results are given in Table 4.9.

Table 4.9 : Level of perception on factors in SWM

Sl. No.	Factors	Mean score			F-Statistics
		LIG	MIG	HIG	
1.	Service quality	2.4182	2.6304	3.0436	2.0862
2.	System	2.0773	2.7366	2.6683	1.9304
3.	Facilities	2.1142	2.0573	2.4542	0.6521
4.	Price	2.7861	3.8843	4.1843	3.1408*

*Significant at five per cent level

The highly perceived factor in SWM among the LIG is 'price' since its mean score is 2.7861 whereas the lesser-perceived factor is 'system' since its mean score is 2.0773. Among the MIG, the higher and lesser-perceived factors are 'price' and 'facilities' since their mean scores are 3.8843 and 2.0573 respectively. Among the HIG, these two factors are 'price' and facilities since their respective mean scores are 4.1843 and 2.4542. Regarding the level of perception on factors, the significant difference among the three income groups has been noticed in the case of 'price since the respective 'F' statistics is significant at five per cent level.

SERVQUAL Scale on the Factors in SWM

The SERVQUAL scale is comprised of two sets of matched items measuring expectations and perceptions (Parasuraman et al., 1985[16]; Bolton and Drew, 1994[17]). The SERVQUAL scale is measured by

$$\text{SERVQUAL Scale} = \Sigma P_{ij} - \Sigma E_{ij}$$

Where P - Level of perception

E - Level of Expectation

ij - Variables and individuals

The results are presented in Table 4.10

Table 4.10. SERVQUAL scale in factors in SWM

Sl. No.	Factors in SWM	Mean score			F-Statistics
		LIG	MIG	HIG	
1.	Service quality	–0.9905	–1.1595	–1.1542	0.9342
2.	System	–1.0219	–0.8058	–1.3094	1.5734
3.	Facilities	–0.8205	–1.3490	–1.4288	1.8687
4.	Price	0.0092	0.0200	0.0286	0.3065

The negative SERVQUAL scale is identified in service quality, system and facilities among the three income groups. It reveals that the respondents are not satisfied upto their level of expectation on these three factors. Regarding 'price', the respondents are satisfied upto their level of expectation since their SERVQUAL scale is positive. Regarding the SERVQUAL scale on factors in SWM, there is no significant difference among the three income groups since their respective 'F' statistics are not significant at five per cent level.

Association between the Profile of Respondents and their SERVQUAL Scale

The level of expectation and perception on the factors in SWM may be highly associated with the profile of the respondents. It is highly essential to find out the significant association between the profile of the respondents and their SERVQUAL scale on service quality, system, facilities and price for some policy implications. The one way analysis of variance has been administered to find out such associations. The results are given in Table 4.11.

Table 4.11 : Association between profile of respondents and their gap between perception and expectation

Sl. No.	Profile Variables	F-Statistics			Price
		Service Quality	System	Facili-ties	
1	Gender	3.0145	2.7332	2.5082	3.1142
2.	Age	2.5086*	2.8184*	2.6086*	2.1142
3.	Nativity	2.6099	2.5165	3.1743*	2.6065
4.	Occupational background	2.7174*	2.6636*	2.5034*	2.7142*
5.	Family size	2.5081	2.8442*	2.7739*	2.8149*
6.	Number of earning member per family	2.8011	2.5114	2.7086	2.1014
7.	Houseownership	3.1414*	2.0868	2.5669	3.8414*
8.	Type of house	2.9099	3.2461*	2.3302	2.1709
9.	ASWI	2.8687*	2.7866*	2.5441*	2.8662*

*Significant at five per cent level.

Regarding the SERVQUAL scale on service quality the significantly associating profile variables are age, occupational background, houseownership and ASWI since their respective 'F' statistics are significant at five per cent level. The significantly associating profile variables with the SERVQUAL scale on 'system' factor are age, occupational background, family size, type of house and ASWI. Regarding the SERVQUAL scale on 'facilities', the significantly associating profile variables are age, nativity, occupational background, family size and ASWI whereas regarding the SERVQUAL scale on 'price, these profile variables are occupational background, family size, house ownership and ASWI. The analysis reveals the importance of the profile variables namely occupational background, ASWI, age and family size in their level of expectation and perception on the services offered by the service provider.

Models on SWM

The methods employed in this research are choice model (CM) and contingent valuation (CV). The aim of CM was to identify marginal values for SWM attributes. This is to allow identification of a desirable SWM plan from the demand side perspective. The researchers used the stated preference approach (Adamovicz, et al., 1994[18]; Bateman, 2002[19]). The CV was used to assess the value of a total SWM package. Results from the two techniques will be contrasted and policy implications offered. Typical profile analysis is conducted to provide insights into respondents' socio-demography, attitudinal, and waste generation and disposal behaviour.

Choice Model

In CM, respondents are presented with multiple choice sets, where each choice set usually contains three or more management options. Respondents are asked to choose their preferred option from each choice set. The option in each choice set contains common attributes, at various levels. The combination of attribute and levels for each option in each choice set is designed using experimental design techniques. Before the choice sets are presented to the respondents, there is a description of the study site, the research issues, the proposed policy changes and its implications on household budgets and the environmental attributes, which are being modelled. In the present study, the choice models are generated from the variables drawn from previous studies (Boxall et al., 1996[20]; Mourato, 1999[21]; Agamuthu, 2001[22]). The model choices are given in Table 4.12.

The models proposed in the present study are based on seven implications namely collection frequency of waste, separation of wastes at source, time of waste collection, type of waste disposal, mode of transport, rating system and pricing system. The three different models have been generated with different sets of implications. The respondents are asked to rate each model on the basis of their attitude towards adoption in practice at five-point scale.

Table 4.12 : Proposed models and their features

Sl. No.	Implications	Model-I	Model-II	Model-III
1.	Collection frequency	3 times per week	Alternative days	Daily
2.	Separation of wastes at source	No separation	Provision of free container for separation	Separation at household cost
3.	Time of waste collection	Any time	Fixed timing	Either morning or evening
4.	Type of waste disposal	Open land	Sanitary type	Incinerator type
5.	Mode of transport	Conventional	Manually loaded compactor	Quick mode
6.	Rating system	Flat	Moderate	Volume based
7.	Pricing system	Attached with property rate	Separate fee	Discriminatory pricing system

Reliability and Validity of the Implications in Each Model

The scores of the variables in each model have been included for confirmatory factor analysis to test the reliability and validity of the variables included in each model. The convergent validity of the model has been examined with the help of the level of significance of 't' statistics of the standardized factor loadings. The composite reliability has been tested to verify the construct validity with the minimum threshold of 0.5. The internal consistency of the data has been tested with the help of Cronbach Alpha. The average variance extracted by each model has been computed to test the validity of the construct with the minimum threshold of 50.00 per cent or 0.5. The result of CFA is presented in Table 4.13.

Table 4.13 : Reliability of the variables in each model

Sl. No.	Model	Number of variables included	Range of standardised factor loading	Range of 't' statistics	Cronbach alpha	Composite reliability extracted	Average variance
1.	Model-I	7	0.6937-0.9368	4.6846-14.8026	0.7129	0.7439	54.02
2.	Model-II	7	0.7103-0.8944	5.2149-13.1146	0.8416	0.8902	61.39
3.	Model-III	7	0.7244-0.9414	5.4031-13.9616	0.7632	0.7908	49.91

The standardized factor loading of the variables in each model-I is varying from 0.6937 to 0.9368, which are significant at five per cent level. This confirms the convergent validity of the model. The same situation is identified in model-II and model-III. All the three models consist of seven variables with the reliability co-efficient of 0.7129, 0.8416 and 0.7632. It indicates that the included seven variables in model-I, II and III explain it to the extent of 71.29, 84.16 and 76.32 per cent respectively. The composite validity of model-I, II and III is greater than the minimum threshold of 0.5. The Average Variance Extracted (AVE) by model-I, II and III are 54.02, 61.39 and 49.91 per cent respectively which confirms the validity of the models.

In order to find out the discriminate validity of the models, the inter-correlation between three models has been computed. Since, all inter-correlation co-efficient are not significant at five per cent level, it confirms the discriminate validity among the models.

Evaluation of the Model-I

The respondents are asked to rate the various (implication) variables in model-I at five-point scale in order to exhibit the level of importance attached to each implication in this model. The mean scores of each (implication) variable in model-I among the LIG, MIG and HIG have been computed separately. Regarding the level of importance attached to the variables in model-I, the significant differences among the three income groups have been analyzed with the help of one way analysis of variance.

The highly rated variable in Model-I by the LIG is the fee to be attached with tax since its mean score is 3.7304 whereas for the MIG and HIG, it is flat rate system with respective mean scores of 3.2141 and 3.0646. In short, the LIG rated the Model-I highly compared to MIG and HIG. Regarding the rating on variables in Model-I, the significant differences among the three income groups have been identified in the rating on three times per week, no separation of wastages, anytime collection of wastages, open land fills type of disposal and fee to be attached with tax since their respective 'F' statistics are significant at five per cent level.

Table 4.14. Rating of Model-I

Sl. No.	Variables in Model-I	Mean score			F-Statistics
		LIG	MIG	HIG	
1.	Three times per week	3.6145	2.5081	2.1454	5.0844*
2.	No separation of wastages	3.5084	2.6691	2.5088	3.3969*
3.	Anytime collection of wastages	3.4511	2.7332	2.4114	3.0686*
4.	Open land fills type of disposal	3.6613	2.6069	2.5656	3.1443*
5.	Conventional mode of transport to collect waste	3.4339	3.0141	2.7199	1.3391
6.	Flat rate system	3.6554	3.2141	3.0646	1.5654
7.	Fee to be attached with tax	3.7304	3.0889	2.5696	3.3089*

* Significant at five per cent level.

Score Index on Model-I (SIM-I)

The Score Index on Model-I is the summative view on the model-I. The SIM-I is computed by

$$\text{SIM-I} = \frac{\sum_{i=1}^{n} SVM - I_i}{\sum_{i=1}^{n} M\ SVM - I_i} \times 100$$

Where

SVM-I - Score on the variables in Model-I

MSVM-I - Maximum score on the Model-I

i = 1-n - Number of variables in Model-I

The SIM-I among the respondents is given in Table 4.15.

Table 4.15 : Score Index on Model-I (SIM-I)

Sl. No.	SIM-I (%)	Number of respondents			Total
		Service Quality	System	Facilities	
1.	Less than 21	14	38	19	71
2.	21– 40	21	62	27	110
3.	41 – 60	42	136	43	221
4.	61 – 80	66	65	8	139
5.	Above 80	48	39	11	98
	Total	191	340	108	639

In short, a maximum of 34.58 per cent of the respondents are with 41 to 60 per cent as their SIM-I. It is followed by 21.75 per cent with an index of 61 to 80 per cent. The respondents with an SIM-I of above 80 per cent constitute 15.34 per cent to the total. The number of respondents with an SIM-I of above 60 per cent constitutes 59.68, 30.59 and 17.59 per cent to its total of LIG, MIG and HIG respectively. The analysis reveals that the LIG residents highly rate the Model-I than others.

Evaluation of the Model-II

Model-II consist different implications from model-I in all seven dimensions. The respondents are asked to rate the seven variables in model-II at five point scale on the basis of their importance. The mean scores of the variables in Model-II among the LIG, MIG and HIG have been computed separately to exhibit their level of importance on each variable in the Model-II. Regarding the level importance attached to the variables in Model-II, the significant difference among the three income groups have been analysed with the help of one way analysis of variance. The results are given in Table 4.16.

The highly rated variable in Model-II among the LIG is manually loaded compactor since its mean score is 3.1144, whereas among the MIG and HIG, these are provision of

Table 4.16 : Rating of the Model-II

Sl. No.	Variables in Model-II	Mean score			F-Statistics
		LIG	MIG	HIG	
1.	Alternative days	2.8188	3.6866	2.8969	3.1214*
2.	Provision of free container for separation of wastages	2.9093	3.9803	3.1441	3.4503*
3.	Fixed timing (afternoon)	3.0144	3.8688	3.5644	2.7184
4.	Sanitary type disposal of wastes	2.8138	3.9196	3.7334	3.3039*
5.	Manually loaded compactor	3.1144	3.5059	3.8118	1.0886
6.	Moderate rate system	2.7589	3.7334	3.6163	3.0447*
7.	Separate fee system	2.5144	3.8486	3.8686	3.4502*

*Significant at five per cent level.

free container for separation of wastages and separate fee system since their respective mean scores are 3.9803 and 3.8686. Regarding the level of importance attached to the variables in Model-II, the significant differences among the three income groups have been noticed in the case of importance attached to alternative days, provision of free container for separation of wastages, sanitary type of disposal of wastes, moderate rate system and separate fee system since their respective 'F' statistics are significant at five per cent level.

Score Index on Model-II (SIM-II)

The Score Index on Model-II reveals the overall fixture on the level of importance attached with the model-II by the respondents. The Score Index on Model-II is computed by

$$\text{SIM-II} = \frac{\sum_{i=1}^{n} SVM-II_i}{\sum_{i=1}^{n} M\,SVM-II_i} \times 100$$

Whereas

SVM-II - Score on the variables in Model-II

MSVM-II - Maximum score on the Model-II

i=1-n - Number of variables in Model-II

The distribution of respondents on the basis of their SIM-II is illustrated in Table 4.17.

Table 4.17 : Score Index on Model-II (SIM-II)

Sl. No.	SIM-II (%)	Number of respondents			Total
		LIG	MIG	HIG	
1.	Less than 21	31	13	2	46
2.	21 – 40	36	21	18	75
3.	41 – 60	83	73	29	185
4.	61 – 80	27	129	44	200
5.	Above 80	14	104	15	133
	Total	191	340	108	639

The important SIM-II among the respondents is 61 to 80 and 41 to 60 per cent which is constituted by 31.30 and 28.95 per cent to the total respectively. The number of respondents with the SIM-II of above 80 per cent constitutes 20.81 per cent to the total. The number of respondents with the SIM-II of above 60 per cent constitutes 21.47, 68.53 and 54.63 per cent to its total of LIG, MIG and HIGs respectively. The analysis reveals that the MIG rate Model-II highly than the LIG and HIG.

Evaluation of the Model-III

Model-III consists of seven different (implication) variables. The respondents are asked to rate the seven variables in Model-III at five-point scale on the basis of the level of importance given to them. The mean scores of the seven variables in Model-III among the LIG, MIG and HIG have been computed separately to exhibit the level of importance attached to these variables by the respondents. The mean scores of the variables are illustrated in Table 4.18.

Table 4.18 : Rating of the Model-III

Sl. No.	Variables in Model-III	Mean score			F-Statistics
		LIG	MIG	HIG	
1.	Daily collection	2.8614	3.4568	3.8184	3.1449*
2.	Separation at household cost	2.9144	3.2341	3.6994	2.0844
3.	Either evening or morning	2.5054	2.9919	3.4516	3.0141*
4.	Incinerator type	2.7374	3.2141	3.3991	1.9196
5.	Quick mode of transport	2.8134	3.5661	3.8184	2.9969*
6.	Volume based rating system	2.9194	3.4408	3.9092	3.1447*
7.	Discriminatory pricing system	3.0214	3.3345	3.3969	0.8941

* Significant at five per cent level.

The highly rated variables in Model-III by the LIG is discriminatory pricing system since its mean score is 3.0214 whereas among the MIG and LIG, these two are quick mode of transport and volume-based rating system since their respective mean scores are 3.5661 and 3.9092. Regarding the level of importance attached to the variables in model-III, the significant differences among the three income groups have been noticed in the case of importance attached to daily collection, collection of wastages at either evening or morning, quick mode of transport and volume based rating system since their respective 'F' statistics are significant at five per cent level. In total, the LIG residents are highly rating the Model-III compared to other two groups of respondents.

Score Index on Model-III (SIM-III)

The Score Index on Model-III represents the respondents' overall view on model-III according to the level of importance attached to all variables in it. The SIM-III is calculated by

$$\text{SIM-III} = \frac{\sum_{i=1}^{n} SVM - III_i}{\sum_{i=1}^{n} M\ SVM - III_i} \times 100$$

Where

SVM-III - Score on the variables in Model-III

MSVM-III - Maximum score on the Model-III

i = 1-n - Number of variables in Model-III

The SIM-III among the respondents is presented in Table 4.19.

Table 4.19 : Score Index on Model-III (SIM-III)

Sl. No.	SIM-III (%)	Number of respondents			Total
		LIG	MIG	HIG	
1.	Less than 21	19	12	1	32
2.	21 – 40	32	44	11	87
3.	41 – 60	104	93	19	216
4.	61 – 80	17	118	53	188
5.	Above 80	19	73	24	116
	Total	191	340	108	639

The important SIM-III among the respondents is 41 to 60 and 61 to 80 per cent, which constitute 33.80 and 29.42 per cent to the total respectively. The respondents with the SIM-III of above 60 per cent constitute 18.85, 56.18 and 71.29 per cent to the total of LIG, MIG and HIG respectively. The analysis reveals that the HIG residents highly rate the Model-III compared to MIG and LIG.

Association between the Profile of Respondents and their Evaluation of Models

The profile of the respondents may be associated with their evaluation of models for SWM. It is highly essential to analyze the rating on three models among the different groups of respondents under each profile variable for some policy implications. The included profile variables are gender, age, nativity and occupational background. The mean score of each model (SOM) among the different groups has been computed by the grand mean score of the variables in each model.

Regarding the score on each model, the significant difference among the different groups in each profile has been examined with the help of one way analysis of variance. The results are given in Table 4.20.

Table 4.20 : Association between the profile variables and their evaluation of models

Sl. No.	Variables in Model-I	Mean of SOM			F-Statistics
		Model-I	Model-II	Model-III	
I	**Gender**				
	Male	2.6894	3.56821	3.6143	3.1144*
	Female	3.6701	3.2517	2.4339	3.5616*
	F-Statistics	3.0144*	0.9698	3.5446*	—
II	**Age**				
	Less than 30	2.8518	3.0657	3.6349	3.0145*
	30-40	2.9096	3.2451	3.4518	2.0861
	41-50	2.8341	4.1355	3.2333	3.5604*
	51-60	3.2568	3.0844	2.9906	1.4508
	Above 60	3.4471	2.9291	2.8149	2.1718
	F-Statistics	2.0145	3.1145*	2.9965*	—
III	**Nativity**				
	Urban	2.4416	2.8434	3.6339	3.5142*
	Semi-Urban	3.0332	3.8604	3.2300	2.6431
	Rural	3.5857	3.6052	2.8145	2.4114
	F-Statistics	3.6841*	3.1042*	3.0996*	—
IV	**Occupational background**				
	Private employment	2.4511	3.7164	3.6343	3.4109*
	Government employment	2.8669	3.7811	3.3085	3.1142*
	Business	3.3746	3.4545	2.7965	2.0962
	Agriculture	3.4969	2.7611	2.8914	2.2241
	Others	3.5643	2.8247	3.1016	2.3946

* Significant at five per cent level.

The male respondents rate the Model-III highly since the mean score is 3.6143 whereas the female respondent rate model-I highly since its mean score is 3.6701. Regarding the rating on three different models, the significant difference is noticed among the male and female respondents separately since their respective 'F' statistics are significant at five per cent level. The significant differences among the male and female respondents have been noticed in evaluation of model-I and Model-III since their respective 'F' statistics are significant at five per cent level.

Model-I is highly rated by the respondents aged above 60 years whereas model-II and III are highly rated by the respondents within the age range of 41 to 50 years and less than 30 years respectively since their respective mean scores are 4.1355 and 3.6349. Regarding the rating on three financial models, significant differences have been identified among the respondents within the age group of less than 30 years and 41 to 50 years respectively since their respective 'F' statistics are significant at five per cent level. The significant differences among the different age group of respondents have been noticed in the evaluation of Model-II and Model-III since their respective 'F' statistics are significant at five per cent level.

Model-I is highly rated by the rural respondents whereas Model-II is highly rated by the semi-Urban respondents since their respective mean scores are 3.5857 and 3.8604. The urban respondents rating model-III highly since its mean score is 3.6339. Among the urban respondents, the significant difference on the evaluation of three models has been since its 'F' statistics is significant at five per cent level. Regarding the evaluation of all three financial models, the significant differences among the respondents with three district nativity have been noticed since their respective 'F' statistics are significant at five per cent level.

The respondents with private employment are highly rating Model-I whereas the respondents with Government employment are highly rating Model-II since their respective mean scores are 3.5643 and 3.7811. The respondents engaged in business and agriculture highly rate Model-II and Model-I since their respective mean scores are 3.4545 and 3.4969. Regarding the rating of three models, the significant difference among the three models has been identified among the respondents with private and government employment. Regarding the evaluation of Model-I and II, the significant differences among the respondents with different occupational background have been noticed since their respective 'F' statistics are significant at five per cent level.

The association between the profile variables namely family size, number of earning members per family, house-ownership, type of house and ASWI and their evaluation of financial models has been examined with the help of one way analysis of variance. The results are given in Table 4.21.

Model-I is highly rated by the respondents with the family size of above 7 whereas model-II is highly rated by the respondents with the family size of 4 to 5 members since their respective mean scores are 3.5542 and 3.7106. Model-III is highly rated by the respondents with the family size of upto 3 members. Regarding the evaluation of three models, the significant difference is identified among the respondents with the family size of upto 3 members and above 7 members. Regarding the evaluation of model-I, II and III, the significant differences among the respondents with different family size have been noticed since their respective 'F' statistics are significant at five per cent level.

The respondents with only one earning member in the family highly rate the model-I since its mean score is 3.6091 whereas among the respondents with two or more than two earning members per family, these are model-II and model-III since their respective mean scores are 3.6164 and 3.6091. The significant difference regarding the evaluation of three models has been identified among the respondents with the earning members of more than two. Regarding the evaluation

Table 4.21 : Association between profile of respondents and their evaluation of models

Sl. No.	Profile	Mean of SIM			F-Statistics
		Model-I	Model-II	Model-III	
I	**Family size**				
	Upto 3 members	2.7378	3.2144	3.6296	3.1441*
	4 – 5 members	2.9361	3.7106	3.1833	0.9337
	6 – 7 members	3.3667	3.6096	2.9336	1.2641
	Above 7 members	3.5542	2.4547	2.8017	3.2693*
	F-Statistics	3.0141*	3.6033*	2.9969*	
II	**Number of earning members per family**				
	One	3.6091	3.3519	2.8189	2.1492
	Two	3.2063	3.6164	2.9728	2.0144
	More than Two	2.5124	3.1562	3.5448	2.9963*
III	**Houseownership**				
	Owned House	2.5268	3.5227	2.8657	1.4581
	Leased	3.0046	3.6145	3.2089	1.3192
	Rented	2.5195	3.3376	3.5816	2.8033
	F-Statistics	2.7081*	0.4456	1.8022	—
IV	**Type of House**				
	Individual	3.4913	3.4761	3.842	60 9604
	Apartments	2.6869	3.4561	2.8091	1.8943
	F-Statistics	1.8441	0.3459	2.7336	—
V	**ASWI (%)**				
	Less than 21	3.1441	3.3858	2.9317	1.1096
	21 – 40	3.0684	3.6516	3.5023	1.4334
	41 – 60	2.5201	3.7137	3.3445	3.2169*
	61 – 80	2.6691	2.9196	3.5334	3.0617
	Above 80	2.5089	2.7229	3.6406	2.9969
	F-Statistics	1.1442	2.9909*	2.0245	—

*Significant at five per cent level.

of Model-III only the significant difference among the respondents with different number of earning members has been identified since its 'F' statistics is significant at five per cent level.

The respondents in individual house highly rate the model-III since its mean score is 3.8426 whereas for respondents in apartments, it is model-II since its mean score is 3.4561. There is no significant difference among the two groups of respondents regarding the evaluation of models. The respondents in owned house highly rate model-I whereas those living in leased house highly rate the model-II since its mean score 3.5268 and 3.6145 respectively. The respondents in rented house highly rate the model-III since its mean score is 3.5816. There is no significant difference among the three groups of respondents regarding their evaluation of three models.

The Awareness on Solid Waste Management Index (ASWI) is also taken as one of the profile variables of the respondents. Model-I is highly rated by the respondents with the ASWI of less than 21 per cent since its mean score is 3.1441. Those respondents with the ASWI of 41 to 60 per cent highly rate model-II since its mean score is 3.7137. Model-III is highly rated by the respondents with an ASWI of above 80 per cent. Regarding the evaluation of three models, the significant difference is identified among the respondents with the ASWI of 41 to 60, 61 to 80 and above 80 per cent. Regarding the evaluation of Model-II alone, the significant difference among the respondents with different ASWI has been noticed.

Factors Influencing the Model Choice

The respondents prefer the models generated mainly depending upon their profile and also various attributes in SWM. In the present study, the level of importance attached to the various attributes of model to select it has been revealed for some policy implications. The attributes (factors) in the models have been drawn from the previous studies (Brisson, 1997[10]; Miranda et al., 1994[11]; Repetta et al., 1992[12] and

Sugdev, 1999[13]). The identified factors are tariff, frequency of collection of wastes, timing of collection, disposal method, service quality, customer care and quantum of disposal. The respondents are asked to rate these factors at five-point scale according to their order of importance attached to these factors to select the model. To mean score of the model among the respondents with different profile have been measured to exhibit their importance attached with the factors. The multiple discriminate analyses have been used to identify the important discriminate factors among the various groups in each profile.

Based on gender, the respondents are classified into Male and female respondents whereas by the age, they are classified into less than 30 years, 30 to 40, 41 to 50, 51 to 60 and above 60 years. The mean score of the factors among these groups and the standardized discriminate co-efficient of the factors in the above-said two profiles are given in Tables 4.22 and 4.23.

Table 4.22 : Mean and standardized discriminate function co-efficient of the factors (Gender)

Sl. No.	Factors	Gender		Standardized Discriminate co-efficient
		Male	Female	
1.	Tariff	3.0451	3.5412	–0.45*
2.	Frequency of collection	3.5144	3.8917	–0.33*
3.	Timing of collection	3.3093	3.9304	–0.68*
4.	Disposal method	2.9667	2.5672	0.51*
5.	Service quality	4.1142	3.1411	1.82*
6.	Customer care	3.9194	3.2568	1.33*
7.	Quantum of disposal	3.7081	2.7086	1.96*
8.	Cluster size	429	210	
9.	Eigen value		18.34	
10.	Per cent of variation explained		91.36	
11.	Canonical correlation		0.7317	

* Significant at five per cent level.

Table 4.23 : Mean and standardized discriminate function co-efficient of the factors (Age)

Sl. No.	Factors	Age					Standardized discriminate co-efficient
		<30	30-40	41-50	51-60	>60	
1.	Tariff	2.7631	2.5142	3.1142	3.6562	3.8914	−1.49*
2.	Frequency of collection	3.3068	3.4511	3.4811	2.9086	2.9969	2.08
3.	Timing of collection	3.4506	3.2191	3.0969	2.8616	2.5731	0.96*
4.	Disposal method	3.6867	3.8082	3.3081	2.7168	2.5616	1.23*
5.	Service quality	3.8098	3.7314	3.5619	3.0181	2.6861	1.07*
6.	Customer care	4.1124	3.9161	3.4568	3.0861	3.1143	0.83*
7.	Quantum of disposal	3.8919	3.6012	3.8114	3.2314	3.4516	0.21
8.	Cluster size	78	131	223	136	73	
9.	Eigen value			17.04			
10.	Per cent of variation explained			84.46			
11.	Canonical correlation			0.6934			

The male respondents rate highly the service quality and customer cares to select the model since their respective mean scores are 4.1142 and 3.9194. The significant discriminate factors to select the model among the two groups are all seven factors since then respective standardized discriminate co-efficient are significant at five per cent level. The eigen value, per cent of variation explained and canonical correlation justify the validity of fitted multiple discriminate analysis.

Customer care is the highly rated factor among the respondents aged less than 30 years and 30 to 40 years since their respective mean scores are 4.1124 and 3.9161. Among the respondents within the age range of 41 to 50 and 51 to 60 years, these factors are quantum of disposal and tariff since their respective mean scores are 3.8114 and 3.6562. Among the respondents aged above 60 years, this factor is tariff since its respective mean score is 3.8914. The significant discriminate factors among the various age group of respondents are tariff, timing of collection, disposal method, service quality and customer care since their respective discriminate co-efficient are significant at five per cent level.

Discriminate Factors among the Respondents Based on their Nativity and Occupational Background

By their nativity, the respondents are classified into urban, semi-urban and rural respondents whereas by occupational background, they are classified into respondents in private employment, government employment, business, agriculture and others. The mean score of various factors among the different group of respondents regarding their nativity and occupational background and their respective standardized discriminate co-efficient are given in Table 4.24 and 4.25.

Table 4.24 : Mean and standardized discriminate function co-efficients of the factors (Nativity)

Sl. No.	Factors	Nativity			Standardized Disc. co-efficient
		Urban	Semi-Urban	Rural	
1.	Tariff	2.7314	3.0661	3.4568	–1.43*
2.	Frequency of collection	3.5678	2.9108	2.671	1.29*
3.	Timing of collection	3.0114	3.2146	2.8314	0.33
4.	Disposal method	3.5669	2.9617	2.6516	1.14*
5.	Service quality	3.9108	3.0617	3.2142	0.67*
6.	Customer care	3.8969	3.1442	3.0687	0.84*
7.	Quantum of disposal	3.8144	3.0629	2.9141	1.17*
8.	Cluster size	199	241	199	
9.	Eigen value	14.46			
10.	Per cent of variation explained	76.39			
11.	Canonical correlation	0.6454			

Table 4.25 : Mean and standardized discriminate function co-efficients of the factors (Occupational Background)

Sl. No.	Factors	Occupation Background					Standard-ized discrimi-nate co-efficient
		Private employ-ment	Gpvt. Employ-ment	Busin-ess	Agricul-ture	Other	
1.	Tariff	2.6942	3.0245	2.8145	3.6865	3.0414	−1.49*
2.	Frequency of collection	3.0451	3.3451	3.2546	3.0969	3.1446	0.17
3.	Timing of collection	3.2344	3.5084	3.0865	3.4514	3.2141	0.24
4.	Disposal method	3.6866	3.1446	2.8686	2.7568	2.4541	1.26*
5.	Service quality	3.8086	3.0447	3.8143	2.6817	2.6842	1.59*
6.	Customer care	3.9341	3.2411	3.0868	2.9393	2.6814	1.44*
7.	Quantum of disposal	3.8144	3.0846	2.9316	2.8141	2.9343	1.06*
8.	Cluster size	189	161	142	52	95	
9.	Eigon value			19.44			
10.	Per cent of variation explained			92.42			
11.	Canonical correlation			0.7686			

The important factor determining the model among the urban respondent is service quality since its mean score is 3.9108 whereas among the semi-urban and rural respondents, these are timing of collection and tariff since their mean scores are 3.2146 and 3.6568 respectively. The significant discriminating factors among the three groups of respondents are tariff, frequency of collection; disposal method, service quality, customer care and quantum of disposal since their respective discriminate co-efficient are significant at five per cent level.

Among the respondents with private and government employment, these factors are customer care and timing of collection since their mean scores are 3.9341 and 3.5084 respectively. The important factors among the respondents engaged in business and agriculture, are customer care and tariff since their respective mean scores are 3.0868 and 3.6865. Among the respondents with other employment, it is timing of collection since its mean score is 3.2141. The significant discriminate factors among the differently occupied respondents are tariff, disposal method, service quality, customer care and quantum of disposal.

Discriminate factors among the respondents with different family size and number of earning members per family

The respondents are classified as those with the family size of upto 3, 4 to 5, 6 to 7 and above 7 members whereas on the basis of number of earning members per family, they are grouped into respondents with one, two and above two earning members in the family. The mean scores of the factors among the different group of respondents based on their family size and number of earning members per family and the standardized discriminate co-efficient of the factors are summarized in Tables 4.26 and 4.27.

Table 4.26 : Mean and discriminate co-efficient factors among the respondents (Family Size)

Sl. No.	Factors	Family Size				Standardized disc. Co-efficient
		Upto3	4-5	6-7	Above 7	
1.	Tariff	2.5681	2.6816	3.1681	3.4541	–1.84*
2.	Frequency of collection	3.4514	3.0862	3.6811	3.7312	0.49
3.	Timing of collection	3.6814	3.7142	2.9161	2.5868	1.56*
4.	Disposal method	3.5086	3.4044	2.6144	2.4133	1.43*
5.	Service quality	3.8661	3.4142	2.8616	2.5168	1.72*
6.	Customer care	3.7332	3.8114	3.0864	2.7341	1.29*
7.	Quantum of disposal	3.6412	3.1147	3.0146	2.9616	0.34
	Cluster size	171	298	122	48	
	Eigen value			17.08		
	Per cent of variation explained			85.14		
	Canonical correlation			0.7013		

* Significant at five per cent level.

Table 4.27 : Mean and discriminate co-efficient factors among the respondents (Number of earning members per family)

Sl. No.	Factors	Number of earning members per family			Standardized Disc. co-efficient
		One	Two	Above two	
1.	Tariff	3.8144	3.0673	2.5616	1.39*
2.	Frequency of collection	3.0446	3.4568	3.9097	–0.68*
3.	Timing of collection	2.9968	3.0144	3.0676	–0.14
4.	Disposal method	3.1144	3.2868	3.2086	–0.39
5.	Service quality	3.3444	3.6566	3.5778	–0.09
6.	Customer care	3.6508	3.7341	3.8682	–0.12
7.	Quantum of disposal	2.8061	3.8566	3.9142	–1.36*
	Cluster size	199	343	97	
	Eigen value		19.36		
	Per cent of variation explained		92.68		
	Canonical correlation		0.7506		

* Significant at five per cent level.

The highly expected factors among the respondents with the family size of upto 3 and 4 to 5 members are service quality and customer care since their respective mean scores are 3.8661 and 3.8114. Among the respondents with the family size of 6 to 7 and above 7 members, frequency of collection since their respective mean scores are 3.6811 and 3.7312. The significant discriminate factors among the four groups of respondents are tariff, timing of collection, disposal method, service quality, customer care and quantum of disposal.

Among the respondents with only one earning member in the family, the most important factor is tariff since its mean score is 3.8144 whereas among the respondents with two and more than two earning members in their family, it is quantum of disposal since their respective mean scores are 3.8566 and 3.9142. The significant discriminate factors among the three groups of respondents are tariff, frequency of collection and quantum of disposal since their respective discriminate co-efficient are significant at five per cent level.

Discriminate Factors among the Respondents Based on House-ownership and Type of House

On the basis of house-ownership, the respondents are classified into those who are in owned house, leased house and rented house. By the type of house, they are classified into those who are in individual house and in apartments. The mean score of the factors among the respondents with different house-ownership and type of house have been computed to exhibit their level of importance attached to the factors. In order to identify the significant discriminate factors among these groups, the multiple discriminate analyses have been executed. The results are presented in Tables 4.28 and 4.29.

Table 4.28 : Mean and discriminate co-efficient of the factors (House-Ownership)

Sl. No.	Factors	House-ownership			Standardized Disc. co-efficient
		Owned house	Lease	Rental	
1.	Tariff	3.6514	3.0145	2.8914	0.54*
2.	Frequency of collection	2.8684	2.9414	3.1456	0.17
3.	Timing of collection	3.0433	3.1456	3.3317	0.22
4.	Disposal method	3.8145	3.0661	3.2334	0.34
5.	Service quality	3.1456	3.5318	3.8617	–0.68*
6.	Customer care	2.9616	3.0868	3.8108	–1.33*
7.	Quantum of disposal	2.9088	3.2344	3.8644	–1.42*
	Cluster size	253	123	263	
	Eigen value		17.33		
	Per cent of variation explained		86.18		
	Canonical correlation		0.7196		

* Significant at five per cent level.

Table 4.29 : Mean and discriminate co-efficient of the factors (Type of House)

Sl. No.	Factors	Type of House		
		Individual	Apartment	Standardized Discriminate co-efficient
1.	Tariff	3.8168	2.9616	1.29*
2.	Frequency of collection	3.4561	3.8168	0.14
3.	Timing of collection	3.3342	3.9144	−0.22
4.	Disposal method	3.5168	3.0642	0.27
5.	Service quality	2.9664	3.8646	−1.14*
6.	Customer care	3.2445	3.3081	0.17
7.	Quantum of disposal	3.0844	3.9142	−1.52*
	Cluster size	258	381	
	Eigen value	16.44		
	Per cent of variation explained	81.48		
	Canonical correlation	0.6909		

The highly rated factor among the respondents living in the owned house is disposal method since its mean score is 3.8145 whereas among the respondents living in leased house and rented house, these are service quality and quantum of disposal since their respective mean scores are 3.5318 and 3.8644. The significant discriminate factors among the three groups of respondents are tariff, service quality, customer care and quantum of disposal.

Among the respondents living in individual house, the important factors are tariff and disposal method since their respective mean scores are 3.8168 and 3.5168. The important factors for the respondents living in apartments are timing of collection and quantum of disposal since then respective mean scores are 3.9144 and 3.9142. The significant discriminate factors among the two groups of respondents are tariff, service quality and quantum of disposal since their respective discriminate co-efficient are significant at five per cent level.

Discriminate Factors among the Respondents with Different ASWI

The awareness of solid waste management among the respondents are summated with the help of an index namely ASWI. In the present study, ASWI among the respondents is classified in terms of age less than 21, 21 to 40, 41 to 60, 61 to 80 and above 80. The important factors influencing the model choice among the respondents with different ASWI groups have been examined with the help of their mean score. The important discriminate factors among these groups are analysed with the help of multiple discriminate analysis. The results are given in Table 4.30.

Table 4.30 : Mean score and discriminate co-efficient of the factors

Sl. No.	Factors	ASWI (%)					Standardized discriminate co-efficient
		Less than 21	21-40	41-60	61-80	Above 80	
1.	Tariff	3.8586	3.6168	3.0811	3.2114	3.0086	–0.89*
2.	Frequency of collection	2.7087	2.5083	3.0114	3.8064	3.6884	1.41*
3.	Timing of collection	2.5159	2.6224	3.1449	3.6146	3.5081	1.08*
4.	Disposal method	2.7331	2.9063	3.1774	3.8216	3.8914	1.24*
5.	Service quality	3.1496	3.0144	3.2443	3.5919	3.6804	1.57*
6.	Customer care	2.8617	3.2146	3.2041	3.4509	3.8189	1.88*
7.	Quantum of disposal	3.1447	3.0451	3.3991	3.8664	4.1214	1.33*
	Cluster size	290	196	91	47	15	
	Eigen value			20.22			
	Per cent of variance explained			98.83			
	Canonical correlation			0.8146			

* Significant at five per cent level.

For respondents with an ASWI of less than 21 and 21 to 40 per cent the most important factor is tariff since its respective mean scores are 3.8586 and 3.6168. Among the respondents with the ASWI of 61 to 80 and above 80 per cent, it is quantum of disposal since its mean scores 3.3991 and 4.1214 respectively. The significant discriminate factors among the respondents with different group of ASWI are all the seven factors since their respective discriminate co-efficient are significant at five per cent level.

Privatization of SWM

Over the last decade the global movement towards involving of the private sector in provision of SWM services has been rapidly gaining momentum and so has the political opposition. The real question facing of the local bodies is whether to hand over the SWM services to private people. What should be the regulated pricing on SWM services? And in what way can the social welfare and justice be maintained by the government in the privatization of SWM. Before answering all the three questions, the most important issue is whether the people are willing to privatize the SWM services. Hence the present study has made an attempt to analyze the people's willingness to privatize the SWM at five scales. The number of respondents with different degrees of favour on privatization of SWM is illustrated in Table 4.31.

Table 4.31. Opinion on privatization of SMW

Sl. No.	Degree of favour on privatization of SWM	Number of respondents			Total
		LIG	MIG	HIG	
1.	Very high	45	83	52	180
2.	High	63	96	26	185
3.	Moderate	42	86	16	144
4.	Low	27	34	14	75
5.	Very low	14	41	---	55
	Total	191	340	108	639

The important degrees of favour on privatization among the respondents are high and very high which constitute 28.95 and 28.17 per cent of the total respectively. The respondents with low and very low degree of favor on privatization constitute 11.73 and 8.61 per cent to the total respectively. The most important degree of favour on privatization among the LIG and MIG is high which constitutes 32.98 and 28.24 per cent to its respective total of 191 and 340 respondents. Among the HIG, it is very high which constitutes 48.15 per cent of its total.

Reasons for Privatization of SWM

The reasons for privatization may be related to the existing poor service, lack of response to the customer call by the public sector, environmental awareness, etc. The reasons are identified by previous studies (Mc.Fadden, 1976[27]; Fullerton and Kinnaman, 1996[28]; Hug and Adams, 1993[29]) were tested in the present study. In total there are 17 reasons for privatization have been identified. The respondents are asked to rate the reasons at five-point scale on the basis of their attitude towards the reasons. The mean score of all reasons among the LIG, MIG and HIG have been computed separately to highlight the important reasons for privatization among the respondents. The one-way analysis of variance has been executed to analyse the significant difference among the three income groups regarding their attitude towards the reasons for privatization. The results are given in Table 4.32.

The highly rated reasons for privatization among the LIG are reliability and efficient complaint handling of private sector since their mean scores are 3.6943 and 3.6166 respectively. Among the MIG, these reasons are reputation of the private company and reliability of private service since their respective mean scores are 3.9691 and 3.8968 whereas among the HIG, these are reliability of private service and red-tapism in public service since their mean scores are 4.3142 and 4.2962 respectively. In total, the HIG are highly rating the various reasons for privatization than the MIG and HIG. Regarding the attitude towards the reasons for privatization, the significant differences among the three income groups have been noticed in the case of flexibility in timing, customized service by private agency, timely collection of wastages,

Table 4.32 : Reasons for privatization

Sl. No.	Reasons	Mean score among customers			F-Statistics
		LIG	MIG	HIG	
1.	Reliability of private service	3.6943	3.8968	4.3142	1.5668
2.	Flexibility in timing	2.5669	3.2109	3.6049	3.2464*
3.	Customized service	3.0617	3.6244	4.1408	3.3961*
4.	Timely collection of wastages	2.9688	3.4942	4.2403	3.4082*
5.	Frequency of collection	3.2214	3.5908	4.0893	3.0044*
6.	Volume based tariff	2.4045	3.6999	4.1164	3.6021*
7.	Complaint handling of private system	3.6166	3.8234	3.8066	0.7368
8.	Responsiveness	3.5645	3.8686	3.9192	0.6919
9.	Easy procedure	2.8641	3.0341	3.5646	1.4568
10.	Reputation of private company	2.6779	3.9691	3.8183	3.4021*
11.	Dissatisfaction on existing system	3.0444	3.8142	4.1236	3.1199*
12.	Poor service in existing system	2.9193	3.6083	4.0863	3.3344*
13.	Non-existence of any system in public	2.6079	3.2344	3.8644	3.5161*
14.	Red-tapism in public service	2.7144	3.3969	4.2962	3.7334*
15.	Political intervention	3.0496	3.6868	3.9193	2.9161

*Significant at five per cent level.

frequency of collection, volume-based tariff, reputation of the private company, dissatisfaction on the existing system, poor service in existing system, non-existence of any system in public agency and red-tapism in public service since their respective 'F' statistics are significant at five per cent level.

Important Reasons for Privatization

The scores on various reasons for privatization among the respondents have been included for Exploratory Factor

Analysis (EFA) in order to enumerate the reasons in term of their importance. Before conducting EFA, the test of validity of data for factor analysis with the help of KMO measure of sampling adequacy and level of significance of chi-square satisfy the validity of data for analysis since the KMO measure is greater than 0.5 and the level of significance of chi-square value is at zero per cent level. The executed EFA results in four important reasons. The (reasons) variables in each important reason, its reliability co-efficient, eigen value and the per cent of variation explained are shown in Table 4.33.

Table 4.33 : Important reasons for Privatization

Sl. No.	Important Reasons	Number of variables	Crown-bach alpha	Eigen value	% of variation explained	Cummu-lative per cent of varia-tion explained
1.	Existing system	5	0.7224	3.8616	28.11	28.11
2.	Office Methods	4	0.7609	3.0414	20.68	48.79
3.	Collection system	3	0.8114	2.6962	18.42	67.21
4.	Service quality	3	0.8321	1.9833	16.17	83.38
	KMO: Measure of Sampling Adequacy: 0.7331			Bartletts test of sphericity: chi-Square: 91.09*		

* Significant at five per cent level.

The enumerated four important reasons for privatization explain the reasons to the extent of 83.38 per cent. The most important reason for privatization is 'existing system' since its eigen value and the per cent of variation explained are 3.8616 and 28.11 per cent respectively. This 'existing system' consists of five reasons with the reliability co-efficient of 0.7224. The second and third important reasons are 'office methods' and 'collection system' since their eigen values are 3.0414 and 2.6962 respectively. The per cent of variation explained by these two factors are 20.68 and 18.42 per cent respectively.

The last factor identified by the factor analysis is 'service quality' since its eigen value is 1.9833. It consists of four reasons with the reliability co-efficient of 0.8321.

Reliability and Validity of the Important Reasons

The reliability and validity of the factors in each important reason have been examined with the help of Confirmatory Factor Analysis (CFA). The convergent validity has been estimated with the help of the significance of standardized factor loading of the reasons whereas the construct validity is ratified with the help of composite reliability. The Average Variance Extracted (AVE) of the construct has been also computed. The results are given in Table 4.34.

Table 4.34 : Reliability and validity of variables in each important reasons

Sl. No.	Important reasons	Range of standardized factor loading	Range of 't' statistics	Composite reliability	Average variance extracted
1.	Existing system	0.6454–0.9029	4.6818–14.1415	0.7309	51.42
2.	Office methods	0.7217–0.8446	6.0899–12.6891	0.7817	54.08
3.	Collection system	0.7303–0.9114	6.4214–14.2917	0.8409	61.24
4.	Service quality	0.6768–0.9342	4.8027–15.6027	0.8724	69.39

The convergent validity of the reasons in each construct has been confirmed since the standardized factor loadings are significant at five per cent level. The standardized factor loading of the reasons in the construct vary from 0.6454 to 0.9342. Since the composite reliability of all constructs are greater than 0.5, the construct validity has been confirmed. The AVE of each construct has confirmed the validity and reliability of the constructs since the AVE of the constructs are greater than the minimum threshold of 0.5.

Discriminate Validity of the Constructs

The discriminate validity of the constructs has been examined with the help of inter correlation between the four important reasons. The correlation matrix is given in Table 4.35.

Table 4.35 : Inter-relationship between important reasons

Factors	Existing system	Office Methods	Collection system	Service quality
Existing system		–0.1817	–0.1033	.2017
Office methods			–0.2247	.1386
Collection system				.1568
Service quality				

The correlation co-efficient between the constructs varies from 0.1033 to -0.2247. There is higher correlation between the office methods and collection system whereas the lesser correlation is noticed between the existing system and collection system. No correlation co-efficient is significant at five per cent level. It shows the discriminate validity among the constructs. It reveals that there is a mutual exclusiveness of the important reasons for privatization.

Respondents' Perception on Important Reasons for Privatization

The respondents' perception on important reasons for privatization is computed by the mean score of various factors in each important reason. The mean score of important reasons among the LIG, MIG and HIG has been computed to exhibit the level of opinion on the important factors for privatization among the respondents. Regarding the opinion on important factors for privatization, the significant differences among the three income groups have been examined with the help of one-way analysis of variance. The results are given in Table 4.36.

The highly regarded important reasons for privatization among LIG are service quality since its mean score is 3.4402. Among the MIG and HIG the important reason is service quality since its mean scores are 3.7966 and 4.1247 respectively. Regarding the perception on important reasons for privatization,

Table 4.36 : Level of opinion on important reasons for privatization of SWM

Sl. No.	Important Reasons	Mean score among			F-Statistics
		LIG	MIG	HIG	
1.	Existing system	2.8671	3.5481	4.0579	3.4869*
2.	Office methods	2.8901	3.6316	3.8265	3.1302*
3.	Collection system	2.9190	3.4319	3.9782	3.0214*
4.	Service quality	3.4402	3.7966	4.1247	2.1089

* Significant at five per cent level.

the significant difference among the three income groups have been found in the perception on existing system, office methods and collection system since their respective 'F' statistics are significant at five per cent level.

Association between the Profile of Respondents and their Opinion on Important Reasons

The profile of the respondents may be associated with their opinion on important reasons for privatization. In order to analyse such association, profile variables included are gender, age, nativity, occupational background, family size, number of earning members per family, house-ownership, type of house and ASWI. The one-way analysis of variance has been employed to analyse such associations. The results are given in Table 4.37.

Regarding the perception on 'Existing System', the significantly associating profile variables are age, occupational background, family size and ASWI since their respective 'F' statistics are significant at five per cent level. The significantly associating profile variables with the perception on office methods are age, occupational background number of earning members per family and ASWI whereas regarding the perception on collection systems, the significantly associating profile variables are age, occupational background, family size, number of earning members per family and ASWI.

Table 4.37. Association between profile of respondents and their opinion on privatization

Sl. No.	Profile	F–Statistics			Service quality
		Existing system	Office methods	Collection system	
1	Gender	2.1403	2.9144	3.2641	3.6566
2.	Age	2.5086*	2.8447*	2.9039*	2.5144*
3.	Nativity	2.5081	2.0443	2.6162	2.8616
4.	Occupational background	2.7339*	2.6344*	2.5034*	2.7311*
5.	Family size	2.7108*	2.0866	2.8184*	2.8336*
6.	Number of earning member per family	2.0686	3.1443*	2.9397*	3.1246*
7.	House ownership	2.1145	1.9692	2.0463	2.7546
8.	Type of house	2.8908	3.1443	2.7365	3.1007
9.	ASWI	2.8684*	3.2408*	2.7369*	2.6266*

*Significant at five per cent level.

The significantly associating profile variables with the perception on 'service quality' are age, occupational background, family size, number of earning members per family and ASWI since their respective 'F' statistics are significant at five per cent level. The analysis reveals the importance of age, occupational background and ASWI in their perception on important reasons for privatization among the respondents.

Impact of Important Reasons for Privatization on their Overall Degree of Favour for Privatization among the Respondents

The important reasons for privatization among the respondents exist system, office methods, collection system and service quality. The perception on the important reasons may have its own influence on the degree of favour for privatization among the respondents. The included independent variables are the score on above said four important reasons whereas the score on the degree of favour for privatization are 5, 4, 3, 2 and 1 for very high, high, moderate, low and very low respectively. The multiple regression analysis has been administered to analyse the impact of independent variables on dependent variable. The fitted regression model is

$$Y = a + b_1X_1 + b_2X_2 + b_3X_3 + b_4X_4 + e$$

Where Y - Degree of favour for privatization

X_1 - Score on existing system

X_2 - Score on office methods

X_3 - Score on collection systems

X_4 - Score on service quality

$b_1, b_2 \ldots b_4$ - Regression co-efficient of independent variables

a - Intercept and

e - Error term

The impact of independent variables on dependent variable has been analysed among LIG, MIG, HIG and also for pooled data separately. The results are given in Table 4.38.

Table 4.38 : Impact of important reasons for privatization on the overall attitude towards privatization

Sl. No.	Important variables	Regression co-efficients			
		LIG	MIG	HIG	Pooled
1.	Existing system	0.1844*	0.2488*	0.2711*	0.2219*
2.	Office methods	0.0968	0.1244	0.1908*	0.1017
3.	Collection system	0.1414*	0.1603*	0.2411*	0.1722*
4.	Service quality	0.0933	0.1443*	0.2603*	0.1649*
	Constant	0.5684	0.9368	1.3969	0.9774
	R2	0.7142	0.8142	0.6931	0.8346
	F-Statistics	0.4968*	10.9697*	7.6642	12.1461*

* Significant at five per cent level

The significantly influencing reasons on degree of favour for privatization among the LIG is existing system and collection system. A unit increase in the perception on above said reasons results in an increase in degree of favour for privatization by 0.1844 and 0.1414 units respectively. Among the MIG, these significant reasons are existing system, collection system and service quality. A unit increases in the perception on above three reasons result in an increase in degree of favour for privatization by 0.2488, 0.1603 and 0.1443 units respectively. Among the HIGs, a unit increases in the perception on existing system, office methods, collection systems and service quality results in an increase in degree of favour for privatization by 0.2711, 0.1908, 0.2411 and 0.2603 units respectively. The changes in the perception on the reasons for privatization explain the degree of favour for privatization to the extent of 69.31 per cent.

Reasons for not Supporting Privatization

Out of 639 respondents, 236 respondents are not in favour of privatization. Out of the 236 respondents, 74.17 per cent are of LIG whereas the remaining are of MIG and HIG. Since there are some reasons for not supporting privatization among the respondents, they are asked to rate the reasons for not supporting privatization at five-point scale. The mean scores of each reason among the LIG, MIG and HIG have been computed separately (Table 4.39).

Table 4.39. Reasons for not supporting privatization

Sl. No.	Reasons	Mean score			F-Statistics
		LIG	MIG	HIG	
1.	Higher tariff	3.9144	3.2342	2.8616	3.1449*
2.	No consideration for poor	3.6608	3.3911	2.9011	3.3096*
3.	Profit motive of private	3.7417	3.0612	3.1441	2.3614
4.	No public welfare	3.3342	2.8611	2.4516	2.6869
5.	Higher establishment cost	2.5643	3.1443	3.6168	3.0144*

* Significant at five per cent level.

The highly viewed reasons for not supporting privatization among the LIG is higher tariff and profit motive of private since their mean scores are 3.9144 and 3.7417 respectively. Among the MIG, these are no consideration for poor and higher establishment cost and profit motive of private since their respective mean scores are 3.3911, 3.1443 and 3.0612. Regarding the perception on the reasons, the significant difference among the three income groups have been noticed in the case of perception on higher tariff, no consideration for poor and higher establishment cost since their respective 'F' statistics are significant at five per cent level.

Evaluation of Financial Model for SWM System

The finance model for SWM system represents the pricing of SWM. The pricing of essential Services fixed by the public service provider should be based on the public welfare in their mind. Even though, the local bodies are having several options to price on their SWM services to the people they are charging either flat rate on marginal cost pricing. The available pricing models for SWM have been identified from the review of previous studies (Billings and AGthe, 1980[30]; Fisher et al., 1995[31]; Hewitt and Hanemam, 1995[32] and Revwick and Archibad, 1998[33]). The identified pricing models in the present study are marginal cost pricing, full cost pricing, cost plus profit pricing, discriminatory pricing, volume-based pricing, service quality-based pricing and flat rate pricing. The respondents are asked to rate the above-said pricing at five point scale on the basis of their willingness. The mean score of each pricing among the LIG, MIG and HIG have been computed separately and shown in Table 4.40.

The highly rated financial model for SWM among the LIG is flat rate pricing and marginal cost pricing since their mean scores are 3.8184 and 3.6817 respectively. Among the MIG, these two financial models are service quality-based pricing and volume-based pricing since their respective mean scores

Table 4.40 : Rating on financial model for SWM system

Sl. No.	Basis of financial model	Mean score			F-Statistics
		LIG	MIG	HIG	
1.	Marginal cost pricing	3.6817	3.0684	2.6861	3.1441*
2.	Full cost pricing	2.4083	2.8144	3.6864	3.4089*
3.	Cost plus profit pricing	2.3366	2.6033	3.7233	3.8904*
4.	Discriminatory pricing	3.7442	2.5144	3.1144	3.6644*
5.	Volume-based pricing	2.5616	3.2868	3.9168	3.7336*
6.	Service quality based pricing	3.0444	3.3361	4.1248	3.8184*
7.	Flat rate pricing	3.8184	3.0445	2.6662	3.5651*

* Significant at five per cent level.

are 3.3361 and 3.2868. Among the HIG, these financial models are service quality- based pricing and volume-based pricing since their mean scores are 4.1248 and 3.9168 respectively. Regarding the attitude towards the financial models for SWM, the significant differenced among the three income groups have been identifie in their perception on marginal cost pricing, full cost pricing, cost plus profit pricing, discriminatory pricing, volume-based pricing, service quality-based pricing and flat rate pricing since their respective 'F' statistics are significant at five per cent level.

Profile of the Respondents and their Choice on Financial Model

Since the profile of the respondents has its own role in the choice of financial model for SWM among them the present study has made an attempt to analyze the level of preference on each financial model among the different group of respondents in each of their profile variable with help of its mean score. The one-way analysis of variance has been employed to analyse the significant difference on the evaluation of financial model among each group of respondents and also among the different group of respondents.

Table 4.41 : Profile of respondents and their preference on finance model for SWM

Sl. No.	Profile	Mean Score							F-statistics
		Marginal cost pricing	Full cost pricing	Cost plus profit pricing	Discriminatory pricing	Volume based pricing	Service quality based pricing	Flate rate pricing	
1	2	3	4	5	6	7	8	9	10
I.	**Gender**								
	Male	3.3705	3.0751	2.9961	2.7461	2.9272	3.9616	2.8352	4.618*
	Female	3.567	2.3961	2.1341	3.4681	3.6861	2.1986	3.9812	3.7103*
	F-Statistics	0.9197	2.5082	3.1415*	2.4199	2.3316	4.1708*	4.0614*	—
II	**Age**								
	Less than 30	2.9688	3.9092	3.4149	3.6344	3.8564	4.2183	1.8056	6.8541*
	30-40	3.5059	3.4163	3.0452	3.5911	3.5616	3.9604	3.0166	1.2399
	41-50	3.7859	2.6869	2.7019	2.9422	3.1016	3.2625	3.1403	2.9904*
	51-60	3.9622	2.1689	2.3392	2.3092	2.6869	2.9666	3.8586	4.1706*
	Above 60	3.6759	2.4142	2.1144	2.5969	2.9185	2.6141	4.0394	5.9081*

Cont...

1	2	3	4	5	6	7	8	9.	10
III	**Nativity**								
	Urban	3.6715	3.2969	3.0415	3.2141	3.8909	3.9603	2.0627	3.8161*
	Semi-Urban	3.4563	2.9163	2.8681	2.3297	3.0141	3.1144	3.3144	3.5099*
	Rural	3.8842	2.2900	2.1961	3.5443	2.6586	3.1284	4.2366	6.8183*
	F-Statistics	1.1427	3.1086*	3.8081*	3.7024*	3.1144*	4.5062*	6.1717*	—
IV	**Occupational background**								
	Private employment	3.6351	2.7681	2.7914	2.4232	3.3563	3.5457	2.9429	6.0339*
	Government employment	3.4903	2.7314	2.8182	3.2084	3.2091	3.2676	3.1443	2.1596
	Business	3.6646	3.0171	2.7617	3.3166	2.8684	3.1441	3.3068	2.5033
	Agriculture	3.9567	2.8143	2.3396	3.8189	2.4091	2.5617	3.9696	4.1242*
	Others	3.8028	2.9193	2.5089	2.7611	3.6441	2.9099	3.3044	5.0261*
	F-Statistics	0.5141	0.6021	0.4417	4.2172*	3.8146*	3.1719*	3.0696*	—

* Significant at five per cent level

Table 4.41 explains the mean score of various financial models among the different groups of respondents based on their gender, age, nativity and occupational background. The male respondents highly rate the service quality-based pricing since its mean score is 3.9616 whereas among the female respondents, it is flat rate pricing since its mean score is 3.9812. Regarding the choice of various financial models, the significant difference among the models have been noticed among the male and female respondents since their respective 'F' statistics are significant at five per cent level. Regarding the evaluation of various financial models, the significant differences among the male and female respondents have been noticed in the case of cost plus profit pricing, service quality-based pricing and flat rate pricing since their respective 'F' statistics are significant at five per cent level.

The respondents aged less than 30 years and between 30 and 40 years prefer the service quality-based pricing since their respective mean scores are 4.2183 and 3.9604. Among the respondents with the age of 41 to 50, 51 to 60 years and above 60 years it is marginal cost pricing since their respective mean scores are 3.7859, 3.9622 and 3.6759. Regarding the evaluation of financial model, the significant difference among the financial models has been identified among the respondents aged less than 30 and above 40 years. The significant difference among the different age groups of respondents has been noticed in the evaluation of all seven financial models.

The urban respondents highly rate the service quality-based pricing whereas the semi-urban respondents rate the marginal cost pricing highly since their mean scores are 3.9603 and 3.4563. The rural respondents rate the flat rate pricing highly since its mean score is 4.2366. Regarding the evaluation of financial models, the significant difference among the seven models has been identified among the three groups of respondents separately. Regarding the evaluation of financial models, the significant differences among the three group of respondents based on their nativity have been identified in the evaluation of full cost pricing, cost plus profit pricing, discriminatory pricing, volume based pricing and flat rate pricing since their respective 'F' statistics are significant at five per cent level.

The respondents with private and government employment highly rate the marginal cost pricing since their mean scores are 3.6351 and 3.4903 respectively. The respondents engaged in business and agriculture highly rate the marginal cost pricing and flat rate pricing since their respective mean scores are 3.6646 and 3.9696. The respondents with other occupations highly rate the marginal cost pricing. The significant difference in the evaluation of seven financial models has been seen among the respondents with private employment, agriculture and others. Regarding the evaluation of financial models, the significant differences among the respondents with different occupations have been identified in the evaluation of discriminatory price, volume-based pricing, service quality-based pricing and flat rate pricing.

The evaluation of the financial models by the different groups of respondents based on their family size, number of earning members per family, house-ownership, type of house and ASWI has been analyzed and shown in Table 4.42.

The most important financial model identified by the respondents with the family size of upto 3 and 4 to 5 members is service quality-based pricing and volume-based pricing since their respective mean scores are 3.7139 and 3.3370. Among the respondents with the family size of 6 to 7 and above 7 members, this is marginal cost pricing since its mean scores are 3.9144 and 4.3196 respectively. The significant difference among the various group of respondents based on their family size have been noticed in the evaluation of all seven financial models.

Table 4.42 : Profile of respondents and their preference on financial model for SWM

Sl. No.	Profile	Mean Score							F-statistics
		Marginal cost pricing	Full cost pricing	Cost plus profit pricing	Discriminatory pricing	Volume based pricing	Service quality based pricing	Flate rate pricing	
1	2	3	4	5	6	7	8	9	10
V.	**Family size**								
	Upto 3	2.9318	3.2596	3.3361	2.5153	3.4194	3.7139	3.1514	7.0332*
	4-5	3.2856	2.8569	2.4723	3.2080	3.3370	3.1763	2.8365	4.1391*
	6-7	3.9144	2.4017	2.5462	2.8144	2.7334	2.6863	3.8604	5.3968*
	Above 7	4.3196	2.3596	2.4086	3.6861	2.4406	2.5092	4.1086	8.1442*
	F-Statistics	3.9091*	3.0616*	2.9969*	3.1447*	3.0061*	3.3096*	3.0199*	—
VI.	**Number of earning members per family**								
	One	3.9244	2.0481	2.3075	3.6341	2.4049	3.0141	3.8284	8.0443*
	Two	3.7196	3.0845	2.8036	2.7864	3.4948	3.5111	2.9518	2.9091
	More than two	2.8823	3.6026	3.2233	2.3463	3.6339	3.6816	2.8661	4.5162*
	F-Statistics	3.1446*	3.7174*	2.7192	3.2641*	3.3441*	3.9024*	3.2161*	—

Cont...

1	2	3	4	5	6	7	8	9	10
VII.	**House ownership**								
	Owned house	3.4211	3.3031	3.1969	2.7672	2.4566	3.1026	3.6063	3.1406*
	Lease	3.0446	2.6542	2.1605	2.5450	3.5102	3.3062	3.4301	3.0239*
	Rental	4.1686	2.4824	2.5054	3.3964	3.7129	3.6867	2.7302	4.1734*
	F-Statistics	3.2091*	2.9969*	3.0141*	2.5617	3.5156*	1.9891	2.8686	—
VIII.	**Type of House**								
	Individual	3.9863	2.2175	2.1116	2.3634	2.5309	2.9071	3.8962	5.0869*
	Apartments	3.4328	3.2622	3.1199	3.4032	3.6137	3.7039	2.7483	1.4542
	F-Statistics	1.1454	3.0146*	3.1443*	3.2144*	3.1089*	2.5146	3.3145*	—
IX.	**ASWI**								
	<21	4.5618	2.7451	2.8275	2.7625	2.9172	3.0162	3.4636	7.1403*
	21-40	3.0445	2.7516	2.7941	3.1456	3.1211	3.2044	3.0991	2.3319
	41-60	2.8033	2.9084	2.3962	2.9968	3.5054	3.3386	2.9417	1.9416
	61-80	2.6562	3.3391	2.4103	3.4102	4.1086	3.9099	2.8332	2.9969*
	Above 80	2.4511	3.8682	2.3019	3.7147	3.9968	4.1341	2.6411	5.0863*
	F-Statistics	5.1408*	3.1417*	2.0661	3.0671*	3.4502*	3.1496*	2.8182	—

* Significant at five per cent level

The respondents with one and two earning members per family highly rate the marginal pricing since their respective mean scores are 3.9244 and 3.7196. The respondents with more than two earning members per family highly rate the service quality-based pricing since its mean score is 3.6816. The significant difference among the evaluation of seven financial models has been identified among the respondents with one and more than two earning members per family. The significant differences among the three group of respondents have been noticed in the evaluation of marginal cost pricing, full cost pricing, discriminatory pricing, volume-based pricing; service quality-based pricing and flat rate pricing.

The respondents living in owned house and leased house highly rate the flat rate pricing since its mean scores are 3.6063 and 3.4301 respectively. The respondents living in rented house highly rate the marginal cost pricing since its mean score is 4.1686. Regarding the evaluation of financial models, the significant difference among the three group of respondents have been noticed in the evaluation of marginal cost pricing, full cost pricing, cost plus profit pricing and volume-based pricing.

The respondents living in individual house highly rate the marginal cost pricing whereas the respondents in apartment highly rate the service quality-based pricing since their respective mean scores are 3.9863 and 3.7039. The significant differences among the two group of respondents have been identified in the evaluation of full cost pricing, cost plus profit pricing, discriminatory pricing, volume-based pricing and flat rate pricing. Among the respondents in individual house, the significant difference on the evaluation of seven pricing has been identified.

The highly rated pricing among the respondents with the ASWI of less than 21 per cent, 21 to 40 and 41 to 60 per cent are marginal cost pricing, service quality-based pricing and volume-based pricing since their mean scores are 4.5618, 3.2044 and 3.5054 respectively. Among the respondents with the ASWI of 61 to 80 and above 80 per cent it is volume-base pricing and service quality-based pricing since their mean scores are 4.1086 and 4.1341 respectively. The significant differences among the evaluation on seven financial models have been noticed among the respondent with the ASWI of less than 21 per cent, 61 to 80 and above 80 per cent. The significant difference among the respondents with different ASWI have been identified in the evaluation of marginal cost pricing, full cost pricing, discriminatory pricing, volume based pricing and service quality-based pricing.

Contingent Valuation Model (CVM)

The Contingent Valuation Model elicits the consumers' willingness to pay (WTP) for different service options. The contingent valuation method describes an ideal system to the customers, where the services of SWM would be at their maximum levels. The willingness-to-pay (WTP) for a proposed improved SWM services to the consumers has to be measured among the respondents. Usually, the survey of discrete choice experiments is used to value attributes of SWM options. Several designs options generated in choice model are used here also. The only difference is that the respondents are asked to mention their willingness-to-pay for each model generated in choice model by an addition (Kabana and Jair 2001[34]; Boxall et al., 1996[35]; Van and Morris, 1999[36]). In the present study, the WTP of the respondents has been measured for the proposed enriched SWM services in general. The respondents are asked to mention their WTP in near future for SWM services. The results are given in Table 4.43.

The important WTP among the respondents for SWM services per month is Rs. 101 to 125 and Rs. 76-100, which constitutes 21.28 and 16.43 per cent of the total respectively. The respondents with the WTP of above Rs. 200 per month constitute 8.76 per cent to the total. Among the LIG, the important WTP are upto Rs. 50 and Rs. 51 to 75 which constitute 36.13 and 20.42 per cent of its total. Among the MIG, these are Rs.101 to 125 and Rs. 126 to 150, which

Table 4.43 : Willingness to pay for SWM per month

Sl. No.	Willingness to pay (in Rs.)	Number of respondents			Total
		LIG	MIG	HIG	
1.	Upto 50	69	12	–	81
2.	51-75	39	46	7	92
3.	76-100	36	58	11	105
4.	101-125	25	90	21	136
5.	126-150	13	65	23	101
6.	151-200	9	42	17	68
7.	Above 200	–	27	29	56
	Total	191	340	108	639

constitutes 26.47 and 19.12 per cent of its total respectively. The important WTP among the HIG are above Rs.200 and Rs.126 to 150 which constitutes 26.85 and 21.29 per cent of its total respectively.

Profile of the Respondents and their WTP

The WTP for SWM services per month may be associated with the profile of the respondents since the socio-economic and demographic characteristics of respondents play an important role in specifying the WTP for SWM among the respondents. The WTP per month for SWM among the various groups in each profile of the respondents is given in Table 4.44.

The male respondents are willing to pay more than the female respondents since their respective mean values of WTP are Rs.129.11 and Rs.64.97. The significant difference among the male and female respondents has been identified regarding their WTP on SWM services. The same situation is also noticed among the various age groups of respondents. The respondents aged less than 30 years are willing to pay a mean of Rs.141.08 whereas the respondents with the age of above 60 years is willing to pay a mean of Rs.58.62 only per month on the SWM services. The mean of urban respondents' WTP

Table 4.44 : Profile of the respondents and their willing to pay of the for SWM per month

Sl. No.	Profile	Mean	Standard deviation	Co-efficient of variation	F-Statistics
I.	**Gender**				
	Male	129.11	34.28	26.55	6.8894*
	Female	64.97	10.04	15.45	
II.	**Age**				
	Less than 30	141.08	21.77	15.43	
	30-40	130.66	22.08	16.89	
	41-50	119.93	17.39	14.50	8.0846*
	51-60	74.69	12.64	16.92	
	Above 60	58.62	8.19	13.97	
III.	**Nativity**				
	Urban	139.43	20.04	14.37	
	Semi-Urban	114.39	16.61	14.52	5.0114*
	Rural	68.93	9.09	13.19	
IV.	**Occupational background**				
	Private employment	120.39	17.14	14.24	
	Government employment	108.62	22.49	20.70	
	Business	127.09	26.06	20.51	6.6734*
	Agriculture	56.72	7.46	13.15	
	Others	82.03	10.08	12.29	

* Significant at five per cent level.

for SWM per month is Rs.139.43 whereas among the semi-urban and rural respondents, it is Rs.114.39 and Rs.68.93 respectively. Regarding the WTP of three groups of respondents, the significant difference among them have been noticed since their respective 'F' statistics is significant at five per cent level.

Based on occupational background, the respondents with private employment are willing to pay a mean of Rs.120.39 per month for SWM services whereas the government employees and businessmen are willing to pay Rs.102.62 and Rs.127.09 respectively. Among the farmers, it is only Rs.56.72. Regarding the WTP, the significant differences among the respondents with different occupational background have been noticed since their respective 'F' statistics is significant at five per cent level.

The association between the profile variables namely family size, number of earning members per family, house-ownership, type of house and ASWI and the WTP among the respondents have been examined with the help of mean, standard deviation, co-efficient of variation of WTP and its respective 'F' statistics. The results are given in Table 4.45.

For respondents with the family size of upto 3 members and 4 to 5 members, the mean of WTP for SWM services per month is Rs.112.11 and 120.83 whereas among the respondents with a family size of above 7, it is Rs.67.69. Regarding the WTP, the significant differences among the respondents with different family size have been noticed whereas the same trend is identified among the respondents with different earning members per family. For respondents with one earning member per family, the mean of WTP is Rs.100.36 whereas it is Rs.149.03 among the respondents with more than two earning members per family.

The mean of WTP among the respondents in owned house and leased house is Rs.88.31 and Rs.117.79 respectively. Among the respondents with rented house, it is Rs.122.24. The respondents living in individual house are willing to pay a mean of Rs.71.04 whereas for those who are living in apartments, it is Rs.133.08. Regarding the WTP, the significant differences among the respondents have been identified when they are classified on the basis of house-ownership and type of house.

Table 4.45 : Profile of respondents and their willing to pay for SWM per month

Sl. No.	Profile	Mean	Standard deviation	Co-efficient of variation	F-Statistics
I	**Family size**				
	Upto 3	112.11	16.79	14.98	
	4-5	120.83	19.33	15.99	
	6-7	86.94	10.69	12.29	4.6684*
	Above 7	67.69	8.44	12.46	
II	**Number of earning members per family**				
	One	100.36	14.44	14.39	
	Two	100.89	10.69	10.59	3.9145*
	More than two	149.03	13.31	8.93	
III	**House ownership**				
	Owned House	88.31	10.14	11.48	
	Leased	117.79	8.33	7.07	3.0633*
	Rented	122.44	14.45	11.80	
IV	**Type of house**				
	Individual	71.04	9.33	13.13	3.2142*
	Apartments	133.08	12.69	9.54	
V	**ASWI**				
	Less than 21	89.90	8.11	9.02	
	21-40	104.45	17.45	16.71	
	41-60	129.07	16.39	12.69	4.1142*
	61-80	142.69	18.41	12.90	
	Above 80	153.34	21.46	13.99	

* Significant at five per cent level.

The ASWI plays an important role in the WTP among the respondents. The respondents with an ASWI of less than 21 and 21 to 40 per cent are willing to pay a mean of Rs.89.90

and Rs. 104.45 for SWM respectively. The respondents with an ASWI of above 80 and 61 to 80 per cent are willing to pay a mean of Rs. 153.34 and Rs. 142.69 respectively. The significant 'F' statistics reveals that there is a significant difference among the respondents with different ASWI regarding their WTP on SWM services.

REFERENCES

1. World Bank (1996), Urban Environment Solid Waste Management Study: Bagnio city, Olongapo city and Batangas city.
2. Cointreau-Levine, Sandara and Prasad Gopalan (2000), "Tools for preparing for private sector participation in Municipal Solid Waste Management", Part III.
3. Sumalde, Zenaida, M (2005), Financing Solid Waste Management, Program and Implementation Constraints of the Local Government units. EEPSEA Research Report No. 2005-RRI.
4. Kreith, Frank (1994), *Handbook of Solid Waste Management*, NY. USA. Mc.Graw, Hill, Inc.
5. Morrison, M.D., Bennett, J.W., and Blamey, R.K (1998), "Valuing Improved wetland quality using choice modeling. Choice modeling Research Reports, No.6. School of Economics and Management, University College, The University of NSW, Australia.
6. Kwabena, A. Anaman and Rashidah M. Jain (2001), "Contingent valuation of solid waste collection services for rural households in Burunei Daussalam", *The Singapore Economic Review*, 45(2), pp. 223-240.
7. Adamowicz, W. J. Louviere and M. Williams (1994), "Coin bing revealed and stated preference methods for valuing Environmental Amenities", *Journal of Environmental Economics and Management*, 26(2), pp. 271-292.
8. Othman, Janal, (2002), "Household preferences for solid waste management in Malaysia, EEEPSEA Research Report, No.2002-RR8.
9. Gottinger, Hans-Wermer 1991, Economic Models and Applications of solid waste management, Germany.
10. Van Houten, G.L and G.E. Morris (1999), "Household Behaviour under Alternative pay – As – You – throw systems for solid waste disposal", *Land Economics*, 75(4), pp. 515-537.
11. Chau, P.Y.K. (1997), Reexamining a model for evaluating information centre success using a structural equation modeling approach", *Decision Sciences*, 28(2), pp. 309-304.

12. Nunnally, J.C (1978), *Psychometric Theory*, Mc.Graw-Hill, New York.
13. Fornell, C and Lancker, D.F. (1981), "Evaluating Structural Equation models with unobservable variables and measurement error", *Journal of* Marketing Research, 18(1), pp. 39-51.
14. Segars, A.H., Grova, V. (1993), "Re-examining perceived case of use and usefulness: a confirmatory factor analysis", *MIS quarterly*, 17(4), pp. 517-525.
15. Skerlavaraj, M., Stembagera, M.I., Skrinjara, R., Dimovskia, V (2007), "Organisational learning culture the missing link between business process change and organizational performance", *International Journal of Production Economics*, 106 (2), pp. 346-347.
16. Parasuraman, A. Zeithmal, V.A. and Berry, L.L. (1985), "A conceptual model of service quality and its implications for future research", *Journal of Marketing*, 49(fall), pp. 41-50.
17. Bolton, R. N. and Drew, J.H. (1994), The Impact of Service Quality, in Rust, R.T and Oliver, R.L (Eds) *Service quality: New Directions in Theory and Practices*, Sage, Thousand Oaks, CA, pp. 173-200.
18. Adamovicz, W., J. Louviere, and M. Williams (1994), "Combining revealed and stated preference methods for valuing environmental amenities", *Journal of Environmental Economics and Management*, 21(1), pp. 271-292.
19. Bateman, I., (2002), *Economic valuation with stated preference techniques: A mannal*, Cheltenhan, UK: Edward Elgar.
20. Boxall, P., W. Adamowicz, J. Swait, M. Williams and J. Louviere (1996), "A comparison of stated preference methods for environmental valuation", *Ecological Economics*, 18(2), pp. 243-253.
21. Mourato, S. (1999), "Household Demand for Improved Solid Waste Management in Malaysia," Paper presented in the workshop on Economic Valuation of Environmental Resource, organized by EPU and DANCED, Renaissance Palm Garden Hotel, Puchong, May 13-15.
22. Agamuthu, P., (2001), *Solid Waste: Principles and Management, Institute of Biological Sciences*, University of Malaya, Kulalumpur.
23. Brisson, I.E. (1997), "Factors influencing to choose the solid waste management in European Union", *Institute of Local Government Studies*, Denmark.
24. Miranda, M.L., J.W. Everett, D. Blume and B.A.Roy, Jr (1994), "Market based incentives and residential municipal solid waste", *Journal of policy analysis and management*, 13(4), pp. 681-698.

25 Repetto, R., R. Dower, R. Jenkins and J. Geoghegan (1992), "Household preferences of the various SWM models, Resources for future, Inc. November.

26. Sugdev, Robert (1999), "Public goods and contingent valuation", Bateman, and Willis, eds., *Valuing Environmental Preferences*, Oxford University Press, USA.

27. Mc.Fadden, D. (1976), "The Revealed Preferences of a Government Bureaucracy: Empirical Evidents", *Journal of Economics*, 7(1), pp. 55-72.

28. Fullerton, D and T.C. Kinnaman (1996), "Household responses to privatization of SWM", *American Economic Review*, 86(1).

29. Hug, S and R.M. Adams (1993), "The peoples' preferences to privatization of solid waste management in Malaysia", *Journal of Environmental Economics and Management*, 25(1), pp. 136-146.

30. Billings, R.B. and Agthe, D.E. (1980), "Price Elasticizes for SWM: A Case of Increasing Rates", *Land Economics*, 56(1), pp. 73-84.

31. Fisher, A., Fullerton, D., Hatch, N.W. and Revinelt, P (1995), "Alternatives for Managing Solid Wastes: A Comparative Cost Analysis", *Journal of Environmental Economics and Management*, 29(1), pp. 304-320.

32. Hewitt, J.A. and Hanemam, M. (1995), "A discrete/continuous choice approach to SWM demand under different pricing", *Land Economics*, 71(2), pp. 173-192.

33. Renwick, M.E. and Archibald, S.O. (1998), "Demand side Management Policies for Residential SWM: who hears the burden?", *Land Economics*, 74(3), pp. 343-359.

34. Kwabana, A. Anaman and Rashidah M. Jair (2001), "Contingent valuation of solid waste collection service for rural households in Brunei Darussalam", *The Singapore Economic Review*, 45(2), pp. 223-240.

35. Boxall, P., W. Adamowicz, J. Swait, M. Williams and J. Louviere (1996), "A Comparison of Stated Preference Methods for Environmental Valuation", *Ecological Economics*, 18(2), pp. 243-253.

36. Van Houtven, G.L and G.E. Morris (1999), "Household Behaviour under alternative Pay-As-You-Throw systems for solid waste disposal", *Land Economics*, 75(4), pp. 515-537.

5 Summary of Findings, Conclusion and Policy Implications

The present study is accomplished in three stages. First of all, the profile of the respondents and their attitude towards drinking water facilities in the existing system is analysed. It is followed by the development of the financial models for drinking water through choice model and contingent valuation methods. In the third, the solid waste management system and the financial models and their appraisal have been discussed. The confined objectives of the study are (*i*) to reveal the profile of the respondents, (*ii*) to analyse the respondents' attitude towards the existing system of drinking water; (*iii*) to examine the willingness to pay for improved service on drinking water and its association with the profile of the respondents, (*iv*) to generate the finance models and evaluation of the financial models by the respondents' perspective; (*v*) to study the switching behaviour among the respondents and its correlates; (*vi*) to generate the choice models in SWM and its evaluation; (*vii*) to examine the various pricing methods for SWM; (*viii*) to analyse the respondents' willingness towards privatization of SWM and its reasons; and (*x*) to evaluate the willingness to pay for SWM services.

Concepts and methodology were formulated according to the objectives of the study with the help of comprehensive review of previous studies. The secondary data about the details of the population and the infrastructural facilities were collected from the Government records. For collecting primary data, Chennai city has been selected purposively for the present study since it is consistently facing the shortage of drinking water scarcity problems, poor in SWM and also has a consistent increasing in the population. Zero point one per cent of the population at Chennai city is selected as the sample size for the present study. The sample size is distributed to ten zones of the Chennai city at a proportionate manner. Further, the random sampling method has been followed to identify the sample in the population of each zone. Out of the total population of 43.43 lakhs, the sample size is determined as 4344. Only 24.84 per cent of the samples responded the questionnaire sent to them. Out of the 1079 responded questionnaires, only 639 questionnaires are found in reusuable form. Hence, the sample size taken for the present study is 639. The appropriate statistical tools have been used to analyse the data to fulfill the objectives of the study. The results are summarized below:

The important annual income among the respondents is Rs. 2.01 to 4.0 lakhs and Rs. 4.01 to 6.00 lakhs. The number of respondents with an annual income of less than Rs.2.01 lakhs is grouped as Lower Income Groups (LIG), whereas the respondents with an income of Rs. 2.01 to 6.00 lakhs are named as Middle Income Group (MIG). The respondents with an annual income of above Rs. 6.0 lakhs are considered as Higher Income Group (HIGs).

The predominant gender among the respondents is male. The dominant age groups among the respondents are 41 to 50 and 51 to 60 years. The most important age groups among LIG, MIG and HIG are 51 to 60 years, 41 to 50 years and 41 to 50 years respectively. Most of the respondents belong to semi-urban areas as their native place. The most important nativity among the LIG, MIG and HIG is semi-urban, urban and urban respectively.

The pre-dominant occupational background among the respondents is private employment and Government employment. The most important occupational background among the LIG, MIG and HIG is private employment, private employment and business respectively. The important family size among the respondents is 4 to 5 members and upto 3 members. The most important family size among the three income groups is 4 to 5 members.

The most important number of earning members per family among the respondents in all three income groups is 'two'. The important house-ownership among the respondents is rental. The most important among the LIG, MIG and HIG is rental, owned house and owned house respectively. The important type of house among the respondents in LIG and MIG is 'apartments' whereas among the HIG, it is 'Individual' house.

Most of the respondents are having only one drinking water pipe connection at their house. The important means used to get the drinking water at their residences are pipe and stand pipe. Most of the respondents are using 'Borewell Water' for their drinking water. The important frequency of water supply perceived by the respondents is 'irregular'. The dominant availability of water supply per week is 48.01 to 84 hours per week. No one is getting 24 hours of water supply per day. The important tariff systems on drinking water among the respondents are 'meter based' and 'flat rate'.

The important years of experience in using the metro water among the respondents are 7 to 10 and above 10 years. The most important years of experience among the LIG, MIG and HIG are 7 to 10 years, 3 to 6 years and above 10 years respectively. Most of the respondents in all three income groups are using the drinking water supply not only for drinking purposes but also for all purposes.

The important sources of drinking water apart from metro water among the LIG are 'buying from neighbours' and 'buying through tanker supplies' whereas among the MIG and HIG these are 'own bore well' and 'buying bottled waters.

Regarding the usage of other sources of drinking water, the significant differences among the three income groups have been noticed in the case of buying from neighbours, buying through tanker supplies, engagement of labour to carry water and buying of bottled water.

Most of the respondents are buying bottled water frequently for their drinking purposes. The frequency of buying of bottled water is more among HIG compared to MIG and LIG. The important reasons for buying bottled water for drinking purposes among LIG and MIG are non-availability of metro water and higher consumption of water whereas among the HIG, these are non-availability of metro water and status. Regarding their perception on reasons for buying bottled water, the significant differences among the three income groups have been noticed in the case of perception on lack of confidence on metro water, accessibility of bottled water, branding of bottled water, convenient mode of buying, quality of water, affordability and status.

The highly viewed expectations from the metro water supply providers among the LIG are regular water supply and responsiveness of officials whereas among the MIG, these are complaint handling and sufficient water supply. Among the HIG, these are reliability of water service and non-defective meter. Regarding the expectations from their service providers, the significant differences among the three income groups are noticed in the case of nominal bill, non-defective meter and emphasized service.

The important expectations by the respondents from the metro water supply providers are quality of water, water supply, service quality, problem maintenance, customer care and price. The highly expected aspects among the LIG is water supply and service quality of water supply whereas among the MIG, these are customer care and service quality. Among the HIG, these are service quality and customer care. Regarding the level of expectations, no significant differences among the group of respondents have been noticed.

Regarding the level of perception on the important aspects of metro service providers, the highly anticipated aspects are price and service quality among the LIG whereas among the MIG, these are price and quality of water. Among the HIG, these are price and problem maintenance. The significant differences among the three groups of respondents have been noticed in the perception on 'water supply' alone.

The negative 'SERVQUAL scale' is identified in all five important aspects of metro water supply providers. It reveals that the respondents are not satisfied up to their level of expectations. Only in the matter of price, they are satisfied at their par. Regarding the level of perception, the significant differences among the three income groups have been noticed in the perception on quality of water, service quality and problem maintenance. The significant associating profile variables with the SERVQUAL scale on the various aspects of metro water supplier are age, occupational background and frequency of water supply availed.

The important monthly expenditure on drinking water among the LIG, MIG and HIG are Rs.82.39, Rs.191.46 and Rs.265.24 respectively. The higher consistency of spending more on drinking water is noticed among HIG. The female respondents stated that they have spent more on drinking water compared to males. The younger respondents are of the view that they are spending more on drinking water compared to the aged respondents. The urban respondents are of the view that they are spending more on drinking water than the rural respondents. The respondents with private employment are concerned about their higher spending on drinking water than the other respondents. The respondents with lesser family size are spending more on drinking water than the respondents with greater family size.

The respondents with more earning members per family are spending more on drinking water compared to others. The respondents living in owned houses are spending more than the respondents living in rented houses. The respondents living in individual houses spend more on drinking water than those respondents living in apartments. The respondents with more pipe connections are spending only the fees on drinking water compared to others. The respondents availing irregular water supply are spending more on drinking water compared to others. The significantly associating profile variables with their amount of expenditure on drinking water are gender, age, nativity, occupational backgrounds, number of earning members per family, house-ownership, number of pipe connections and frequency of water supply availed.

The higher willingness-to-pay for drinking water is identified among HIG compared with MIG and LIG. The male respondents are willing to pay more than the female respondents. The youngsters are ready to pay more on drinking water than the elders. The urban respondents' WTP is greater than the WTP of rural respondents. The respondents with private employment are willing to pay more than the farmers.

The WTP among the respondents with the lesser family size is greater than the WTP among the respondents with higher family size. The respondents with more earning members per family are ready to pay more than other respondents. The respondents living in owned houses are willing to pay more than the respondents in rented houses. The respondents in individual houses are ready to pay more than the respondents in apartments. The respondents with only one water pipe connection are willing to pay more than the respondents with more pipe connections. The respondents availing irregular water supply are willing to pay more for the drinking water in future. The significantly associating profile variables with the WTP among the respondents are gender, age, nativity, occupational background, number of earning members per family, number of pipe connections and frequency of water supply availed.

The respondent's monthly expenditure on drinking water is greater than their WTP for the improved drinking water supply in future. The greater difference is noticed among the HIG compared to MIG and LIG. The significantly associating profile variables with the difference between their monthly expenditure on drinking water and their WTP on it are gender, age, nativity, occupational background, number of earning members per family, number of pipe connection and frequency of water supply availed.

The important reasons for willingness-to-pay more for drinking water among LIG are environmental awareness and reliability of water service whereas among MIG, these are quality of water and labour problem. Among the HIG, these are affordability and labour problem. Regarding the perception on reasons for higher WTP, the significant differences among the three income groups have been noticed in the case of perception on reliability of water service, quality of water, problem with local government, labour problem and assured service.

The important reasons for their WTP shown by the factor analysis are environment and service factors. The highly perceived factor among the three income group is 'environment' factor. But the significant differences among the three income groups have been noticed on the perception on both environment and service factors.

The highly perceived reasons for not willing to pay more for drinking water among the LIG are unaffordability and high tariff whereas among MIG, these are non-reliability of government service and poor service quality. Among the HIG, these reasons are government mismanagement of resources and non-reliability of government service. Regarding the perception on these reasons, the significant differences among the three income groups have been noticed in the case of perception on un-affordability, high tariff, government irresponsibility, government mismanagement of resources, non-reliability of government service, poor service quality and political intervention.

The important reasons for not willing to pay more for drinking water identified by the factor analysis are political, mismanagement and economic factors. The highly viewed factors among the LIG, MIG and HIG are Economic and Political factors.

The significantly associating profile variables with the perception on 'political and mismanagement factors are age, occupational background, number of earning members per family, number of pipe connections and frequency of water supply availed. Regarding the perception on 'economic factor', these profile variables are age, occupational background, family size, number of earning members per family, number of pipe connections and frequency of water supply availed.

Most of the respondents are willing to switch over to private corporate for getting drinking water supply. The number of respondents not willing to switch over to private suppliers is identified as higher among the LIG compared to MIG and HIG. The highly viewed reasons for their switching among LIG are lesser switching cost and complaint handling. Among the MIG, these are 'Losing of confidence on existing supplier and reputation of the new service provider whereas among the HIG, these are feedback from foreign practices and cost of water holidays. Regarding the perception on the reasons for switching, the significant difference among the three income groups have been noticed in the perception on good quality of water, good service, poor service of existing service provider, knowledge about the new services, mental effort to accept the changes, reputation of the new service providers, social cost being greater than social welfare, simple procedure to get connection and method of payment of tariff.

The important reasons for switching identified by the factor analysis are price, office management, new service provider, supplementary cost, present service provider, personal and quality of water. The highly perceived factors for switching among the LIG are better office management and dissatisfaction with present service provider. Among the MIG and HIG, these are preference to new service provider over present service provider. Regarding the perception on important reasons for switching, the significant differences among the three income groups have been identified in the perception on new service provider and personal factor.

The significantly associating profile variables on the price are age, nativity, occupational background, number of earning members per family and frequency of water supply availed. Regarding the perception on office management, the significantly associating profile variables are age, nativity and occupational background of the individuals whereas regarding the perception on 'new service provider', the significantly associating profile variables are nativity, occupational background, family size, number of water pipe connections and frequency of water supply availed.

The significantly associating profile variables regarding the perception on 'supplementary cost' are age and nativity of the individual respondents whereas regarding the perception on present service provider, these profile variables are age, nativity, family size and frequency of water supply availed. Regarding the perception on 'personal' factor, the significantly associating profile variables are age, occupational, background and house-ownership of the respondents whereas regarding the quality of water, these profile variables are age, occupational background, family size, number of earning members per family and house-ownership.

The significantly and privately influencing factors leading to switching and their rate of switching to new service provider among the LIG are new service provider, present service provider and quality of water whereas among the MIG, these are new service provider, supplementary cost, present service provider and quality of water. The significantly and positively influencing factors on the rate of switching among the HIG are office management, new service provider, supplementary cost, present service provider, personal and quality of water.

The highly rated financial model on the basis of low tariff by the LIG is model-I which represents the role of government and local bodies in providing drinking water at a tariff below cost which is also mentioned by the MIG. But HIG respondents highly rate Model-V which includes privatization and the discriminatory pricing of drinking water. Regarding the rating of five financial models, the significant differences among the three income groups have been identified in the evaluation of Model-I and V on the basis of low tariff.

On the basis of regular water supply, the highly rated model by the LIG is Model-III which represents the privatization and regulated price by the government whereas the MIG and HIG highly rate the financial Model-V. Regarding the evaluation of financial models, there is no significant difference among the three income groups. But among the LIG and HIG, there is a significant difference regarding the rating of all five financial models.

The highly rated financial model by the LIG on the basis of convenient timing of water supply is financial Model-V whereas among MIG and HIG, these are Model-III and Model-IV. The significant difference among the rating of all five financial models among the LIG, MIG and HIG are as follows:

On the basis of quality of water, the highly rated financial models by LIG and MIG are Model-V and Model-III whereas by the HIG, it is Model-V. Among the MIG and HIG, the significant differences among the rating on five financial models have been noticed.

On the basis of 'responsiveness', the highly rated financial model by LIG and MIG is Model-IV whereas among HIG, it is Model-V. Among the LIG, MIG and HIG, the significant differences among the evaluation of all five financial models have been noticed. The highly rated financial model on the basis of complaint handling for all three income groups is Model-V. The significant differences in rating of five financial models among LIG, MIG and HIG have been identified.

Regarding the reliability of water supply, the highly rated financial model by LIG is model-V whereas among MIG and HIG, it is model IV. The significant differences on rating of five financial models have been identified among MIG and HIG. The highly rated financial model by LIG on the basis of assurance of water supply is model-V whereas among MIG and HIG, these are model-V and model-IV. Among all three income groups, significant differences among the evaluation of five financial models have been noticed.

On the basis of quantum of water consumed, the highly rated financial model by LIG is Model-II whereas among the MIG and HIG, it is Model-V. Regarding the rating of financial models, significant differences among the three income groups have been identified in the evaluation of Model-I, IV and V. Among the three income groups, significant differences on evaluation of five financial models have been identified.

Regarding the government subsidy, the highly rated financial model by LIG and MIG is Model-I whereas for HIG, it is Model-II. The significant differences in rating of five financial models have been identified among all three income groups. On the basis of discriminatory pricing, the highly rated financial model by LIG and MIG is Model-II whereas for LIG, it is Model-II. On the basis of privatization, the highly rated financial model by all three income groups is model-V.

On the basis of overall dimensions, the highly rated financial model by all three income group is Model-IV. There is no significant difference in evaluating of all five financial models among the LIG. Among MIG and HIG, the significant difference has been identified.

The significantly associating profile variables in evaluating the financial Model-I are age, occupational background, family size, number of earning members per family and house-ownership. Regarding the evaluation of financial Model-II, these profile variables are age, occupational background, house-ownership and type of house. The significantly associating profile variables with the evaluation of financial Model-III are age, nativity, occupational background, family size, number of earning members per family and house-ownership of the respondents whereas in evaluation of financial Model-IV, these profile variables are age, occupational background, family size, house-ownership, type of house, number of pipe connections and frequency of water supply availed. Regarding the evaluation of Model-V, the significantly associating profile variables are gender, age, occupational background, family size, number of earning members per family, house-ownership number of pipe connection and frequency of water supply availed.

The important factors leading to the choosing of the financial models among the LIG is tariff whereas among MIG and HIG, it is regular water supply. The significant discriminant factors among the three income groups to choose the financial model are tariff, quality of water and service quality. The LIG highly rate tariff whereas the MIG and LIG highly rate the quality of water and service quality. The important factor among the males is nature of service provider whereas for the females, it is quality of water. The significant discriminant factors among the male and female respondents to choose the financial model are tariff, customer care, nature of service provider and proper maintenance.

The highly rated factors among the youngsters are quality of water and regular water supply whereas among the elders, it is tariff and nature of service provider. The significant discriminant factor among the various age group of customers to choose the financial model are tariff, quality of water, service quality, customer care, nature of service provider and proper maintenance. The highly rated factors among the urban and rural respondents are customer care and quality of water. The significant discriminant factors among the urban, semi-urban and rural respondents are tariff, service quality, customer care and nature of service provider.

The most important factors leading to the choosing of the financial model among the respondents with private and government employment are service quality and regular water supply whereas among the respondents in business and agriculture, these are regular water supply and tariff. The significant discriminant factors among the five groups based on their occupational background are tariff, regular water supply, service quality, customer care and nature of service provider. The respondents with smaller family size highly rate the customer care as the most important factor whereas the respondents with bigger family size rate, tariff as the most important factor. The significant discriminant factors among these groups of respondents are tariff, quality of water, service quality, customer care, nature of service provider and proper maintenance.

The respondents with only earning member and more than two earning members rate the service quality and proper maintenance as the most important factors of water supply system. The significant discriminant factors are tariff, quality of water, nature of service provider and proper maintenance.. The respondents in individual house highly rate tariff whereas among the respondents in apartments it is service quality. The significant discriminant factors among them are tariff, service quality, customer care and nature of service provider.

The highly known variables in Solid Waste Management (SWM) among the LIG and MIG are type of solid wastes and collection fees whereas among the HIG, these are systems of collection in foreign countries and collection timing. Regarding the awareness of SWM, the significant differences among the three income groups have been noticed in the case of awareness on disposal system. The HIG respondents are having more awareness on SWM than the MIG and LIGs. The significantly associating profile variable with their level of awareness on SWM among the respondent are age, nativity and occupational background.

The important variables in SWM which are highly expected by the LIG are frequency of collection and assured service whereas among the MIG, this is assured service and responsiveness on the customer call. Among the HIG, this is responsiveness on customers call and complaint handling. Regarding the level of expectation on variables in SWM, the significant differences among the three income groups have been noticed in the case of expectations on collection time, separation of wastages, street sweeping, disposal of wastages, number of workers engaged, complaint handling, reliability of service, discriminatory pricing and fine on violation of rules and regulations.

The important factors in SWM identified by the factor analysis are service quality, system, facilities and price. The highly expected factors among the LIG is service quality whereas among the MIG and HIG, these are price and service quality. Regarding the level of expectation factors in SWM, the significant differences among the three income groups have been noticed in the expectation on system, facilities and price.

Regarding the level of perception on these factors in SWM, the significant differences among the three income groups have been noticed in the level of perception on 'price'. The highly perceived factors among the LIG, MIG and HIG are price, only in price, the SERVQUAL scale is positive. It reveals that the respondents are satisfied upto their level of expectation on price factor alone. Regarding the remaining three factors, the respondents are not satisfied upto their level of expectation.

The significantly associating profile variables with SERVQUAL scale on service quality are age, occupational background, house-ownership and ASWI whereas the case of 'system' these profile variables are age, occupational background, family size, type of house and ASWI. Regarding the SERVQUAL scale on 'facilities, the significantly associating profile variables are age, nativity, occupational background, family size and ASWI whereas in the case of 'price', these profile variables are occupational background, family size, house-ownership and ASWI.

The choice model for SWM in the present study consists of seven variables related to collection of wastes, frequency of collection, timing of collection, waste disposal, mode of transport used, rating system and pricing system. Three models have been generated which are confined with the reliability and validity. The highly rated variable in Model-I by the LIG is 'fees with tax' whereas among the MIG and HIG, these are conventional mode of transport and flat rare system. Regarding the rating on variables in Model-I, the significant differences among the three income groups have been noticed are: collection system, separation of wastages, timing of collection and type of disposal. The model-I is highly rated by the LIG compared to MIG and HIG.

The highly rated variable in Model-II by the LIG is 'timing of collection' whereas among the MIG and LIG, these are type of disposal and mode of transport. Regarding the rating of the variables in Model-II, the significant difference among the three income groups have been noticed in the case of collection of wastages, separation of wastages, disposal of wastages, mode of transport and rating system. In total, the Model-III is highly rated by the HIG compared to MIG and LIG.

The highly rated models among the male and female respondents are Model-III and Model-I. Regarding the evaluation of three models, the significant differences among the male and female respondents have been identified. Similarly, the significant differences on the rating of all three models have also been noticed among the male and female respondents. The highly rated model among the youngsters is Model-III whereas among the elders, it is Model-I. Regarding the evaluation of Model-II and Model-III, the significant differences among the different age group of respondents have been identified.

The urban respondents are highly rating the Model-III whereas the semi-urban and rural respondents are highly rating the Model-II. Regarding the rating of three models, the significant differences among the three groups of respondents have been noticed. Only among urban respondents, the significant differences on the evaluation of three models have been identified. The respondents with private and government employment highly rate the Model-III and Model-II respectively. The respondents with agriculture background highly rate the Model-I. Regarding the rating on Model-I and Model-II, the significant difference among the respondents with different occupational background is identified. Among the respondents with private and government employment, the significant differences on the evaluation of three models have been noticed.

The highly rated model among the respondents with a smaller family size is model-III whereas among the respondents with the bigger family size, it is Model-I. Regarding the evaluation of all three models, the significant differences among the respondents with different family size have been noticed. The highly rated model among the respondents with one earning member in their family is Model-I whereas among the respondents with two earning members and more than two earning members, it is Model-II and III. Regarding the evaluation of models, the significant differences among the respondents with different earning members per family have been identified.

The highly rated model by the respondents with owned house is Model-I whereas among the respondents with leased and rented house, it is Model-II and Model-III respectively. Regarding the rating on models, there is no significant difference among the respondents with different types of house. The same trend is also identified among the respondents in different types of house. The highly rated model among the respondents in individual house is Model-III whereas among the respondents in apartments, it is Model-II.

The respondents with lesser awareness on SWM, are highly rating the Model-II whereas among the respondents with high awareness on SWM, it is Model-III. Regarding the rating of Model-II, the significant differences among the respondents with different levels of awareness on SMW have been noticed. Among the respondents with high level of awareness on SWM, the significant difference on the evaluation of three models is also noticed.

The important factors leading to the model choice among the male and female respondent are service quality and timing of collection of wastes. The significant discriminant factors among them leading to choose the model is tariff, frequency of collection, timing of collection, disposal method, service quality, customer care and quantum of disposal. The important factor among the youngsters is customer care whereas among the elders it is tariff. The significant discriminant factors among different age groups of respondents to choose the model is tariff, timing of collection, disposal methods, service quality and customer care.

The important factors identified by the urban and semi-urban respondents to choose the model are customer care and timing of collection, whereas among the rural respondents it is tariff. The significant discriminant factors among the three groups of respondents are tariff, frequency of collection, disposal method, service quality, customer care and quantum of disposal. For respondents with private and government employment the important factor is timing of collection whereas among the respondents with business and agriculture, they are service quality and tariff. The significant discriminant factors among the respondents with different occupational backgrounds are tariff, disposal method, service quality, customer care and quantum of disposal.

The respondents with smaller family size highly rate customer care whereas the respondents with bigger family size highly rate the frequency of collection and tariff. The significant discriminant factors among the respondents with different family size are tariff, timing of collection, disposal method, service quality, and customer care. The highly rated factor among the respondents with only one earning member is tariff whereas among the respondents with two or more earning member per family, it is quantum of disposal and customer care. The significant discriminant factors among the respondents with different numbers of earning members per family are tariff, frequency of collection and quantum of disposal.

The highly rated factor leading to the model choice among the respondents living in owned house and leased house is disposal method and service quality whereas among the respondents living in rented house, it is quantum of disposal. The significant discriminant factors among the three groups of respondents are tariff, service quality, customer care and quantum of disposal. The respondents in individual house highly rate the 'tariff' factor whereas among the respondents living in apartments, it is timing of collection. The significant discriminant factors among the above-said two groups are tariff, service quality and quantum of disposal.

The respondents with low awareness on SWM highly rate the tariff whereas the respondents with high awareness on SWM highly rate the quantum of disposal. The significant discriminant factors among the respondents with different levels of ASWI are all seven factors leading to choose the model.

The majority of the respondents highly favour the privatization of SWM system in the study area. The important reasons for opting of privatization among the LIG and MIG are reliability of private service whereas among the HIG is also the reliability of the private service. Regarding the perception on the reasons for privatization, the significant difference among the three income groups have been noticed in the case of flexibility in timing, customized service by private, timely collection of wastages by private, volume based tariff, reputation of private company, dissatisfaction on existing system, non-existence of any system in public service and red-tapism in public service.

The important reasons for privatization of SWM elicited by the factor analysis are existing system, office methods, collection system and service quality. The important reason identified by LIG, MIG and HIG is service quality. Regarding the perception on reasons, the significant differences among the three income groups have been identified in the perception on existing system, office methods and collection system.

The significantly associating profile variables on the perception on existing system are age, occupational background, family size and ASWI whereas in the perception on office methods, these profile variables are age, occupational background, number of earning members per family and ASWI. The significantly associating profile variables with the perception on collection system is age, occupational background, family size, number of earning members per family and ASWI whereas in the perception on service quality, these are age, occupational background, family size, number of earning members per family and ASWI.

The significantly and positively influencing factors leading to opt for privatization or the overall attitude towards privatization among LIG also existing system and collection system whereas among the MIG, these are existing system, collection system and service quality. Among the HIG, these factors are existing system, office methods, collection system and service quality.

The important reasons for not favouring privatization among the LIG is higher tariff whereas among the MIG and HIG, these are non-consideration for the poor and higher establishment cost. Regarding the perception on the reasons for not supporting privatization, the significant differences among the three income groups have been noticed in the perception on higher tariff, non-consideration for poor and higher establishment cost.

The highly favoured financial model by the LIG is flat rate pricing whereas among the MIG and HIG, this is service quality based pricing. Regarding the rating on various financial models, the significant differences among the three income groups have been noticed in the rating on marginal cost, full cost, cost plus profit, discriminatory pricing, volume based pricing, service, quality based pricing and flat rate pricing.

The highly rated financial models among males and females are service quality based and flat rate pricing for SWM respectively. Regarding the evaluation of various financial models, the significant differences among the males and females have been identified in the case of cost plus pricing, service quality based pricing and flat rate pricing. Among the male and female respondents, the significant differences on rating on all seven financial models have been identified.

The highly rated financial model among the youngsters is service quality based pricing whereas among the elders, it is flat rate pricing. Regarding the evaluation of all financial models, the significant differences among all age groups have been noticed. The highly rated financial model among the urban respondents is service quality based pricing whereas among the rural respondents, it is flat rate pricing. The significant differences among the urban, semi-urban and rural respondents have been noticed in the rating of full cost pricing, cost plus profit pricing, discriminatory pricing, volume-based pricing and flat rate pricing.

The respondents in private and government employment highly rate the marginal cost pricing whereas for the respondents in business and agriculture, these two are marginal pricing and flat rate pricing. Regarding the rating of financial models of SWM the significant differences among the three income groups have been noticed in the case of discriminatory pricing, volume based pricing, service quality based pricing and flat rate pricing. The respondents with smaller family size highly rate the service quality based pricing whereas the respondents with bigger family size are highly rating the marginal cost and flat rate pricing. Regarding the rating on financial models, the significant difference among the respondents with different family size is identified in the case of all seven financial models.

The highly rated financial model among the respondents with one earning member per family is marginal cost pricing whereas among the respondents with two or more earning members, they are service quality based and volume based pricing. Regarding the rating of financial models, the significant difference among the respondents with different earning members per family is identified in the case of all seven financial models.

The respondents in owned house highly rate flat rate pricing whereas the respondents in leased and rented house highly rate the volume based and marginal cost pricing of SWM respectively. Regarding the valuation of financial models, the significant differences among the three groups of respondents have been noticed in the case of marginal cost pricing, full cost pricing, cost plus profit pricing and volume based pricing. The respondents in individual houses and apartments highly rate the marginal cost pricing and service quality based pricing respectively. Regarding the evaluation of financial model, the significant difference among the two group of respondents have been noticed in the case of full cost pricing, cost plus profit pricing, discriminatory pricing, volume based pricing and flat rate pricing.

The respondents with low awareness on SWM highly rate the marginal cost pricing whereas the respondents with high awareness on SWM, it is service quality based pricing and volume based pricing. Regarding the rating on financial models, the significant differences among the respondents with different levels of awareness have been noticed in the case of marginal cost pricing, full cost pricing, discriminatory pricing, volume based pricing and service quality based pricing.

The higher willingness to pay for SWM services is identified among HIG than the MIG and LIG. The higher WTP is identified among the males than among the females. The youngsters are having higher WTP than the elders whereas urban respondents are willing to pay more than the rural respondents. The respondents with business are willing to pay more than the respondents with other occupations. The higher WTP is noticed among the respondents with small family size compared to others. The respondents with more earning members in their family are willing to pay more for SWM services. The respondents in owned house are willing to pay less than the respondents in rented house whereas the respondents in apartments are willing to pay more than the respondents in individual house. The respondents with lesser ASWI are willing to pay lesser for SWM. Regarding the WTP, the significantly associating profile variables are gender, age, nativity, occupational background, family size, number of earning members per family, house-ownership, type of house and ASWI.

Conclusion

The present study concludes that the existing model and the pattern of services offered regarding the drinking water and SWM is not at the satisfactory level among the respondents. By the choice of model, the respondents are willing to have a private participation in the drinking water service but at the regulated price fixed by the local bodies. The respondents are also in favour of the discriminatory pricing on the water services which should be based on the quantity of water consumed and also on the annual income of the respondents. The contingent valuation method reveals that the respondents are willing to pay more on the improved drinking water services. The optimum financial model for drinking water services is highly associated with the profile of the respondents.

Regarding the solid waste management, the respondents are not satisfied up to their level of expectation with the existing service providers. The choice model analysis reveals that the Lower Income Groups are willing to have flat rate pricing with minimum service quality whereas for the Middle Income Groups and Higher Income Groups, the selected financial models consist of moderate and volume based ratio system with high service quality. The contingent valuation methods reveals that the respondents are willing to pay more for the improved service by the new service provider (Private Corporates) since they are losing confidence on the public service providers. The profile of the respondents is highly associated with the choice of model, pricing system and willingness to pay. The financial model should contain the ingredients of the various attributes which are mostly appearing in different segment. Hence the optimum financial model for the infrastructural facilities should be designed on the basis of the customer segment. Even though the service offered to them is same the price charged on them should be discriminatory.

Policy Implications

Based on the findings of the study, the following policy implications are drawn:

1. Before framing the appropriate financial model for the infrastructural facilities for the respondents, the local bodies should analyse the importance of profile of the respondents. A permanent system should be established at the state level to analyse the willingness of the respondents in a scientific and consistent manner.
2. The local bodies should try to minimize the gap between respondents' perception and expectation on various services offered by them since the respondents are not satisfied upto their level of expectation in all aspects of service except price.
3. Since the respondents' monthly expenditure on drinking water is greater than their willingness to pay for drinking water they have to be provided an enriched service with better service quality. The profile of the respondents has its own role in the determination the WTP among the respondents; the local bodies are advised to follow the discriminatory pricing of water supply especially based on annual income of the respondents and also the quantity of water consumed by them.

4. The privatization of drinking water supply is welcomed by the respondents. The state and local governments should not hesitate to hand over this service to the private corporate. But the government should have a control on these private corporate through its regulated pricing system.
5. Since the important reasons for switching to private corporate are the dissatisfaction on existing service provider and higher expectation on the private service provider, the government should ensure a minimum guarantee on the quality and quantity of drinking water at reasonable price by the private service providers.
6. The highly rated financial model by the all respondents is Model-V which indicates the inclusion of privatization and discriminatory pricing system. The government should guide the private corporates to fix a tariff below cost to the poor people, but they should be allowed to fix a tariff above cost to the rich people. The private corporate are advised to offset the loss incurred in tariff below cost by the tariff above cost. When there is an excess of loss, the government or local bodies should grant subsidy to the private corporate to follow the model.
7. Since the profiles of the respondents play an important role in the selection of financial model, their willingness to pay for enriched service and also for privatization, there is a greater need for customer segmentation analysis to select the appropriate financial model suitable to each customers' segmentation. Even though it is a difficult task, the government should grant more funds to meet the expenses on Research and Development works related to customer segmentation analysis.
8. The awareness on solid waste management has its role in the selection of models, financial model and

willingness to pay more for SWM. Hence, the government has to take steps to increase the awareness on SWM among the respondents. It should conduct many awareness programmes.

9. The choice model reveals that the daily collection of wastages, separation of wastes at household cost, both morning and evening waste collection, incinerator type of waste disposal, quickest mode of transport, volume based rating system and discriminatory pricing system are the most attractive models among the respondents. Hence, the government has to design a model combining the above-said attributes and satisfy their customers.

10. Since the important factor influencing the model choice by the respondents are tariff, service quality, customer care and quantum of disposal, the government has to study on the above-said variables in order to generate the optimum model. The optimum model need not be the single model. It should be an appropriate model to the relevant customer segment.

11. The privatization of SWM is welcomed by the respondents because of the dissatisfaction with existing system and also the faith on the new system. Hence, the government has to provide an enriched service to the respondents or handover the SWM system to the private corporate. Since respondent's perception of higher tariff and profit maximization of the private corporate are the reasons for non-privatization, the government has to formulate some plan to regulate the pricing on SWM by the private corporate.

12. Even though few sections of respondents prefer the flat rate pricing, a majority of the respondents are in favour of service quality based pricing and volume based pricing. Hence the government has to redesign

their pricing system on the basis of the proposed enriched service quality and also the volume of wastages discharged by the respondents. Apart from this, regarding the willingness to pay more on SWM among the respondents, the government should not hesitate to revise its pricing policies if they are ready to provide an enriched and assured service to the respondents.

Directions for Future Research

The present study focuses on the generation of financial model for drinking water and SWM services offered by the local bodies and evaluation of these models according to the customers' point of view namely choice model and contingent valuation model only. This study paves the way for future research on the generation of financial models for other public services. The present study not includes the cost of production, cost of service and cost of maintenance of the plant, machinery, equipments and administrative staffs required for rendering this service. Hence, future studies may focus on that aspect. Since the drinking water and SWM are related to so many engineering concepts and formulae to generate the financial models, they have to cover all engineering aspects related to financial model. The cost and benefit analysis on the proposed financial model as per the officials' point of view may be focused upon in near future. The other models like baseline model and choice model in the socio-economic factors, estimation of implicit prices, and estimation of equilibrium values for non- monetary attributes and estimating the value of a program may be studied in future studies.

Bibliography

BOOKS

1. Bolton, R. N. and Drew, J.H (1994), The impact of service quality, in Rust, R.T. and Oliver, R.L (Eds) *Service quality: New Directions in Theory and Practices*, Sage, Thousand Oaks, CA.
2. Grayson, R.B. and Bloschl, G., (2000), Spatial Patterns in Drinking Water Pricing: Observation and Modelling, Cambridge University Press.
3. Jacques Tacq (1996), *Multivariate Analysis Techniques in Social Science Research*, Thousand Oaks, CA: Sage Publications.
4. Jenkins, R.B. (1993), The Economics of Solid waste reduction: The impact of user fees, Edward Elgar.
5. Jerkins (1993), The measurement of Environmental and Resource value, Resources for the Future, Washington, D.C., U.S.A.
6. Joreskog, K.G. and Sorbom, D. (1993), *"LISREL 8: Structural Equation Modeling with the SIMLIS Command Language*, Scientific Software, Maple, IN.
7. Joseph Hain, Jr. Ralph. E., Runad L. Tatham and W.C. Black, (1999), *Multivariate Data Analysis with Reading*, 5th ed., Prentice Hall, NJ.
8. Kreith, Frank (1994), *Handbook of solid waste Management*, NY. USA. Mc.Graw, Hill, Inc.
9. Nunnally, J.C. (1978), Psychometric Theory, Mc.Graw-Hill, New York.
10. Repetto, R., R. Dower, R. Jenkins and J. Geoghegan (1992), "Household preferences of the various SWM models, *Resources for Future*, Inc. November.

11. Repetto, R., R. Dower, R. Jenkins and J. Geoghegan (1992), "Pay-by the Bag household collection charges to Management solid waste", *Resources for the Future*. Inc. November.

12. *Urban Water Supply and Sanitation: South Asia Rural Development Services* (1999), The World Bank and Allied Publishers, New Delhi.

JOURNALS

13. Adamovicz, W., J. Louviere, and M. Williams (1994), "Combining revealed and stated preference methods for valuing environmental amenities", *Journal of Environmental Economics and Management*, 21(1).

14. Anderson, J.C and Gerhing (1988), "Structural Equation Modeling in Practice: A Review and Recommended Two-step Approach", *Psychological Bulletin*, 103(3).

15. Arrow, K., R. Solow, P.R. Portney, E.E. Leamer, R. Pedner, and H.Schuman (1993), "Report of the NOAA Panel on Contingent valuation", *Federal register*, 58(10).

16. Babakus, E., and Boller, G.W. (1992), "An Empirical assessment of the SERVQUAL scale", *Journal of Business Research*, 24(3).

17. Bates, A.J. (2000), "Water as consumed and its impact on the consumer — Do we understand the variables?", *Food and Chemical Toxicology*, 38(1).

18. Bathurst, J.C. and O'Connel, P.E. (1992), "The future of distributed modeling: The system hydrologique" *European, Hydrol.Proc.*, 6(1).

19. Beck, M.B. (1987), "Water Pricing Model: A Review", *Water Resource Research*, 23(2).

20. Beven, K.J. (1989), "Changing ideas in water pricing — the case of physically based models", *Journal of Hydrology*, 105(4).

21. Billings, R.B and Agthe, D.E (1980), "Price Elasticizes for SWM: A Case of Increasing Rates", *Land Economics*, 56(1).

22. Biswas, A.K., Jayatilaka, R. and Tortajada, C. (2005), "Social perceptions of the impacts of Colombo water supply projects", *A Journal of the Human Environment*, 34(8).

23. Boxall, P., W. Adamowicz, J. Swait, M. Williams and J. Louviere (1996), "A comparison of stated preference methods for environmental valuation", *Ecological Economics*, 18(2).

24. Cameron, T.A., G.L. Poe, R.G. Emier and W.D. Schulze (2002), "Alternative non-market value elicitation methods: Are the underlying preferences the same?", *Journal of Environmental Economics and Management*, 44(3).

25. Cameson, J., and James, M. (1987), "Efficient Estimation Methods for 'Closed-Ended' Contingent Valuation Surveys", *Review of Economics and Statistics*, 69 (2).

26. Chau, P.Y.K. (1997), Reexamining a model for evaluating information centre success using a structural equation modeling approach", *Decision Sciences*, 28(2).

27. Choe, C. and I. Fraser (1999), "An economic analysis of household waste management", *Journal of Environmental Economics and Management*, 38(1).

28. Cronin, J.J. Muchael, B.K., and Thomas, M.K.G. (2000), "Assessing the Effects of Quality, Value and Customer Satisfaction on Consumer behavioural intentions in service environment", *Journal of Retailing*, 76(2).

29. Dale Fodness and Rrian Murray (2007), "Passengers' expectations of airport service quality", *Journal of Services Marketing*, 21(7).

30. Doria, M.F. (2006), "Bottled water versus tap water, understanding consumer preferences", *Journal of Water Health*, 12(3).

31. Falachee, M. and Mackae, A.W. (1995), "Consumer Appraisal of Drinking Water: Multidimensional Scaling Analysis," *Food Quality and Preference*, 6(1).

32. Fewtrell, L, R.B. Kaufmam, D. Kay, W. Enanoria, L. Haller and J.M. Colford (2005), "Water sanitation, and Hygiene Interventions to Reduce Diarrhea in Less Developed Countries: A systematic review and meta-analysis", *Lancet Infections Diseases*, 5(1).

33. Fisher, A., Fullerton, D., Hatch, N.W. and Revinelt, P. (1995), "Alternatives for Managing Solid Wastes: A Comparative Cost Analysis", *Journal of Environmental Economics and Management*, 29(1).

34. Fornell, C. and Lancker, D.F. (1981), "Evaluating Structural Equation models with unobservable variables and measurement error", *Journal of Marketing Research*, 18(1).

35. Fullerton, D. and T.C. Kinnaman (1996), "Household responses to privatization of SWM", *American Economic Review*, 86(1).

36. Fullerton, D. and T.C. Kinnaman (1996), "Household responses to pricing garbage by the Bag", *American Economic Review*, 86(4).

37. Gi-Du Kang, Ferrey fames and Kostas Alexandis (2002), "Measurement of Internal Service Quality: application of the SERVQUAL battery to Internal Service Quality", *Managing Service Quality*, 12(5).

38. Griffin, R.C., and Mjelde, J.W. (2000), "Valuing water supply reliability", *American Journal of Agricultural Economics*, 82(2).

39. Gunatilake, H., J.C. Yang, S.K. Pattanayek, and C.Vandenberg (2006), "*Willingness to pay studies for designing water supply and sanitation project*: A good Practice case study. ERD Technical Note, No.17, Economics and Research Department, Asian Development Bank, Manila. Available: http://www.adb.org/documents/erd/technical-notes/tm019.pdf.

40. Hanemann, W.M., (1984), "Welfare Evaluations in Contingent Valuation Experiments with Discrete Responses", *American Journal of Agricultural Economics*, 66 (3).

41. Hartley, T.W. (2006), "Public perception and participation in water reuse", *Desalination*, 187(6).

42. Hensker, D., Shore, N. and Train, K. (2005), "Households' willingness to pay for water service attitudes", *Environmental and Resource Economics*, 32(4).

43. Hewitt, J.A and Hanemam, M. (1995), "A discrete/continuous choice approach to SWM demand under different pricing", *Land Economics*, 71(2).

44. Hong, S., R. Adams, and H. Love (1993), "An economic analysis of household recycling of solid wastes: The case of Portland, Oregon", *Journal of Environmental Economics and Management*, 25(2).

45. Hug, S. and R.M. Adams (1993), "The peoples' preferences to privatization of solid waste management in Malaysia", *Journal of Environmental Economics and Management*, 25(1).

46. Jebesman A., and Hornberger, G.M. (1993), "Complexity in 'Financial Model' for drinking water", *Water Resource Research*, 26(4).

47. Kathryn, H, Dansky and Diane Brannon (1996), "Discriminate Analysis: A technique for adding value to patient satisfaction surveys", *Hospital and Health Services Administration*, 41(4), Winter.

48. Kitaeff, R. (1994), "Marketing Research Competencies", *Marketing Research: A Magazine of Management and Applications*, 6(3), Summer.

49. Kontogianni, A., Longford, I.H., Papandreou, A., and Skourfos, M.S., (2004), "Social preferences for improving water quality: An Economic analysis of benefits from waste water treatment", *Water Resources Management*, 17(1).

50. Koss, P and Sami Khawaja, M. (2001), "The value of water supply reliability in California, A contingent valuation study", *Water Policy*, 3(1).

51. Kwabana, A. Anaman and Rashidah M. Jair (2001), "Contingent valuation of solid waste collection service for rural households in Brunei Darussalam", *The Singapore Economic Review*, 45(2).

52. Lehtinen, U. and Lehtine, J.R. (1991), "Two approaches to service quality dimensions", *The Services Industries Journal*, 11(1).

53. Levallois, P., Grondin, J., and Gingras, S. (1999), "Evaluation of consumer attitudes on taste and tap water alternatives in Quebec", *Water Science and Technology*, 40(4).

54. Lund, J.R. (1995), "Derived estimation of Willingness to pay to avoid prolalistic shortage", *Water Resources Research*, 31(5).

55. MC Fadden, D. (1976), "The Revealed Preferences of a Government Bureaucracy: Empirical Evidence", *Journal of Economics*, 7 (1).

56. Meens, E.G., T. Brueck, L., Dixm, A., Manning, J. Miles and Patrick, R. (2002), "Drinking water quality in the New Millennium: The risk of underestimating public perception", *Journal of the American Water Works Association"*, June.

57. Merret, S. (2002), "Deconstructing Household's Willingness – to – pay for water in low income countries", *Water Policy*, 4(2).

58. Nielsen, J.B., Gyrd-Hanson, D. Kristiansen, I.S. Nexpe, J. (2003), "Impact of Socio-demographic factors on Willingness-to-pay for the reduction of a future health risk", *Journal of Environmental Planning and Management*, 46(1).

59. Noel Capon, Gavan J, Fitzsimons and Rick Weingarte (1994), "Affluent investors and mutual fund purchases", *International Journal of Bank Marketing*, 12(3).

60. Ntengwe, F.W. (2004), "The impact of consumer awareness of water sector issues on willingness to pay and cost recovery in Zambia", *Physics and Chemistry of the Earth*, 29(15-18).

61. Oestman, E., Schweitzer, L., Tornbulian, P., Corado, A. and Suffet, I.H. (2004), "Effects of chlorine and chloramines on earthy and musty odours in drinking water", *Water Science Technology*, 49(3).

62. Owen, A.J., Colbourse, J.S., Clayton, C.R.I., Fife-Sahaw, C., (1999), "Risk Communication of hazardous processes associated with drinking water quality — a mental models approach to customer perception; part-1-a methodology", *Water Science and Technology*, 39(10).

63. Palmer, K. and M. Walls (1997), "Optional policies for solid waste disposal: Taxes, subsidies and standards", *Journal of Public Economics*, 65(2).

64. Parasuraman, A., Zeithaml, V.A., and Berry, L.L. (1991), "Refinement and reassessment of the servqual scale", *Journal of Retailing*, 67(4).

65. Parasuraman, A., Zeithmal, V.A. and Berry, L.L. (1985), "A conceptual model of service quality and its implications for future research", *Journal of Marketing*, 49(fall).

66. Parasuraman, A., Zeithammal, V.A., and Berry, L.L. (1988), "SERVQUAL: A Multiple Item Scale for measuring consumer perceptions of service quality", *Journal of Retailing*, 64(1).

67. Parasuraman, A., Zeithammal, V.A., and Berry, L.L. (1990), "A Empirical examination of relationship in an extended service quality model", *Cambridge*, MA: Marketing Science Institute.

68. Parasuraman, A., Zeithammal, V.A., and Berry, L.L. (1993), "More on improving service quality measurement", *Journal of Retailing*, 69(1).

69. Pirion, P., Mackey, E.D., Suffet, I.H. and Bruchet, A. (2004), "Chlorinous flavour perception in drinking water", *Water Science and Technology*, 49(4).

70. Po, M., Nancarrow, B., Leviston, Z., Porter, N., Syme, G and Kaercher, J. (2005), *"Predicting Community Behaviour in Relation to Waste Water Reuse: What Drives decisions to accept or reject?,* Melbourne: CSIRO.

71. Portney (1994), "The contingent valuation debate: why Economists should care", *Journal of Economic Perspectives*, 8(4).

72. Prasada Rao, P. and Vedantam Sahia (2006), "Mutual Funds: Exploring the Retail Customer Expectations", *The ICFAI journal of services marketing*, 4(2), June.

73. Raje, D.V., Dhobe, P.S and Deshpande, A.W. (2002), "Consumer's willingness to pay more for municipal supplied water: a case study". *Ecological Economics*, 42(3).

74. Rechovsky J.D. and S.E. Stone (1994), "Market Incentives to Encourage Household Waste recycling: Paying for what you throw away", *Journal of Policy Analysis and Management*, 13(1).

75. Renwick, M.E. and Archibald, S.O. (1998), "Demand side Management Policies for Residential SWM: who hears the burden?", *Land Economics*, 74(3).

76. Segars, A.H., Grova, V. (1993), "Re-examining perceived case of use and usefulness: a confirmatory factor analysis", *MIS quarterly*, 17(4).

77. Skerlavaraj, M., Stembagera, M.I., Skrinjara, R., Dimovskia, V. (2007), "Organisational learning culture the missing link between business process change and organizational performance", *International journal of production economics*, 106 (2).

78. Stenekes, N., Colebatch, H.K., Waite, T.D and Ashbolt, N.J (2006), "Risk and governance in water recycling: Public acceptance revisited", *Science, Technology and Human values*, 31(4).

79. Stiglitz, J., (2002), "Globalison's Discontents", *The American Prospect*, 13(1), January.

80. Teas, K.R. (1994), "Expectations as a comparison standard in measuring Service Quality: An Assessment of Reassessment", *Journal of Marketing*, 58(2).

81. Thomas T. Semon (1996), "Marketing Research Needs Basic Research", *Marketing News*, 28(6), March.

82. Turgeon, S., Rodriguez, M.J., Theniault, M., and Levallois, P. (2004), "Perception of drinking water in Quebec region (Canada): The influence of water quality and consumer location in the drinking water system", *Journal of Environmental Management*, 70(3).

83. Turgeon, S., Rodriguez, M.J., Theniault, M., and Levallois, P. (2004), "Perception of drinking water in Quebec region (Canada): The influence of water quality and consumer location in the drinking water system", *Journal of Environmental Management*, 70(3).

84. Van Houten, G.L. and G.E. Morris (1999), "Household Behaviour under Alternative pay – As – You – throw systems for solid waste disposal", *Land Economics*, 75(4).

85. Whittington, Dale (2002), "Improving the Performance of Contingent Valuation Studies in Developing Countries", *Environmental and Resource Economics*, 22 (4).

86. Willis, K.G., Scarpa, R., Acust, M., (2005), "Assessing water company customers preferences and willingness to pay for service improvements: A stated choice analysis", *Water Resources Research*, 41(2).

87. Yasuo Fujita, Ayumi Fujii, Shgeki Farukawa and Takehiko Ogawa (2005), "Estimation of willingness to pay for water and sanitation services through contingent valuation method (CVM) – A case study in Iquitos city, The Republic of Peru", *JBICI Review*, No. 11.

88. Zafar Khan, Sudhi, K. Chawla and S. Thomas A. Cianuiolo (1995), "Multiple Discriminate Analysis: Tool for effective marketing of computer information systems to small business elicits", *Journal of professional services marketing*, 12(2).

REPORTS

89. Agamuthu, P. (2001), *"Solid Waste: Principles and Management, Institute of Biological Sciences"*, University of Malaya, Kulalumpur.

90. Alison Wedgwood and Kevin Sanson (2003), *"Willingness-to-pay surveys – A Streamlined approach"*, Water, Engineering and Development Centre, Lough Borough University, UK.

91. Benmagen, Eugene and V. Alterz (2004), "Impacts of Unit Pricing Solid Waste Collection and Disposal in Olongopo city, Phillippines, *EEPSEA Research Report*, No.2004-RR4.

92. Brisson, I.E. (1997), "Factors influencing to choose the solid waste management in European Union", *Institute of Local Government Studies*, Denmark.

93. Carson, R. (1992), "A Contingent Valuation Study of Lost Passive use value Resulting from the Exxon Valdez oil spill", Appendices A-D-A Report to the Assorney General of the State of Alaska.

94. Cointreau-Levine, Sandara and Prasad Gopalan (2000), "Tools for preparing for private sector participation in Municipal Solid Waste Management", Part III.

95. David, C. and A.B. Inocencio (2001), "Urban Water Pricing: Metro Manila in Enhancing and sustaining stakeholders' participation in watershed management", General Technical report services-9, University of the Philippines Los Banos.

96. Dumol, M. (2000), *"Manila Water Concession: A Key Government Officials' Daisy of the World's Largest Water Privatisation"*, World Bank Publication, Washington, D.C. July.

97. Francisco, H.A . (2002), "Watershed-Based Water Management Strategy: The Missing Link to sustainable water services", Paper presented during the policy forum on water resource management, Philippine Institute for Development Studies.

98. Gottinger, Hans-Wermer (1991), *Economic Models and Applications of solid waste management*, Germany.

99. Gunatilake, H., J.C.Yang, S.K. Pattanayek, and C.Vandenberg (2006), *"Willingness to pay studies for designing water supply and sanitation project*: A good Practice case study. ERD Technical Note, No.17, Economics and Research Department, Asian Development Bank, Manila. Available: http://www.adb.org/documents/erd/technical-notes/tm019.pdf.

100. Janal Othman (2002), *"Household preferences for solid waste management in Malaysia"*, Department of Agricultural and Resource

Economics, Faculty of Economics, University Kebanysan, Malaysia, through http://www.eepsea.org.

101. Laplante, Benoit (2003), *"Cost-Sharing for solid waste management"*, Economy and Environment: selected readings in the Philippines (2003), H.A. Francisco and M.S. delos Angeles (ed.) Phils: REECS-EEPSEA.

102. Eugenia, M., C. Bemnagen and Vincent Altez (2004), *"Impacts of units pricing of solid waste collection and disposal in Alongapo city, Phillippines"*, Economy and Environment Program for Southeast Asia, Singapore, Available: www.eepsea.org.

103. Ministry of Water Resources (1999), *"Water Resources Development Plan of India: Policy and Issues"*, New Delhi.

104. Morrison, M.D., Bennett, J.W., and Blamey, R.K. (1998), *"Valuing Improved wetland quality using choice modeling. Choice modeling Research Reports*, No.6. School of Economics and Management, University College, The University of NSW, Australia.

105. Mourato, S. (1999), "Household Demand for Improved Solid Waste Management in Malaysia" Paper presented in the workshop on Economic valuation of Environmental resource, organized by EPU and DANCED, Renaissance Palm Garden Hotel, Puchong, May-13-15.

106. Natural Human Development Report (2001), Planning Commission, New Delhi, 2001.

107. Othman, Janal, (2002), *"Household preferences for solid waste management in Malaysia*, EEEPSEA Research Report, No.2002-RR8.

108. Pattanayak, S.K, J.C.Yang, C. Agarwal, H.M. Gunatilake, S.J.H. Bandara and T.Ranasinghe (2004), *Water Sanitation and Poverty in Southwest Srilanka. RTI. International*, Durham, N.C.

109. Sugdev, Robert (1999), *"Public goods and contingent valuation"*, Bateman, and Willis, eds., *Valuing Environmental Preferences*, Oxford University Press, USA.

110. Sumalde, Zenaida, M. (2005), *Financing Solid Waste Management, Program and Implementation Constraints of the Local Government Units*, EEPSEA Research Report No.2005-RRI.

111. Voloerberch, I., Kelay, T., Chenoweth, J., Fife-Schaw, C., Morrison, G., and Lundehn, C., (2007), *"Measuring customer preferences for drinking water services: Methods for water utilities"*, Techneau Report, www.techneau.org.

112. Water Quality Status and Statistics (1996 & 1997), Central Pollution Control Board, New Delhi, 1999.

113. Water Supply and Sanitation (2002), A WHO-UNICEF sponsored study, Planning Commission of India.

114. World Bank (1996), *Urban Environment Solid Waste Management Study: Bagnio city,* Olongapo city and Batangas city.

WEBSITES

115. Candidate Countries Euro barometer (2003), "Consumer's opinions on services of general interest: Public opinion in the acceding and candidate combines",http://ec.europa.eu/publicopinion/archives/cceb/2003/cceb2003. 3sigfullrep-en.pdf.

116. Consumer Council for water (2005), "Shaping the consumer council for water: A report by opinion leader research", http://www.ofwat.gov.uk/ aptrix/ofwat/publish.nsf/attachment by title/pdf.

117. Ebarvia, M.C.M. (2003), *"Pricing for Ground water use of Industries in Metro Manilu, Philippines",* EEPSEA, Research Report. http://203.116.43.77 //publications/research1/ACF4D.html.

118. Ochoa, A.L et al., (1990), "Informe de proyecho Detecciony control de fugase. Impact de micro medicion en Guaymas, Sonora internal report, Mexican Institute of water technology, jutepec, Morelos, Mexico. http://billioteca.unesco.org.uy/collect/billiote/import/lileros/effcient water/wochoa.html.

119. Water Manifesto (2000), 30 Rue Manrose, 1030 Brussels, Belgium, http: //www.f1 boat.com/99/water manifesto.html.

Index

A

ANOVA, 24, 94

Awareness on Solid Waste Management Index (ASWI), 157, 207

C

Candidate Countries Euro Barometer (2003), 10

Central Pollution Control Board (CPCB), 6

Chennai Corporation, 5

Chennai Metropolitan Water Supply & Sewerage Board (CMWSSB), 4

Collection of data, 23

Confirmatory Factor Analysis (CFA), 91

Construct development, 22-23

Consumer acceptance of recycled water, 10-11

Consumer Council for Water, 9

Contingent valuation method, 12-14

Customer preferences on drinking water, 8

D

Development of financial model for drinking water supply, 68-129

- association between profile of respondents and their importance on three reasons for not willing-to-pay more, 85-86
- association between the profile of respondents and their level of importance attached to reasons, 94-96
- association between the profile of respondents and their overall rating of financial models, 115-116
- difference between monthly expenditure and WTP for drinking water, 74-75
- discriminant factors among the respondents, 123-125
  - based on their nativity and occupational background, 120-123
  - with different occupancy status and type of house, 125-127
- discriminant factors to choose the financial model, 118-120
- evaluation of finance models by the respondents, 101-103
  - basis of assurance of water supply, 108-109

compliant handling, 107
discriminatory pricing, 111-112
privatization, 112-113
quality of water, 105
quantum of water consumed, 109-110
regular water supply, 103-104
factors leading to choose the financial models, 116-118
financial models on drinking water services, 98-101
impact of factors of switching on their rate of switching to new service provider, 96-98
important reasons for switching, 90-91, 93-94
– – – unwillingness-to-pay more, 82-83
– – – unwillingness-to-pay more, 84-85
– – – willingness-to-pay more, 80
on drinking water, 78-80
overall rating on financial models, 113-115
privatization of drinking water services, 86-88
profile of the respondents and their difference on monthly expenditure and WTP, 75-76
rating of financial model on the basis of
convenient timing of water supply, 104
government subsidy, 110-111
reliability of water supply, 107-108
responsiveness, 106
reasons for not willing-to-pay more, 81-82
– – switching from public to private service provider, 88-90
– – willing-to-pay more for drinking water, 76-78
reliability and validity of the measures in each construct, 83-84, 91-93
significant difference among the respondents regarding their WTP, 73-74
willingness to pay, 68-69
WTP in different users segments, 69-73

E

Economic and Political Factors, 201
Exploratory Factor Analysis (EFA), 52

G

Government of Tamil Nadu, 5

H

HIG, 97, 196

I

Introduction, 1-31
evolution of water and sanitation sector programs, 3-4
framework of analysis, 23-26
identification of research gap, 17-18

limitation of the study, 26
methodology of the study, 20
need for the study, 5-7
population of the study, 21-22
present scenario of water supply and solid waste management in Chennai, 4-5
research design, 20
– model, 18-19
review of previous studies, 8
sampling framework of the study, 20-21
scheme of the report, 26-27
solid waste management, 14-17
statement of the problem, 7-8
tariff structures on the basic services, 4
water pricing, 11-12
– – and metering, 9-10
– quality, 8-9
– resources quantity and quality, 2-3
willingness to pay for drinking water, 11

K

Khan, Zafar, 118
KMO, 170

L

LIG, 97, 196

M

MIG, 97, 196
Municipal Solid Waste (MSW), 6

N

National Water Policy, 3
Natural Human Development Report, 2001, 1

O

Objectives of the study, 19

P

Policy implications, 216
Profile of the respondents and their behaviour on drinking water facilities, 32-67
age of the respondents, 34-35
annual income among the respondents, 33-34
association between profile of the respondents and their monthly expenditure on drinking water, 65-66
– – – – respondents and their SERVQUAL scale, 59-61
drinking water pipe connection among the respondents, 41-42
family size of the respondents, 37-38
frequency of using bottled water among the respondents, 48-49
– – water supply, 43-44
gender of the respondents, 34
house ownership among the respondents, 39-40
important expectations among the respondents, 52-54
level of expectation on important factors, 56-57

– – perception on factors among the respondents, 57-58
means used to get drinking water, 42-43
monthly expenditure on drinking water, 61-62
nativity of the respondents, 35-36
number of earning members per family, 38-39
occupational background of the respondents, 36-37
profile of the respondents and their monthly expenditure on drinking water, 62-65
reasons for buying bottled water by the respondents, 49-50
reliability and validity of the important expectation, 54-56
respondents' expectation from metro water services, 51-52
– opinion on other important sources of drinking water, 47-48
tariff on drinking water, 45
type of house among the respondents, 40-41
usage of metro water among the respondents, 46-47
water availability per week, 44
years of experience with metro water system, 45-46

R

Reliability and validity of the implications in each model, 145-146
Reliability and validity of the important reasons, 171
Reliability and validity of the variables in each factor, 138-139
Respondents' perception on important reasons for privatization, 172-173

S

SERVQUAL, 207
Solid Waste Management (SWM), 206
Solid waste management and its financial model, 130-193
association between profile of the respondents and their ASWI, 134-135
evaluation of models, 152-157
opinion on important reasons, 173-174
SERVQUAL scale, 142-143
awareness on solid waste management
among the respondents, 131-133
index among the respondents, 133-134
contingent valuation model, 186-187
customers' expectation from SWM service, 135-137
discriminate factors among the respondents based on
different family size and number of earning members per family, 162-164

house-ownership and type of house, 164-165

their nativity and occupational background, 160-162

with different ASWI, 166-167

– validity of the constructs, 139-140, 171-172

evaluation of financial model for SWM system, 177-178

model-I, 146-147

model-II, 148-149

model-III, 150-151

factors influencing the model choice, 157-160

financed model in SWM, 131

financing of solid waste management services, 130-131

impact of important reasons for privatization on their overall degree of favour for privatization among the respondents, 174-176

important factors in SWM, 137-138

– reasons for privatization, 169-171

level of expectation among the respondents, 140

– – perception on factors in SWM, 141

models on SWM, 144

privatization of SWM, 167-168

profile of the respondents and their

choice on financial model, 178-186

WTP, 187-191

reasons for not supporting privatization, 176-177

– – privatization of SWM, 168-169

score index on model-I, 147-148

score index on model-II, 149-150

score index on model-III, 151-152

SERVQUAL scale on the factors in SWM, 141-142

U

Urban Water Supply and Sanitation, 4

W

Water Supply and Sanitation, 2002, 1

Willingness to pay for drinking water, 11

World Bank, 130